REFORM NATION

REFORM NATION

THE FIRST STEP ACT
AND THE MOVEMENT TO END
MASS INCARCERATION

COLLEEN P. EREN

STANFORD UNIVERSITY PRESS
Stanford, California

Stanford University Press
Stanford, California

© 2023 by the Board of Trustees of the Leland Stanford Junior University.
All rights reserved.

No part of this book may be reproduced or transmitted in any form or by any means, electronic or mechanical, including photocopying and recording, or in any information storage or retrieval system, without the prior written permission of Stanford University Press.

Printed in the United States of America on acid-free, archival-quality paper

ISBN 9781503613355 (cloth)
ISBN 9781503636736 (paperback)
ISBN 9781503636743 (electronic)

Library of Congress Control Number: 2022055894

Library of Congress Cataloging-in-Publication Data available upon request.

Cover design and art: Pablo Delcan
Typeset by Newgen in Garamond Premier Pro 11.25/14.75pt

For Mehmet Eren

Sana söylemek istediğim en güzel söz: henüz söylememiş olduğum sözdür.

The most beautiful words I wanted to say to you, are the words I haven't yet said.

—NAZIM HİKMET

CONTENTS

	Preface	ix
	Glossary of Terms and Acronyms	xv
1	The First Step Act Puzzle	1
2	Mainstreamization and the Movement	25
3	Billionaires, Philanthropy, and Reform	55
4	Celebrity Activism in Reform	85
5	Reform®: Corporate Social Activism	107
6	Strange Bedfellows	131
7	Formerly Incarcerated Activists and the Future of Criminal Justice Reform	163
	Acknowledgments	191
	Interviewees, Titles, and Affiliations	193
	Notes	197
	Bibliography	227
	Index	249

PREFACE

Those seeking change in the US criminal justice system, whether incremental or radical, have long had to march forward despite the ever-present threat of the ground swiftly shifting beneath them, of having their often Sisyphean efforts halted or swallowed by unstable political and social landscapes. Hope and optimism have been tempered by a sense of impending tragedy, of caution, of pessimism born of realist knowledge of how, as crime waves or headline-catching incidents come and go, so too does the general public's appetite for more humanistic and less carceral responses to violence and harm. Few are so naïve as to believe that when it comes to crime and punishment, tipping points mean that regression is impossible. The criminal justice system metes out punishments meant to "change" individuals in sentences lasting decades or even lifetimes, but the climate around criminal justice reform can be transformed in months.

I began work on this book in late 2019, in the four months before COVID would roil the world. It was less than a year after the feel-good story of the bipartisan passage of the federal First Step Act—a time of numerous state-level victories for reformers, of low salience of crime for voters, of an unprecedented flood of philanthropic donations to reform-minded organizations, and of a hopeful sentiment that with the nearly 20-year slow retreat away from a widespread "lock 'em up!" sensibility, the history of which is documented in this book, the tide had turned. Nevertheless, in 2019 advocates would point out the precarity of their successes. As one interviewee observed, "there's always going to be a next terrible crime, right?" There was always the threat of an uptick in crime, the political weaponization of "worst of the worst" crimes, or of a reform having easily exploitable instances of failure.

In the first half of 2020, it seemed possible that the national criminal justice reform movement would not experience such a threat imminently. In fact, it seemed to some in the movement that it might have reached an inflection point that would propel it forward. The moment of the crisis of the pandemic presented itself as one of exciting opportunity. The ravages of COVID brought unimaginable social change, disruption, and death. With the prospect of the incarcerated facing a bloodbath in prisons, where physical distancing to avoid contagion was impossible, the question of how many people *need* be in prison became an urgent concern. It was one that was answered with a dramatic reduction in the jail population through lowered arrests and release of those held on low-level charges. During the same period, the horrific video of George Floyd's murder under the knee of a White police officer in Minneapolis, sparked unprecedented engagement by nearly 10 percent of Americans in nationwide protests against racism and police brutality—arguably the largest in the nation's history. Polls conducted at the time indicated widespread support for reforming policing and belief in racial bias in policing.[1]

This fleeting time of hope disappeared as it appeared, in a matter of months, ushering in some of the worst fears of reformers. Though the vast majority of the 140 protests against police brutality across the US did not entail violence, where riot violence, vandalism, arson, and looting did break out, leading to the biggest insurance payouts for civil unrest in US history, they fractured support.[2] Violent crime—in particular the most visible and attention-getting of crimes, homicide—increased dramatically. Murder rose across red and blue cities, in suburbs, and in rural areas beginning in the summer of 2020,[3] up 29 percent from the prior year, reaching a level last recorded in the late 1990s, along with an increase in aggravated assaults.[4] Those rates remained well below their historical peaks, and other violent crimes like robbery and rape declined, and sustained decreases were seen in property crimes. But the issue of crime and reform measures became rapidly more toxic, divisive, and recentered in public and political discourse, especially as the slogan "defund the police" took center stage. The high-profile recall of progressive prosecutorial reformer Chesa Boudin, San Francisco district attorney in 2022; the 2021 election of former police officer Eric Adams as New York City mayor, running on a public safety platform; crime reemerging as a major concern nationally for voters; pushback against decarceratory measures like bail reform at the state level—these seemed to portend a worrisome trend for reformers. The whiplash in penal climate led to a drastic, premature querying in the media: "Is criminal justice reform *dead*?"[5]

There had been a similar rush to check the pulse of the criminal justice reform movement and pronounce its untimely demise with a kind of schadenfreude only a few years earlier. Seven years before, the year 2015 "came to symbolize a nightmare of exploding crime."[6] There had been a large uptick in homicide from the previous year. Then-candidate Donald Trump reported fake statistics showing murders at their highest rate in 45 years, running on a promise to "restore law and order," while a majority of Americans said that they were personally worried a "great deal" about crime. Former FBI director James Comey had created a national stir with his pronouncement that a "chill wind" across law enforcement due to antipolice hostility explained and portended a continued increase in violent crime. In 2016, an article in *New York Magazine* opined that with Donald Trump's Attorney General Jeff Sessions in power, "a painfully constructed bipartisan and cross-ideological movement to "de-incarcerate" many people . . . could soon completely fall apart." Indeed, the article's title proclaimed: "Criminal Justice Reform Is Dead."[7] There was a perception that the momentum especially for bipartisan federal reform may have fizzled out, that the reform "moment" had passed with a whimper. Still, Lenore Anderson, president and cofounder of the Alliance for Safety and Justice, as well as the Heritage Foundation's John-Michael Seibler,[8] argued through op-eds against such a reading of the reform movement's demise. "Criminal Justice Is Dead? Not So Fast" Anderson wrote,[9] describing the momentum seen in state-level initiatives, while Seibler pointed to bipartisan lawmakers still pushing reform in Washington. They were correct. And it's likely that those who pushed back against the "reform is stone-cold dead in the mainstream" reading in 2022, like the Nolan Center for Justice's David Safavian, are also correct.[10]

Upticks in crime are difficult to portend. Are they going to be a limited aberration or part of a longer-term pattern? It is similarly difficult to augur what the post-2020 shift in the tone and tenor of media and public response to crime and "reform" will mean for the reform movement in the decades to come. The 2015–2016 pessimism about federal and even state-level reform cautions against cynicism and hopelessness. Public opinion data from 2022 does not fatalistically determine a long winter of retreat from transformative changes. Approximately 5 percent of Americans in 2022 listed crime as the *most* important problem facing the country, well below economic considerations. Historical surveys showed the percentage of those who said they would be afraid to walk within a mile of their own home at night to be around the same as it had been in 2019. A majority, 53 percent, said they worried about crime a "great deal," but this was the same percentage as in 2016. Fifty-one percent said they had seen more crime in their area than in the previous year, but 51 percent also said this in 2006, 2007, and 2009.[11]

The criminal justice reform movement, more so than almost any other movement for social change around human rights and humanitarian principles, has never had a linear path forward or even a universally accepted teleological aim among participants. The reform ecosystems of states, where most decarceratory and ameliorative change needs to happen, vary tremendously. The relationship between federal-level policy shifts and state-level changes is also complex. All is subject to uncertain political tides.

I don't think these observations reflect a kind of fatalism, that reform is inexorably tied to the whims of social trends and so therefore the movement is merely riding these waves, helpless to steer the ship. What I've documented in this book is the post-2000 movement's mainstreamed character, its nationalized alliances, as well as its harnessing of successful stories appealing to the values of individuals across the political spectrum. These changes mean that it has a greater reach and mobilizing capacity than at any point in US history. Looking forward, there is no reason to see that regressing significantly. However, what I also explore are the characteristics of the national movement that can render it fragile, fractured, and of limited efficacy in making significant dents in mass incarceration. These are considerations that help in evaluating how to ensure its longevity and resilience despite changing headwinds.

Colleen P. Eren, October 2022

GLOSSARY OF TERMS AND ACRONYMS

ACLU	American Civil Liberties Union
ACU	American Conservative Union
BLM	Black Lives Matter
CPAC	Conservative Political Action Conference
CZI	Chan Zuckerberg Initiative
BJS	Bureau of Justice Statistics
BOP	Bureau of Prisons
FAMM	Families Against Mandatory Minimums
FIP	Formerly incarcerated people
FICPFM	Formerly Incarcerated, Convicted People & Families Movement
FSA	First Step Act
IRC	Independent Review Committee
PATTERN	Prisoner Assessment Tool Targeting Estimated Risk and Need
JAN	Justice Action Network
JLUSA	JustLeadershipUSA
LOHM	Ladies of Hope Ministries

NAACP	National Association for the Advancement of Colored People
NIJ	National Institute of Justice
NYPD	New York City Police Department
RAPP	Releasing Aging People in Prison
SCBC	Second Chance Business Coalition
SHRM	Society for Human Resource Management
SORN	Sex Offender Registration and Notification
SRCA	Sentencing Reform and Corrections Act
SSA	Smarter Sentencing Act
TPPF	Texas Public Policy Foundation

REFORM NATION

ONE

THE FIRST STEP ACT PUZZLE

In the minutes before the Oval Office signing ceremony for the First Step Act[1] on December 21, 2018, President Donald Trump addressed one of the issues that had come to define his presidency: the push for tougher security—including a wall—along the southern border of the United States.[2] The wall was about "safety for the country," he said emphatically. He described the "pouring of drugs" into the country and human trafficking as "at the all-time worst in history," and threatened to shut down the government that evening for an extended period unless the Democrats approved $5.7 billion in funding for the wall. "It's an issue of crime, safety, and least importantly, dollars on illegal immigration . . . we're going to get a wall," he concluded, before segueing: "Now to a very positive note. Criminal justice reform. Everybody said it couldn't be done."

The assemblage of individuals who clustered around Trump, filling the Oval Office for the signing was almost as incongruous as the transition from discourses of safety, crime, drugs, and illegal immigration to a discourse of criminal justice reform. Conservative politicians were well-represented. Vice President Mike Pence appeared on Trump's right across the room from Senators Ted Cruz of Texas, Mike Lee of Utah, and Kentucky Governor Matthew Bevin, while Senator Chuck Grassley of Iowa stood in front of Senator Doug Collins of Georgia with his fingertips pressed into Trump's armchair, alongside Martin Luther King Jr.'s niece, Alveda King, a Trump ally and former state representative. These onlookers stood intermingled with Democrats. Representative Bobby Scott of Virginia and Senator Sheldon Whitehouse of Rhode Island were tucked in behind Grassley. Conservative and libertarian advocacy organization leaders standing behind the first row of politicians included the American Conservative Union's Pat Nolan and David Safavian, Justice Fellowship's Craig DeRoche, Right on Crime's John Koufos, and Faith and Freedom Coalition's Ralph Reed. FreedomWorks' Jason Pye looked on from under the portrait of President Andrew Jackson. From the liberal advocacy organization #cut50,[3] founder, activist, and television political commentator Van Jones stood near Ivanka Trump, and #cut50 cofounder Jessica Jackson was alongside Jared Kushner. Representatives of the International Association of Chiefs of Police and the Fraternal Order of Police added to the tableau, with the formerly incarcerated, former NYPD commissioner Bernie Kerik prominently positioned to the left of Trump. Other formerly incarcerated advocates, like founder of Ladies of Hope Ministries' Topeka Sam and Georgetown lawyer Shon Hopwood, stood directly behind Mike Pence. Finally, below the Oval Office painting of President Lincoln stood Doug Deason, Texas philanthropist-activist and major Republican donor.

Trump's opening comments in praise of the First Step Act (FSA) contained what would become familiar motifs: an insistence that the bill was not weak on crime but rather was championed by those committed to being "tough" and keeping the US safe; a concern for unfairly long sentencing for nonviolent drug offenses; the importance of son-in-law Jared Kushner to the bill's passage, and praise for bipartisan cooperation. "Behind me is a cross-section of everybody in our country. . . . We have everybody here, we have everybody wanting this! . . . There are big stars in this room," he noted, describing his surprise at the support for the legislation, especially from "tough" Republican legislators like Senator Grassley, and at the successes seen in criminal justice reform in conservative states. He told of his initial skepticism and his gradual education on the merits of reform. He singled out the stories of Alice Marie Johnson, a grandmother given life without parole for a nonviolent drug-trafficking charge, and of a judge who had left the bench because he was forced to impose a 28-year mandatory minimum on a young man undeserving of that kind of time: "I never forgot it."

As those filling the Oval Office offered their comments, they repeated the themes Trump had invoked. Senator Ted Cruz underscored the bill's "toughness" and safety-preserving attributes: "It keeps murderers and rapists in prison." Keeping with Trump's pointing to a lack of proportionality of punishment, Cruz also mentioned the unfairness of a system which had led young Black men to spend decades in prison for nonviolent crimes. Bipartisan processes were extolled with astonishment, given the unlikelihood of the bill being passed in the current administration and given the polarization of parties. Senator Doug Collins called it a miracle, and Bernie Kerik insisted that he and Van Jones had thought it would never be done under Trump. Senator Mike Lee joked about texting with the liberal Van Jones and Senator Cory Booker while working on the FSA. Jones himself expounded: "There is nothing more important than freedom . . . all the great movements [are] about freedom," before emphasizing the need for bipartisanship: "We have the right to disagree, but we have a responsibility where we do agree to work together hard." Governor Matt Bevin concurred: "This transcends partisanship, this is not a partisan issue, this is a human issue. . . . You don't win political points by doing this, but it's the right thing to do." "It's not a partisan issue, it's a people issue," echoed formerly incarcerated leader Topeka Sam, who spoke of the FSA's banning of shackling during labor and making women's sanitary products available. Others lauded the act's antirecidivist and redemptive promise to help the incarcerated reintegrate into society, employment, family, and faith communities. For them, the act was full of hope.

Although he largely avoided interjection, Trump, when inviting his daughter to speak, quipped that if he had trouble working with Jared Kushner on points of the bill, he would call Ivanka: "She would say, 'Daddy, you don't understand, you *must* do this.'" Ivanka herself praised the formerly incarcerated leaders in the room "whose stories crystallized why [criminal justice reform] is important." Alveda Scott King was the last onlooker to speak prior to the signing: "They asked this man when he was a candidate, what are you going to do for race and racism . . . he said 'we're Americans,

CHAPTER ONE

FIGURE 1.1. First Step Act signing, December 21, 2018, REUTERS/ Alamy Stock photo

we all believe the same, we need for people to be safe, secure, blessed, working if they need to,' so I just want to say thank you, you keep your promises, so keep going, sir."

Acknowledging that there was more room for reform under the conditions articulated—that is, without compromising safety and without letting those with less sympathetic offenses off "easy"—Trump said, "This is a first step, but there's going to be a second and a third and possibly a fourth; it's a great subject, it's a great topic . . . ." He handed of the signing pens to Senator Grassley and the other to Van Jones.[4]

Within moments of the signing, a reporter questioned Trump about the looming shutdown. Smiling, Trump said, "This is such an incredible moment, what we've just done, criminal justice reform, that I just don't think it's appropriate to talk about anything else." The First Step Act had been signed just under the wire. That night at midnight, the government shut down for the longest period in US history because of the impasse over funding for the wall and border security.

The Oval Office signing ceremony presented only a limited glimpse of the unlikely group that had coalesced around the FSA, with varying degrees of commitment and enthusiasm, to move the bill forward. The criminal justice reform advocacy organization #cut50, spearheaded by Van Jones and Jessica Jackson, had compiled an 11-page list of supporters organized by the stakeholder group to which each belonged in lobbying for the bill. The senatorial cosponsors were listed, including 15 Democrats, 16 Republicans, and 1 Independent, but also 200 advocacy organizations representing business, faith-based, civil rights, and criminal justice reform advocacy groups. Among these were the American Civil Liberties Union (ACLU), the American Conservative Union (ACU), the Business Roundtable, the National Association for the Advancement of Colored People (NAACP), Koch Industries, the National Urban League, the National Latino Evangelical Association, the American Legislative Exchange Council Action (ALEC), Families Against Mandatory Minimums (FAMM), Prison Fellowship, Right on Crime, and Dave's Killer Bread. Law enforcement organizations and individuals listed as supporters included the American Correctional Association, the National District Attorneys Association, the Fraternal Order of Police, and the National Organization of Black Law Enforcement Executives. Because the National Sheriffs' Organization did not endorse the FSA, sheriffs across the country signed in their personal capacity.

Newspaper editorial board endorsements were another category of supporter. Twenty-five, from both national and local outlets, representing a spectrum of ideological leanings, were included. Among them were *The New York Times*, *The Washington Post*, *USA Today*, *Fox Broadcasting*, the *Washington Examiner*, *Reason*, and *The Wall Street Journal*. "Don't faint from surprise, but many Democrats and Republicans agree on fixing some of the harder edges of the criminal justice system. A bipartisan proposal would correct some unfair federal sentencing practices, and Congress should grab the chance," *The Wall Street Journal* commented, while *The New York Times* warned: "If Democrats resist the temptation to let the perfect be the enemy of the good, they can seize this opening [through the FSA] to make progress on an enduringly vexing challenge."[5]

Rounding out the list of supporters were two groups. First, there was an amalgamation of 50 "celebrities and public figures" from music, movies, sports, social movements, and politics, including former Green Party vice presidential candidate Rosa Clemente, billionaire Mark Cuban, Alyssa

Milano, Khloe and Kim Kardashian, Alicia Silverstone, Kanye West, and the entire Baltimore Ravens football team. These celebrities had in fact sent a letter directly to congressional leaders urging them to move forward with a vote on the bill before the end of 2018.[6] Last, there was a somewhat atypical constituency: 50 formerly incarcerated activists, including all of those at the FSA signing.

The unique constellation of stakeholders seen in the Oval Office, and reflected in the #cut50 list of supporting individuals and organizations, reconvened several months after the FSA had passed. In April of 2019, the White House hosted a First Step Act celebratory party for 300 guests in the East Room, concurrent with a Prison Reform Summit. Reality star Kim Kardashian, who by that point had announced that she was studying to be a lawyer under the mentorship of #cut50's Jessica Jackson, was invited to participate but declined.[7] In his introductory comments, Trump touted the recently passed reform for its bipartisanship, having the inherent value of being "for the good for the whole nation," changing what he termed outdated systems with unfair sentencing that led to cycles of poverty, and having the practical value of saving money. Six formerly incarcerated people who had been released under the FSA shared the stage with the president. Among them were Alice Marie Johnson, herself granted clemency by Trump and who would later be featured in a controversial 2020 Super Bowl ad touting the president's actions on criminal justice reform, and Matthew Charles, released from prison by the FSA, who emotionally pleaded for more to be done for those left behind in prison, for a "second step" to be taken.

THE FIRST STEP ACT AS SYMBOL

A "second step" and indeed many more steps would be crucial to any serious reduction in the number of incarcerated people in the US, because the FSA was hardly revolutionary. This fact was acknowledged even by those who advocated for it. A common opening comment among the contributors to this project who had worked on the legislation was "it was a first step." Derek Cohen of the Texas Public Policy Foundation, for one, called attention to its being "somewhat lackluster," releasing only a "paltry" number of the federal system's incarcerated people, and Jailila Jefferson-Bullock similarly noted: "[It] is one meager stride in a required marathon to effect true change. Its myriad improvements simply fail to achieve the status of groundbreaking."[8] Certainly, given the highly decentralized nature of the US criminal justice system, where most incarceration, and most change, happens at the state level, even drastic reforms to the federal system—certainly much more drastic than those in the FSA—would have a negligible impact on the nation's incarceration rate.[9]

Yet the relationship between federal and state reforms has long been symbiotic, the influence undeniable. During the frenzied Tough on Crime/War on Drugs time of the 1980s and 1990s, federal legislation ratcheting up sentences was passed, with national politicians goading states, even quasi-bribing them with funding, to move in concert with the federal government. In contrast, by the early 2000s states were becoming sites of so-called ambitious reforms, leading the federal government to reconsider its harsh turn,[10] in a reevaluation strongly signaled by the FSA.[11] Reform-oriented federal reform legislation following 2000 was positioned to influence states; an early example could be seen in Florida's introduction of its own "First Step Act" in 2019.

After all, with its messaging on criminal justice issues, "the federal government has a huge influence," Michael Jacobson, former Vera Institute of Justice director and former New York City corrections commissioner, pointed out.[12] The public, generally uninformed about politics, is even less knowledgeable about state and local political issues and more likely to pay attention to national-level discourse.[13] This doesn't apply only to policy. Work on political elites' rhetoric has furthermore provided evidence that when presidents adopt a punitive tone about crime in speeches this tone may be reflected in public opinion.[14] (Trump's waffling between stirring fear of crime through the "law-and-order" rhetoric that was central to his 2016 campaign[15] and touting "reform" complicates the matter of how the public would interpret his position on the issue and respond to it). And there was some concurrence around the FSA's significance: "It is the most ambitious and aggressive criminal justice reform in generations,"[16] Cohen said. Jefferson-Bullock concurred: "[It is an] ambitious, bipartisan compromise to commence with much-needed, genuine federal sentencing reform."[17] According to Hopwood, it was "an important victory [for] the criminal justice reform community."[18]

What was most significant about the FSA was its symbolism. It was a federal piece of legislation coming at the end of 2018, during a time when US political polarization seemed intractable and the possibility of moving forward with compromise on any issue, least of all something like criminal justice reform, seemed remote. As Holly Harris of Justice Action Network emphasized in our interview, "federal work is not the most impactful, but it is certainly the most symbolic."[19] Hannah Cox of Conservatives Concerned About the Death Penalty said in agreement, "I thought it was a great symbolic event for the country: that we can still come together and get things done. The FSA is small, but it is significant in that it happened at this level."[20] And Van Jones, when I asked about where the FSA fit in the history of criminal justice reform, declared: "It's the Death Star—it's a moment at the end of Star Wars, where they fire the final shot. The heroes pull off something impossible. Is there another trilogy or three more trilogies? Sure. But all by itself it's a victory."[21]

The First Step Act's symbolism lay in its representativeness of the interconnected changes to a *national* ethos and a *nationalized* movement structure. It was one of the few major pieces of federal criminal justice reform since the 1970s, along with the other two federal decarceratory acts enacted within the previous 11 years, to gesture at reversing the incarceration frenzy (Table 1.1). The very name of the act was a tacit admission that the US had gone too far. As such, it signaled a shift in the sociohistorical milieu to one where a national, partially coordinated movement toward a less punitive and less carceral ethos, as well as changes to both federal- and state-level policy, was politically possible. However, with its "strange bedfellow" constellation of stakeholders and advocates outside of government hinted at in this book's opening pages, from a spectrum of political beliefs and interest groups, some of which had previously been only marginally involved in criminal justice issues, the FSA symbolized the reform movement's having reached the crucial point of national social, political, economic, and cultural salience and ubiquity—its mainstreamization.

The individuals standing around the Oval Office desk in December of 2018; those whose names appeared on the #cut50 list of supporters; those who acted behind the scenes to encourage the bill's passage—these new strategic if temporary alliances signaled reform moving beyond a peripheral, local status and even hinted at the creation of a new political constituency: those most impacted by the criminal justice system. I have divided these constituencies into five categories—high-net-worth philanthropists and their philanthropies; celebrities; businesses and corporate leaders; right- and left-leaning national advocacy organizations with reform as an objective, and directly impacted activists.

At the same time, the dynamics behind passage of the FSA represented tensions and divides in the larger movement: the frames used, and by which groups; the stories, voices, and media used; the capital activated among elite participants; the bitter controversies that erupted behind the veneer of trans-partisanship; the groups that withheld their support or actively opposed the bill; the demands made; the amount of change deemed possible. To varying degrees, these fault lines captured what was happening nationally. They were the growing pains of an expanding, and expansive, movement that had found itself waging battle in and being shaped by a specific context, as had other large movements in the first quarter of the twentieth-first century. This was the era of post-democracy, with low sustained civic engagement and a concentration of power.[22] It was also a period marked by philanthrocapitalism, wherein private-sector individuals and businesses adopted market-based strategies to address social problems the government has failed to solve.[23]

STUDYING THE NATIONAL CRIMINAL JUSTICE REFORM MOVEMENT

Sociologist Arlie Russell Hochschild, in describing her research methods, characterizes the impetus for her research as "something bothering me, a little mental itch. Usually, it turns out to be a conflict or contradiction of some sort."[24] As a sociologist, the mental itch of what was afoot in the criminal justice reform movement built gradually as I observed shifts in political and public discourse, in media, in culture, in protests, and even in marketing. The FSA's symbolism and its function as a flashpoint for debate and for illuminating some of the contours and rifts of the reform movement made a fascinating departure point for investigating the larger questions about the movement that led to the writing of this book. How and when did criminal justice reform as a national movement emerge, and what impelled that emergence? What issues are included and excluded under the broad "coalition" umbrella? Who are the stakeholders and who among them have a seat at the decision-making table? What are the ideological differences within the movement, especially between "right" and "left," and how are they negotiated? How are decisions about movement objectives made? What strategies and frames are being used? Does the infusion of capital in its various forms help or hinder the movement? Is the movement driven from above or from below, and how durable is it? What goals are being articulated? How does the movement speak to democratic processes for change in the United States?

To be clear, using the FSA and its passage as a departure point for investigating national movement trends is not to argue that it represents the apex of criminal justice reform or to suggest that it is a major step toward ending America's incarceration addiction. This is not a puff piece on a bipartisan federal bill during a time of polarization, but neither is it a hit piece. I am less interested in the act itself than in using it as a "canary in the coalmine" showing that criminal justice reform was no longer a niche cause, but one that responded to a nationally recognized social problem with a movement that had itself gone national—with all the internal divisions we might expect, divisions that intensified as more resources existed for mobilization and the influence of powerful institutional actors and individuals grew, shifting movement gravity and creating new valences.

The FSA itself is less important than its exemplification of national-level movement dynamics and divisions. However, an exposition of its provisions—and where it fits in the history of federal criminal justice reform in the late twentieth and early twenty-first centuries—gives us critical contextual information for understanding the deeper political and sociological questions raised by the book.

THE FIRST STEP ACT IN A FEDERAL CRIMINAL JUSTICE REFORM CONTEXT

With limitations pointed out by even its staunchest supporters, the FSA still finds itself among the major pieces of federal criminal justice legislation since mass incarceration began in the 1970s. At that time, the incarceration rate was around 200 per 100,000 adults but would sharply rise until its peak of 1,000 per 100,000 between 2006 and 2008.[25] Table 1.1 lays out

TABLE 1.1. Major federal criminal justice legislation, 1968–2010

Legislation	Year/ president (party)	Description
Omnibus Crime Control and Safe Streets Bill	1968/Lyndon Johnson (D)	Part of Johnson's "War on Crime" and broadest federal crime bill passed at that time; established block grant and massive federal investment in penal and juridical agencies.
Comprehensive Crime Control Act	1984/Ronald Reagan (R)	Continued bipartisan "Tough on Crime" push; eliminated federal parole; made bail system more restrictive; increased penalties; gave federal government new authority over range of offenses; made civil asset forfeiture easier but insanity defenses more difficult.
Anti-Drug Abuse Acts	1986, 1988/ Ronald Reagan (R)	Established long mandatory minimum sentences for drug possession; enshrined 100-to-1 sentencing disparity for distribution of powder versus crack cocaine.
Violent Crime Control and Law Enforcement Act	1994/Bill Clinton (D)	Gave funds to states to hire 100,000 police and nearly $10 billion to fund prisons; provided funding for law enforcement–informed prevention programs; expanded federal death

(continued)

TABLE 1.1. (*continued*)

Legislation	Year/president (party)	Description
		penalty; allowed 13-year-olds to be prosecuted as adults for some crimes; established three strikes sentencing; required states to register sex offenders; created new crimes; increased penalties for range of crimes; gave billions to combat illegal immigration.
Prison Litigation Reform Act	1996/Bill Clinton (D)	Applied also to juveniles; limited lawsuits brought by incarcerated persons in federal courts through restrictions including requirement that grievance procedures within jail or prison be exhausted before bringing suit in court; restricted court oversight of prison conditions.
Prison Rape Elimination Act	2003/George W. Bush (R)	Applied to every incarcerated person; requires zero-tolerance policy for sexual violence among incarcerated or between the incarcerated and staff; created prevention, detection, response, reporting standards.

Legislation	Year/president (party)	Description
Second Chance Act	2008/George W. Bush (R)	Focused on promoting reentry/reintegration while reducing recidivism; encouraged new programs including for reentry courts, drug treatment alternatives to prison, drug treatment/mentoring post-release; formalized Prison Reentry Initiative to oversee second chance programming.
Fair Sentencing Act	2010/Barack Obama (D)	Reduced sentencing disparity between crack and powder cocaine to 18-to-1 but did not apply retroactively to those already sentenced.

the chronology of these bills and describes their main provisions. Notable is that from the late 1960s to 2003, so-called reforms to the criminal justice system were in the direction of harsher sentencing and expansion of the incarceration apparatus in the name of the War on Crime/War on Drugs and being "tough on crime," and these gave the federal government more power over criminal justice matters. Also notable is the extent to which federal crime bills in the Tough on Crime era were overwhelmingly bipartisan, championed by Democrats and Republicans alike. As for the sentencing "reforms" of the 1980s that put forth mandatory sentencing, they were often argued on the "liberal" grounds of reducing racial discrimination in sentencing though, perversely, they severely exacerbated precisely that problem.[26]

CHAPTER ONE

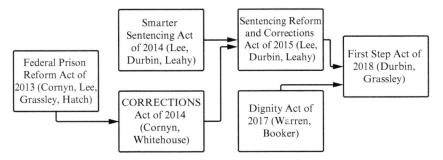

FIGURE 1.2. Senate legislative influences on the First Step Act

The FSA itself was not the product of a single year of effort, but represented a cobbling together of previous pieces of bipartisan legislation that had failed to achieve passage over the five years prior.[27] Figure 1.2 is a chronological presentation of the Senate's legislative influences on the FSA.

Introduced in 2014 by Republican senator Mike Lee and Democratic senators Dick Durbin and Patrick Leahy, the Smarter Sentencing Act (SSA) died when Democratic leaders stalled in bringing it up for a vote before congressional elections. Supported by some of the same criminal justice reform groups that would later champion the FSA, the SSA would have lowered mandatory sentences for drug offenses and expanded "safety valve" exceptions, congressional maneuvers that make mandatory minimums "a little less mandatory by letting a court override [those] required for non-violent, 'low-level' defendants who cooperate with the state with minimal to no criminal involvement previously."[28] Also, the SSA would have permitted thousands of federal prisoners, almost 90 percent of whom were Black, to be resentenced in accordance with the 2010 Fair Sentencing Act.

In 2015 Senator Durbin again tried to introduce legislation containing the provisions of the SSA, this time with Republican senator Chuck Grassley, through the Sentencing Reform and Corrections Act (SRCA). This would have, again, expanded the safety valve, given judges new authority to depart from certain mandatory minimums, limited the instances in which mandatory minimums could be given, made the Fair Sentencing Act retroactive, and ended "stacking."[29]

Additionally, the SRCA incorporated the prison reform provisions from another bill that had failed to be heard around the same time as the

SSA: the 2014 CORRECTIONS Act.[30] Introduced by Senators John Cornyn and Sheldon Whitehouse, the bill attempted to legislate prison reform through risk assessment, recidivism planning, Bureau of Prison (BOP) partnerships with nonprofits and faith-based groups, in-prison re-entry programming, reductions to incarceration expenditures, and credit toward prerelease custody. Furthermore, it tried to reform some juvenile justice matters, including solitary confinement.[31] The SRCA ultimately failed to pass after becoming mired in acrimonious partisan debates. Democrats rejected the Republicans' attempt to include an expansion of *mens rea* through the bill, believing it would make financial, environmental, and other white-collar crimes harder to prosecute. Republicans, for their part, balked at the idea of releasing federal prisoners early.[32]

Finally, elements of Senators Cory Booker and Elizabeth Warren's 2017 Dignity Act were absorbed into the FSA. The Dignity Act mandated that incarcerated people at the federal level be placed in facilities as close to their children as possible, prohibited charging for phone calls, mandated free video conferencing, banned the use of shackling and segregated housing for those pregnant or postpartum, and made feminine hygiene products free in quantities according to individual need.

In its final form, the 132-page First Step Act, authorized at $75 million per year for five years (or about a meager $400 per incarcerated person),[33] had two major categories of reform: corrections and sentencing. These were reflective of the not-so-easy melding, paring back, and expansion of the wish lists in the previously mentioned bills. The process by which the act came together will be explored throughout the book.

MAJOR PROVISIONS OF THE FIRST STEP ACT

The First Step Act's changes to federal corrections policy[34] revolved around a new risk and needs assessment system, to be developed by the US attorney general in consultation with, among others, BOP, the National Institute of Justice (NIJ), and an independent review committee (IRC) of nonprofit organizations.[35] The system was unveiled in 2019. It included an algorithmic assessment tool known as PATTERN, which measured 17 factors[36]—some fixed,[37] such as the nature of the crime, and others dynamic, such as completion of programs or drug treatment while incarcerated—in order to predict the risk of recidivism generally and recidivism involving violent offenses specifically.[38] Almost no public information could be found about the tool's development and effectiveness, which would draw criticism for its perceived baking in of class and racial bias, in addition to its giving different sex-based risk scores for the same factors. Depending on the score, the BOP would classify an incarcerated individual as low, medium, or high risk and, based on that risk, develop evidence-based programs to reduce the likelihood of recidivism.

In-prison incentives were also offered based on participation in programs, such as more visitation time at the discretion of the warden, videoconferencing up to 510 minutes a month, a higher spending cap at the commissary, transfer to a facility closer to home, and vaguely stated "greater" email access.

Key to the correctional reforms were the incentives of "earned time" credits for program participation and "good time" credits for good behavior. For every 30 days of program participation, those incarcerated could earn 10 days of earned time credits. These qualified them for prerelease custody subject to 24-hour electronic monitoring or supervised release after they added up to the remainder of time left in their sentence. However, those whose crimes fell under the broad designation of "violent" (like sex-related crimes, terrorism, some types of fraud, and higher-level drug offenses) were excluded from earned time credit. There were further restrictions on earned time credits. They were not to be issued retroactively. Even if an incarcerated person had earned enough time to be released, they needed to be classified as minimum or low risk based on two PATTERN assessments or with the explicit permission of the warden.

The FSA also made modifications to the stingy calculation of "good time" credits by the BOP, allowing the incarcerated to secure up to an extra week of good time credits per year of the sentence imposed, to be applied retroactively.[39]

As might be anticipated, the new risk and needs assessment process, to be followed by appropriate programming, generated and in fact required, an enormous amount of bureaucracy. The DOJ and the IRC were required to submit reports to Congress, dissecting the effectiveness of programs by their "type, amount and intensity." Identifying disparities among demographic groups and attending to their individual "criminogenic" needs were emphasized. The Government Accountability Office was entrusted with auditing the work of both the BOP and the DOJ.

The second major category of reform in the FSA was sentencing, especially on two fronts. The first front made retroactive the sentencing reforms of the Fair Sentencing Act of 2010. This meant the reduction of glaring sentencing disparities between crack and cocaine offenses applied to the incarcerated before implementation of the law, with the caveat that they would have to petition the court because a reduction would not be automatic. The second front dealt with mandatory minimums, which since the 1980s had contributed to the exponential rise in the number of incarcerated. The FSA expanded the safety valve and lowered mandatory minimums for certain drug offenses, and it replaced the life without parole mandatory minimum with a minimum of 25 years. The bill furthermore tried to narrow the range of offenses for which mandatory minimums kick in, reserving them for drug felonies carrying a sentence of 10 years or a serious violent felony. Lastly, mandatory minimum sentencing was affected by the removal of "stacking provisions" under 924c of the US Code, which triggered lengthy mandatory minimums for the "separate" crime/charge of being in possession of or using a gun during a drug or violent offense. Even the presence of a legally purchased gun in the home of a defendant could result in an enhanced sentence under the old system. Because charges were stacked and sentences were served concurrently, some truly outrageous sentences resulted, as in the case of Weldon Angelos. Angelos received a 55-year sentence as a result of 924c provisions for the sale of $1,000 of marijuana to an informant over a month-long period, keeping a gun with him during the sales, and possessing firearms in his home. According to Jason Pye of FreedomWorks, "Although he was a first-time drug offender, Mr. Angelos was treated as a recidivist by prosecutors through the stacking of the charges under a single indictment."[40]

Beyond its sentencing and corrections reform provisions, which made inroads in reducing the number of federally incarcerated, other provisions gestured toward decarceration. A BOP pilot program of early release to home confinement was reauthorized and expanded (only nonviolent, non-terrorism-related, non-sex-related, and non-espionage-related crimes were included). It lowered the age of eligibility from 65 to 60 and made early release available to incarcerated people who had served two-thirds of their sentence and to the terminally ill of any age. Relatedly, the FSA took some aim at increasing the use of compassionate release by the BOP, which had stood at a paltry 6 percent of all applicants. Requirements put pressure on the BOP to give timely assistance in compassionate release cases, and individuals could now file a motion for release on their own[41] in court after administrative appeals had been exhausted, essentially going over the head of the BOP.

An assorted set of within-prison conditions was slated for improvement through other provisions, and attention was given to the challenges of reentry. The act mandated planning and executing expansion of evidence-based opioid and heroin treatment in prison. The importation of policies originally contained in the Dignity Act of 2017 meant that shackling during pregnancy or postpartum was to be prohibited, feminine hygiene products were to be free and based on individual need, and the incarcerated were, with caveats, to be placed closer to their families (if within 500 driving miles can be considered close). Solitary confinement for juveniles was not abolished, but the FSA enjoined juvenile facilities to "try" less restrictive techniques and never use solitary unless physical risk was imminent. In-prison employment was expanded with Federal Prison Industries (operating under the trade name UNICOR),[42] which was now able to sell products made by the incarcerated to public entities and nonprofits for restricted uses. Fifteen percent of their wages would be paid upon release, a trivial amount considering that in 2021 the pay in federal prison was set at a maximum of $0.40 an hour, coming out to an annual salary, at 40 hours per week, of $832, which would allow at most $125 to be paid per year at release.[43] The BOP was strong-armed through the FSA into also providing the personal identification documents[44] necessary for living and working upon release to the former federally incarcerated.

Finally, the FSA reauthorized the Second Chance Act of 2007, which meant reauthorization of reentry- and antirecidivism-based grants and research programs for those currently incarcerated and those who had returned home. Grants linked to reentry and antirecidivism were renewed, including those tied to family-based substance abuse treatment; drug treatment programs in prisons; mentoring programs in prisons and during

The First Step Act Puzzle

reentry; community-based transitional services; improvement of education in prisons, jails, and juvenile facilities, and career training. As with the research and assessment requirements for correctional reforms we saw earlier, the grants were to be tied to presentation of "measurable performance outcomes" focused on lowering recidivism, and "to the extent practicable, random assignment and controlled studies, or rigorous quasi-experimental studies with matched comparison groups to determine the effectiveness of the program."[45]

Research programs through the NIJ and the Bureau of Justice Statistics (BJS) focused overwhelmingly on recidivism-related questions. One NIJ study was to "identify the number and characteristics of children [of] incarcerated parents and their likelihood of engaging in criminal activity."[46] The FSA mandated a Prisoner Statistics Program to alleviate some of the massive holes in data on the incarcerated. The looked at their personal conditions, as well as the conditions of confinement (how many have been placed in solitary confinement, how many have children or are pregnant, the number in recidivism programs, and so forth).

In the several years following the FSA's passage, some of the organizations most responsible for pushing the legislation lauded its accomplishments. #cut50 put out the booklet "#HomeForTheHolidays: A Celebration of Freedom Made Possible by the First Step Act" presenting the stories of incarcerated people who were released and quantifying in bold the act's impact: 7,000 people earning time off their length of incarceration, 17,000 years of freedom added, 20,000 of the released benefiting from FSA provisions, and the lowest number of people in federal prison since 2003.[47] A more measured assessment from The Sentencing Project declared that the act had "mixed outcomes" but noted among its achievements the reduction of an average six years' time for the 1,691 people who had their sentences retroactively lowered under the Fair Sentencing Act, with Black people making up 91 percent of those receiving reductions.[48] Several hundred people were approved for the home confinement pilot program for the elderly, and 100 people received compassionate release. The good time credit expansion furthermore led to the federal release of 3,100 people.[49]

The full impact of the FSA was not immediate evident. Characteristically slow-moving, bureaucratic, and recalcitrant, the BOP dragged out implementation and made "letter of the law versus spirit of the law" proposals for interpreting vaguely defined earned time provisions in the way least advantageous to the incarcerated peoples' ability to secure their freedom through good-faith participation in eligible programming. Shortages in staffing, reducing the amount of earned time credit available, and delays due to the COVID-19 pandemic further intervened. It took until January of 2022, under President Joe Biden, for a final DOJ rule to detail how earned time credit release would work, with more generous BOP interpretations of what would count as a "day" for the purpose of this accounting and with earned time becoming retroactive to the passage of the FSA. Instantly, thousands were made eligible for release. Attorney General Merrick Garland, announcing the new DOJ rule, stated: "The First Step Act, a critical piece of bipartisan legislation, promised a path to an early return home for eligible incarcerated people who invest their time and energy in programs that reduce recidivism. Today, the DOJ is doing its part to honor this promise, and is pleased to implement this important program."

However one views the FSA and its ongoing outcomes—perhaps as a combination of "somewhat lackluster,"[50] "meager stride in a required marathon to effect true change,"[51] "modest but meaningful,"[52] and a "major step" while major steps remained to be taken[53]—it is of vital importance to understand how it came to pass, who supported and opposed it, and what that revealed about the national criminal justice reform movement at that moment in time, the changes the movement witnessed, and the stakeholders it comprised. In that understanding, the implications for the future of reform may be seen, along with a discernment of the opportunities, advantages, constraints, and perils of movements in philanthrocapitalist and post-democratic environments more broadly.

REFORM NATION? STUDYING THE REFORM MOVEMENT

While this book leans on research from sociologists, historians, and political scientists to provide context and analytical insights—especially sociologists who have studied social movements—few examples exist of work dedicated solely to understanding the criminal justice reform movement *as* a movement, especially during the 20 years between the critical years of

2000 and 2020. Most "reform" literature elucidates problems within the system and their etiology, and proposes solutions to those problems.[54] As exploratory, hypothesis-generating research such as that envisioned by sociologist Arlie Hochschild, this book does not present representative samples to show how common a phenomenon is, but rather to discover and describe *what* something is, in this case the national criminal justice reform movement, and why it assumed its characteristics at this point in history. To understand this picture—"what it is"—I sought in-depth interviews with individuals purposively chosen for their positions of leadership who were heavily engaged in the movement, who came from the stakeholder groups I identified outside of government: billionaire philanthropists and their philanthropies; celebrities; businesses and corporations; right- and left-leaning advocacy groups and nonprofit organizations, and directly impacted activists. Those who had special experience/expertise with the FSA, or who could speak to the history and context of the movement and its frames were also consulted.

I conducted 53 interviews between October 2019 and December 2021 (the Appendix has a full list of participants and their affiliations/titles). Of those, over a third were with those either formerly incarcerated or directly impacted by having a spouse/partner or parent who was incarcerated. Until April of 2020, the interviews were mostly conducted in person in or near the participant's place of work, during criminal justice reform events, or in their home. However, as the COVID-19 pandemic led to shutdowns, the remaining interviews were conducted via teleconferencing. Additionally, I was a participant observer at dozens of in-person and virtual events organized by national and state reform organizations, including the abolitionist Critical Resistance's "Organizing Against Toxic Imprisonment in the Face of COVID-19" conference in March 2020; the American Conservative Union's "Prison CPAC" in November 2019, and #cut50's "Day of Empathy" in April 2020. These events gave more insight into the frames, alliances, tactics, and social connections among participants.

Emerging from this research are several central ideas to which the book will return in the chapters to follow.

First, beginning in approximately the year 2000, the criminal justice reform movement went through a process of mainstreamization, which meant it could become nationalized. Disparate submovements, such as the reentry movement and the anti-death-penalty movement, were brought under a national, discursive "reform" umbrella in the media and by most participants, though many prison abolitionists actively eschewed the term. Different subfields within this space may have been more or less centered and thickly embedded, and so inclusion and prominence were open to contestation. Prior to this period, while certainly there were many organizations involved in these issues, particularly at the state and local level, and many of the same demands were articulated, the phrase *criminal justice reform* was not used universally, and when it was used prior to the 2000s it often connoted *regressive* policies. By 2018, it connoted a collective understanding of the necessity of amelioration—making things less harsh and punitive—but also support for decarceration. Criminal justice reform was, at the start of the 2020s, popularly understood to mean at least both of those things, even if the extent of decarceration sought was not agreed upon.

Mainstreamization meant that the reform movement had entered a new stage, distinct from earlier iterations. What impelled this new era was the scale of the problem of mass /overincarceration, and the accompanying broadening of support across sectors, especially well-resourced ones. What was furthermore new was that the scale of the problem coincided with the sociohistorical and political context of post-democracy and philanthrocapitalism, converting it from a niche issue into one championed by celebrities and entrepreneurs, and giving it the resources to create professionalized nonprofit infrastructures and leadership. Because of its expansion, mainstreamization, and nationalization, the movement's internal dynamics of contradiction, tension, and conflict have sometimes been writ large on the national stage, as is characteristic of any large social movement. The book explores these tensions and contradictions in each of the five stakeholder groups it investigates.

Despite the scaling up of reform apparatuses, and unlike with other mainstreamed social causes like gay marriage, the movement possessed a tenuousness threatening its longevity and relentless forward progress. The history of cyclical shifts in public sentiment and pushes for reform around prisons and punishment caution against lofty thinking that something mainstreamed will necessarily lead to a break in those cycles. It is uncertain whether even the configuration evident at the start of the 2020s has the ability to return levels of incarceration to what they were in the 1970s, even if it had the imagination and will to do so.

ORGANIZATION OF THE BOOK

Departing from the groundwork of this introductory chapter, Chapter 2 further lays the foundations for understanding the national reform movement by presenting the phenomenon of mainstreamization theoretically and descriptively. It gives evidence, rooted in firsthand accounts of movement actors, of how and why reform *as a movement* evolved post-2000 to become national and took on such an influential role in political and social discourse. The large umbrella of this movement and its constituent subgroups and issues are delineated, as are subgroups and issues that are more peripheral and fighting for inclusion, such as those organized around the intersection of immigration and criminal justice or victims/survivors or women and gender-nonconforming people.

Chapters 3 through 7 are individually structured around one nongovernmental stakeholder/interest group in the national movement whose influence can be discerned in the passage of the FSA. Each chapter begins with an insider account of how the stakeholder/group came to have a role in passage of the act, before moving into dynamics, internal tensions, opportunities, and changes created by them in criminal justice reform broadly. Chapter 3 explores the roles of high-net-worth philanthropists who have leveraged their financial and political capital and their philanthropies. Chapter 4 focuses on celebrities and "influencers" in the movement. Chapter 5 discusses corporate leaders and businesses. Chapter 6 deals with "right" and "left" national advocacy organizations. Finally, Chapter 7 presents the role of directly impacted activists nationally, before offering parting thoughts about the post-2000 reform movement.

Throughout this book and in my analysis, I do not attempt, with a kind of academic omniscience, to suggest the "best" way for the movement, and those giving their lives or resources to it, to proceed. I do not argue for what the best reforms are to end or severely curtail the incarceration rate while at the same time ensuring harm reduction for larger communities; nor do I wax quixotic. In a system so vast, bureaucratic, and balkanized as the criminal justice system, along with the complexities of the US political landscape and the need for effectively dealing with harm to real people and communities, there can be no single template. Pontificating is easy without having to live through actual changes on the ground. What I try to do instead is chart the movement's meteoric rise over a period of 20 years. I explore the contexts, tensions, fault lines, constraints, possibilities, and contradictions that shaped its progress, insights into which should speak to other movements as both inspirational roadmaps and cautionary tales. This may give more intentionality and self-consciousness to the choices that are being made while raising much larger questions—questions about our democratic processes and how they inform criminal justice policy, how social change is enacted generally, and where we are going.

TWO

MAINSTREAMIZATION AND THE MOVEMENT

In the year after the First Step Act's passage, then-presidential candidate Joe Biden insisted in a statement to *The New York Times* that too many people of color were incarcerated and that, if he were president, he would champion ending mandatory minimums, private prisons, and cash bail, and advocate for automatic expungement for marijuana offenses.[1] He verbally committed to a self-identified ACLU voter, in fact, to cutting incarceration by more than 50 percent.[2] It was quite the about-face. In the late 1980s, then-Senator Joe Biden had complained that President George H. W. Bush was remiss in not putting enough "violent thugs" behind bars. He touted his own tough-on-crime record into the 1990s, including his work on the 1994 Crime Bill, which accelerated the pace of incarceration, declaring: "Lock the S.O.B.s up!" and used the racially coded, fear-instilling language of "predators" to describe these criminal Others. Biden's language while campaigning in 2019 sounded like not only an evolution but a reversal. He admitted that his previous positions on crime, especially his support of the 1994 Crime Bill, were "a mistake."[3]

Biden's stance on criminal justice reform was an individual example of the dramatic shift being writ nationally, and not only in federal policies, between 2000 and 2020. Most states—whether Republican- or Democrat-leaning—passed reforms aimed at decarceration or at least ameliorating the "hidden punishments" of a criminal record.[4] In the business world, JP Morgan Chase, Walmart, McDonalds, Bank of America, Best Buy, and others would form a Second Chance Business Coalition to integrate more formerly incarcerated people into their workforce,[5] and PUMA would create its own criminal justice reform–themed sneakers. In philanthropy, where criminal justice reform had previously received little attention, big funders poured unprecedented dollars into the space, like the Chan Zuckerberg Initiative's $350 million commitment in 2021,[6] and high-net-worth philanthropists were publicly vocal about their support for reform.[7] Celebrities, like Kim Kardashian and Alyssa Milano and some who had been directly impacted by the criminal justice system like singer John Legend and rap artist Meek Mill, contributed star power and their platforms of millions of followers to the cause.

The very language used to describe what had happened during the excessively punitive turn in the United States changed: widespread acknowledgment that "mass incarceration" or "overincarceration" was a problem and "criminal justice reform" was a needed solution was by 2018 a ubiquitous idea and—at least as a slogan—was devoid of much controversy. In 2016, the Pew Research Center showed that 44 percent of Americans thought criminal justice reform should be a *top* priority.[8] More telling of mainstreamization, perhaps, was a 2020 poll from the Associated Press–NORC Center for Public Affairs Research reporting that an overwhelming 94 percent of US residents surveyed thought criminal justice reforms were needed, with 69 percent supporting a "major" or "total" overhaul[9]: "Nearly all in the US back criminal justice reform." On police reform specifically, this poll showed widespread support for various measures, among them penalizing officers for racially biased policing and prosecuting officers for excessive force—but not for reducing their funding. In a 2020 poll conducted jointly by a Democratic and a Republican firm, two-thirds of voters said they would be more likely to vote for candidates who advocated criminal justice reforms that included police reform. The data was so remarkably favorable that it led James Williams of Arnold Ventures to say, "The only comparable things that come to mind are ice cream and puppies."[10]

Thus the playing field for those working on ratcheting down the excesses of the criminal justice system had changed—dramatically—since 2000, with two key and overlapping alterations, normative and structural.

While perspectives on and assessments of the movement and interpretations of the origin of that sociopolitical and cultural shift varied among the reform leaders interviewed for this book, on this point there was consensus.

Normatively, the meaning of "criminal justice reform" itself in the late 2010s to the early 2020s was a complete reversal from the late 1970s through the 1990s, when the phrase was used in discussions of *more* prisons, with longer and more draconian sentences. What these previous bills were "reforming," in a punitive direction, were the pre-1970s rehabilitation-focused sentencing and corrections policies. In 1983, for instance, a book optimistically titled *Criminal Justice Reform: A Blueprint* was released. With contributions from academics, administration officials, and politicians, it advocated for tougher sentencing for drug crimes, wider use of the death penalty, and restricting bail, Freedom of Information Act (FOIA) requests, and appeals processes.[11]

The post-2000 reform movement's accumulation of national social, political, economic, and cultural salience and ubiquity—its mainstreamization—meant that the *general* claims of reform—to decarcerating and ameliorating the widespread harms of the criminal justice system—appeared taken for granted. This was true even as the demands remained battlefields of contention among political allies and opponents alike, and as the victories remained drastically short of what would bring the US back to its 1970s incarceration level.

Structurally, though much work necessarily remained state-focused or regional, the movement itself was nationalized and professionalized, as was seen in the immigrants' rights movement in the early 2010s.[12] Organizing around disparate aspects of criminal justice (reentry, capital punishment, sentencing reform, bail reform, drug legalization) was brought together discursively and in some cases through coalitional work under the unified banner of criminal justice reform.

INCARCERATION NATION TO REFORM NATION?
THE MAINSTREAMIZATION PROCESS

Even interviewees for this book who, because of youth or later engagement with the issue, lacked historical memory stretching back pre-2000, noted the striking pace of shifting social and cultural understandings of the issue in the US at the start of the 2020s compared with the mid-2010s. The United States, after all, was the "Incarceration Nation"[13] that binge-incarcerated its residents in its punitive fury, going from around 200,000 people in prison in 1970 to around 1.5 million by the mid-2000s. There was no amount of being "tough on crime" that was tough enough for decades. Yet, at the end of the 2010s especially and the beginning of the 2020s, "criminal justice reform" and "ending mass incarceration" were not only mainstream —"It's kind of mom and apple pie-ish now to say let's end mass incarceration," said former Vera Institute of Justice president and New York City corrections commissioner Michael Jacobson.[14] They were presented by interviewees as vogueish and marketable: a "popular" topic,[15] a "shiny object,"[16] a "cushy, kind of safe thing to say nowadays,"[17] "a sexy word."[18] "The movement has evolved so that it is much more respectable to say you're in criminal justice reform. It's suddenly fashionable for the candidates to talk about it," recalled Sue Ellen Allen, founder of Reinventing Reentry.[19] Robert Rooks, a veteran in the space as cofounder of the Alliance for Safety and Justice, concurred: "For most of my 22 years in this work, the issue was not mainstream. I remember at socials, people ask what you do, you say 'criminal justice reform' and it would be a conversation stopper, like—why are you doing that for criminals? But now, the issue is being mainstreamed right before our eyes."

It would be hard to imagine a scenario in which #cut50's list of supporters of the FSA, discussed in Chapter 1, would exist were it not for this popularity and the perceived safety of making overtures toward criminal justice reform.

The criminal justice reform movement did not undergo, nor did it have the potential to undergo, mainstreamization overnight. That development involved five interconnected structural and normative processes playing out between US society and movement participants. The first and most fundamental of these, collective acknowledgment, took almost 30 years to achieve. Figure 2.1 is a model of these processes, not always proceeding linearly, containing inherent tensions/conflicts among those in the movement and externally represented by arrows leading away.

Collective acknowledgment, quite simply, is the majority acceptance of the idea that the criminal justice system in the United States has significant

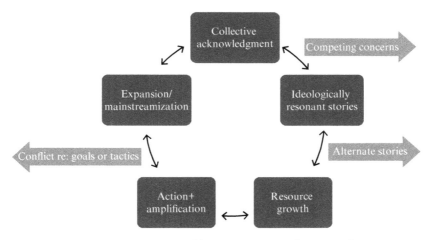

FIGURE 2.1. Mainstreamization and barriers to criminal justice reform

problems in need of remedy.[20] This is of course very general and schematic. For the moment, we can leave aside the more substantive questions (In what ways is it dysfunctional? Is there the possibility of a system *ever* being functional? Which components are in most need of reform or should be included in this discussion?). There can be no coalitional mass movement for change without that basic acknowledgment of a major problem in need of intervention. Leading away from this acknowledgment stage are *competing social concerns* (such as those of increasing crime) that can have the effect of elevating them above concerns of tackling reform, in effect, of neutralizing the idea of a problem existing. The mainstreamization of reform took place during a historic, sustained, and dramatic drop in violent and nonviolent crime beginning in the 1990s and a consequent reduction in public punitiveness that could be directly linked to declining rates of incarceration.[21] It was also taking place during a period of low unemployment and a very tight labor market, which helped whet corporate interest. This socioeconomic milieu helped create an environment where ample space existed for questioning the primacy of prisons in US life, and there was openness to ideologically resonant stories supportive of alternative visions.

Collective acknowledgment and *ideologically resonant stories/frames* are so closely interlinked, there often is a chicken-and-egg feedback loop between them. Ideologically relevant stories are a way of telling or illustrating the problems of the criminal justice system and its impacts. They provide familiar narrative arcs, coherence, resonance, and, importantly, motifs and logics that cohere with different ideological positions and identities, which inspire individuals and organizations to support change. People need to see how someone like themselves is affected and/or how someone like themselves can and should uphold their values by contributing to change. Social movement scholars sometimes refer to the related concept of frames and framing, but I prefer "story" here, which was used more frequently by movement actors and organizations. Indeed, careers that carried the title "storyteller" and the phrase "leveraging storytelling" were common in the proliferating nonprofit sector built around the sprawling harms of overincarceration. On the other hand, if stories do not speak to large ideological groups of their underlying values, stir empathy, or help individuals see a role for themselves in change or the benefits that will accrue, future growth may be prevented as alternate stories prevail. For example, there may be acknowledgment of problems in the system and its effectiveness, but more, not less, "law and order" and being "tough on crime" may be an appealing counter-story.

With several ideologically resonant stories that can position reform within a worldview that inspires change, particularly as public relations risks and backlash against involvement diminish under the cover of more widespread support, there is both *resource growth and action/amplification*. Resources coming into the arsenal of reform include the accruing of crucial social, political, economic, and cultural capital from philanthropy, engaged high-net-worth individuals, and celebrities. These aid in amplifying (a buzzword also adopted by the movement) resonant stories, which can lead to more acknowledgment while also providing expanded movement infrastructure. As actions are taken, mainstreamization again has the possibility of being hindered. Conflict over policy goals or tactics, reflective of internal divisions within the broader movement, may increase reputational risk and dissuade participation, or frustrate coalition-building. While debate and differences in objectives and stories can invigorate and strengthen criminal justice reform, too much discord, disagreement on end goals, and distrust can splinter efforts.

Last, *expansion/mainstreamization* describes a normative acceptance of criminal justice reform as a legitimate vehicle for solving problems in the system. As more issues are brought within the general framework of reform, as its presence can be found in more sectors, as more topics are de-risked and become better resourced, as members of the public accept non-"lock-'em-up" alternatives, and have stories aligning with their ideologies that lead them to identify as supporters of reform, expansion/mainstreamization occurs. As part of this expansion, there is a natural opening of the Overton window, a concept that describes the range of ideas politicians can support that are widely accepted as legitimate.[22]

Important to emphasize about this model is that it presents mainstreamization as a cycle of building normative consensus and resourced networks, which does not easily predict the effectiveness of the movement. It has resulted in a decarceratory, ameliorative meaning of "reform" gaining national prominence and ubiquity from 2000 to 2020. But it is not suggestive of various stakeholders' success in planting that sensibility durably in US soil, the rolling back of incarceration to 1970s rates, or any other substantive goals. As Baz Dreisinger, founder of the Incarceration Nations Network said, "we have a movement [around criminal justice reform]: it is a critical mass of people engaging around the same thing. It doesn't necessarily lead to anything. We can be talking about the same thing until the cows come home. But what does it *do*?"[23]

Yet the softening of the US public across all sectors in the 20 years between 2000 and 2020 toward the idea of reform through mainstreamization might have been a necessary if not sufficient step. Punishment in the US is more heavily influenced by the public will than it is in continental Europe.[24] From elected prosecutors and judges to state and local representatives who craft laws to ballot initiatives that allow direct democratic input, how Americans *feel* and think about crime and crime control is enormously important. In *Incarceration Nation*, his study of the influence of public opinion on criminal justice policy over 50 years, Peter Enns concluded: "Increasingly the evidence suggests that to fully understand the US legal system, we must consider the public's preferences. The public played a prominent role in the rise of mass incarceration, and it will play a central role if mass incarceration is to end . . . the public has been moving in a less punitive direction for more than a decade and policies have begun to change. The time is right for reform."[25]

CHAPTER TWO

A MATTER OF MAGNITUDE: GETTING TO ACKNOWLEDGMENT

Even before prisons existed in the US as we would recognize them, there was a modicum of acknowledgment among some sectors that reforms were necessary. The Quakers' 1787 Philadelphia Society for Alleviating the Miseries of Public Prisons, for instance, advocated for a more "humanitarian system" than the Penal Code of 1786, which had led to hard labor as a punishment, often in the streets, or flogging.[26] There was nothing new about limited opposition to carceral regimes in the US. However, the scope of acknowledgment from policy leaders and, most important, the public, beginning in the 2000s departed necessarily from these earlier iterations because of the magnitude of the carceral system, the therefore expanded proximity to those impacted, and the association of the criminal justice system with increasingly unpopular, regressive attitudes and responses to substance abuse and/or mental health problems.

The magnitude of incarceration post-1970s—its human and financial costs—was indeed a principal element in the awakening of previously untapped constituencies. With a mere 200,000 people in prison in the early 1970s, with the War on Drugs yet undeclared, the US prison system was "roughly on par" with its European counterparts like those in Finland, Denmark, Norway, and Sweden, not only in scale but also in severity of punishments.[27] Many of these nations retained capital punishment at the time, while in the mid-1970s the US had not had an execution for almost 10 years. But post-2000—with 7 million people under correctional supervision daily; 70–100 million with a criminal record, and spending on police, courts, and corrections at $250 billion, or 40 percent of the national defense budget,[28] and untold opportunity costs—it was abundantly evident that the justice system was seriously off-track. It violated a wide range of moral and political principles. Some of these were deeply humanistic and rights-based, but others were utilitarian concerns about fiscal austerity, such as those offered by politicians and advocates in the passage of the Second Chance Act and in their advocacy of a slate of post-2000 state-based sentencing reforms.[29] "We are reaching a tipping point," Robert Rooks conveyed. "It's the net widening of the system. Everyone has a loved one, or they themselves have been involved, in the criminal justice system, impacting everyday people more than before. The average American today sees the criminal justice system as large and bureaucratic and cumbersome. It's holding people back, and not helping us get real safety."

Juan Cartagena, president of LatinoJustice PRLDEF,[30] emphasized that, for organizations like his, which was founded to protect the civil rights of Puerto Ricans, getting involved in the criminal justice space was almost inevitable given "the sheer numbers of mass incarceration.... There is no group I've talked to in the last 25 years of any persuasion—any race, of any economic strata—that doesn't have a member of their family or very, very close friend ensnared in the criminal justice system."[31] Topeka Sam, in the Harlem office of her Ladies of Hope Ministries, spoke optimistically of the potential of this larger ensnaring for movement expansion: "Criminal justice reform is the one thing in this country at this particular time that is bringing everyone together.... I think people are understanding this is starting to impact *everyone*. It's no longer "their" problem. It's now become *our* problem that looks like *everyone*. The numbers show it's one in three people that are impacted. That's not one of three Black people. That's the country."[32]

As Cartagena, Rooks, and Sam pointed out, by 2000, and especially by the 2010s, the incarceration binge had become a nationwide issue in the US.[33] Incarceration had become decoupled from the crime rate. It was reflective of policy and prosecutorial choices, from those requiring incarceration for a broader range of offenses to the lengthening of prison sentences[34] to vast increases in criminal justice system budgets. As a result, national survey data from the peak years of incarceration showed that, by age 23, 49 percent of Black men, 44 percent of Hispanic men, and 38 percent of White men had been arrested, along with 18 percent of Black women, 16 percent of Hispanic women, and 20 percent of White women (excluding arrests for minor traffic violations).[35] Proximity—which I define here as closeness through either personal experience of the harms of the carceral system or through that of a close loved one—was forced upon a sizable portion of the American population. Indeed, 64 percent of US adults in 2018 had an immediate or extended family member incarcerated. One in 5 had a parent locked up, and more than 1 in 10 had either a spouse or a child incarcerated. Nearly 30 percent had a sibling incarcerated.[36]

For all the discussion of American exceptionalism in punitiveness, the US prison system, while having a long history of unequally affecting racial minorities and the poor, was not so exceptional in scale in the 1970s. Incarceration had not directly impacted a large enough swath of the American population for the issue to be directly, personally felt by a critical majority. It *would* be felt as proximate to middle class White people post-2000, simultaneously as a destructive incursion of the carceral system and as a failure of public health support for the comorbid problems of substance abuse and mental illness. This was especially pronounced as the opioid/heroin epidemic of the late 1990s had been "largely a White person's scourge," with 90 percent of people trying heroin for the first time at the turn of the twenty-first century being White, altering the perception of addiction from an "inner city" and "minority" problem, as crack-cocaine addiction was, to one that could involve suburban and rural Whites.[37] That those addicted to opioids and caught up in the criminal justice system were given sympathetic depiction in popular media, not producing the same moral panic,[38] and in fact were leading to a reevaluation of the War on Drugs, was pointed out by DeAnna Hoskins of JustLeadershipUSA (JLUSA). "Now that the face of addiction has changed to White America, it's a public health issue," she observed wryly. "They'll just say we were unfair when we created a system that attacked the Black community because of the crack epidemic, but no one wants to go to the root of the structural racism this system was built on."

In her office on the grounds of a small Catholic college in Brentwood, New York, Serena Liguori, the executive director of New Hour for Women and Children, spoke of having a front row seat to this changed sensibility, as the War on Drugs came to White communities. "I talk to correctional officers who have family members incarcerated because the opioid epidemic is happening on Long Island, and it's impacting White families and upper-middle-class families. We're going suddenly—wait! We have to decriminalize because it's impacting everyone."[39]

Cliff Maloney, director of the libertarian organization Young Americans for Liberty, spoke candidly of how the proximity of White Americans to drug addiction affected their relationship with the criminal justice system: "I hate to say this. I think the opioid crisis in a way helped [reform efforts]. It helped introduce conservative America to the idea that good people can get addicted to this stuff." He was himself an example of that

Mainstreamization and the Movement

shift: "My dad did three years for PCP—drug possession with intent to sell. My dad runs a small business with five employees. I look at my dad, I don't think 'he's a felon.' He's a good member of society. I think it [became] easier for me when I started to share these ideas. Like—I *know* my dad, I love and respect my dad. Other people are having those experiences, they're finding and connecting just by sheer numbers."[40]

Leaders of other libertarian and conservative-leaning national organizations pointed to this widening of impact as a major underlying factor for criminal justice reform's salience among right-leaning White people. Marc Levin, founder of the influential conservative reform campaign Right on Crime, remarked: "The opioid epidemic has been pernicious in rural areas, and it's broadened the constituency for criminal justice reform. I see that continuing to gather steam. We're seeing emerging in rural areas and suburban areas a kind of appetite for things like bail reform and pretrial diversion. There's been a fundamental shift in how society looks at issues of addiction and to some degree mental health as well."[41] Holly Harris, executive director of Justice Action Network (JAN), noted that much of the advocacy for the First Step Act was done by JAN in Kentucky, home state of Republican Senator Mitch McConnell (who had an outsized say in whether to call a vote on the First Step Act), and that the state's openness to reform was direct result of the opioid crisis. "Kentucky is a place where— look, man—everybody is sick," she described. "This is a very conservative commonwealth. People love Donald Trump. But they're really supportive of reform and are willing to put aside partisan differences because almost everybody's had a friend, family member, or themselves, who has struggled with addiction."[42]

Personal proximity through an impacted loved one such as Harris described may have been one of the key drivers of public acknowledgment. However, national policy leaders at the beginning of the 2000s began to sound the alarm on the need to acknowledge that the scale of incarceration meant that the scale of concerns about post-incarceration for individuals and communities also had metastasized with unmet needs. "[Before 2000], people had not thought about—what about people coming home from prison? Prisons were out of sight, out of mind," Jeremy Travis reflected in his office at Arnold Ventures, with Central Park providing a dramatic backdrop through the window. Former director of the National Institute of Justice (NIJ) under President Clinton, Travis described with astonishment the changes in the reform movement he had witnessed during his 40-year tenure in that space. "As the [Clinton] administration was ending, as a product of the executive session on sentencing and corrections, I wrote the paper: 'But They All Come Back: Rethinking Prisoner Reentry.' Obviously, it was a reality, but 'reentry' didn't exist as a word before: that paper was the first time. [And in] 1999, Attorney General Reno and I released a concept paper calling for partnerships on reentry between police, corrections . . . communities, and reentry courts. It was the launch of what, in retrospect we would call—and I'm not objective here—the reentry movement." The attitude of "out of sight, out of mind" Travis described was possible in the early 1980s, when only 200,000 people left prison and jails every year. But by 2009, over 700,000 were leaving.[43] Acknowledgment was no longer the purview of the marginalized, or the "enlightened." It had become a societal imperative.

EXODUS AND REDEMPTION: IDEOLOGICALLY RESONANT STORIES

Many leaders in the reform movement would point to the influx of philanthropic resources, expanded attention and reach on media platforms in presenting issues (even if, as Serena Liguori noted, it was a "watered-down version" of them) as reasons for mainstreaming from 2000 to 2020. Before exploring this infusion of money and attention in depth, it is crucial to understand the ideologies[44] that fueled it: the deliberately cultivated, cohesive, and emotionally resonant narratives on why large-scale incarceration exists and why criminal justice systems should be reformed. "What I want to do is not try to pass a law. I want to change the narrative, the basis of how America talks about criminal justice," former Republican politician and president of Justice Fellowship Craig DeRoche, who stood near the Oval Office desk during the signing of the FSA, emphasized. "That's what we've set about to do in Prison Fellowship—reconstruct the argument differently so it can succeed. I believe that helped contribute to the passage of the First Step Act as well as other reforms."[45] Udi Ofer, director of the ACLU's Justice Division, viewed narrative shifts as even more essential to the criminal justice reform movement than to other movements, such as for marriage equality: "It's the greatest challenge of the movement. We're not going to win this with a Supreme Court decision, or with an act of Congress. You literally have to win peoples' hearts and minds."[46] Bill Cobb, former deputy director of the ACLU's Campaign for Smart Justice, pointed to the viral quality of "reform" as evidence of the success of some of those narratives at the end of the 2010s. "You have to have people talking about you," he related. "These were the conversations we had at the national ACLU. We were intentional. This is why we rolled out projects in the manner in which we did. This is why we spread like a virus, quietly. And so today *everybody's* talking about criminal justice reform."[47]

Helping propel viral reform messages were dramatic structural changes to media and corresponding shifts in consumption behaviors in the mid-2000s. Social media juggernauts like Facebook in 2004, Twitter in 2006, and Instagram in 2010 came into existence. But most important were narratives that converged into two "stories," which I label "exodus" and "redemption" following social movement scholar Francesca Polletta, who argues "Insurgents have always known that stories of exodus and redemption, of chosen people and returning prophets, are powerfully motivating of collective action."[48] Such stories are replete with culturally familiar arcs and archetypes that were deeply moving to individuals adhering to right- and left-leaning political ideologies, impelling reform forward. "Humans are storytelling animals . . . the implications for politics of the human impulse to think and communicate in stories, with plot and drama, heroes and villains—are profound. . . . Politics revolves around a contest of stories," professor of public policy Frederick Mayer posited.[49] In the context of social movements, "story" does not imply that the accounts are fictional but rather that facts or events are connected, intelligible, and inspire change. Certainly other frames—or ways of focusing attention on the problem of overincarceration—have been used, like the exorbitant costs of the carceral system, primarily but not exclusively by advocates on the right (see Chapter 6). However, the criminal justice system purports to ensure safety and justice—outcomes that most voters are instinctually reluctant to place a price cap on. Cost in itself is a low priority in determining support if unconnected to other core values and morally laden stories.

CHAPTER TWO

EXODUS: FROM OPPRESSION TO FREEDOM, FROM OVERINCARCERATION TO MASS INCARCERATION

By far the most successful story used to capture what was at stake in the criminal justice reform movement for those with left ideological leanings can be shorthanded here as the exodus: a story of struggle, violence, oppression and enslavement of an entire people, who would seek freedom led by one of their own. That incarceration in the US and globally unequally affects racial/ethnic minorities and the poor is not a new understanding, nor is the critical criminological argument that crime control and incarceration exist as a way of diverting attention away from the law breaking of the powerful and toward the marginalized and powerless. But in 2010, civil rights lawyer Michelle Alexander's *The New Jim Crow*[50] laid out a compelling, easily understandable narrative of these facts that intellectually and emotionally resonated, moving away from the more class-based arguments of the 1970s toward identity-linked arguments. Alexander provided a sometimes religiously framed origin story (indeed, it was called the "bible of a new social movement" by the *San Francisco Chronicle*)[51] of why *mass* incarceration exists in the US, using critical race theory to trace that *why* directly to the desire for racialized systems of social control of Black people beginning with slavery, then transmogrified into Jim Crow laws, then into the War on Drugs and beyond. "The original sin of policing in this nation is its attachment to the nation's first and most devastating sin: chattel slavery," ACLU director Anthony Romero opined in 2020 discussing his organization's role in advocating for major changes to policing, and in which we can hear echoes of Alexander's arguments.[52]

In this exodus recounting in *The New Jim Crow* and elsewhere, the criminal justice system is functioning "as it was intended, and . . . is not broken, it's doing what it was designed to do" as many left-leaning interviewees stated and repeated in abolitionist and left-leaning reform panels. And because it was functioning as intended, as part of this continuing legacy of White supremacist oppression of a people still living a form of slavery, resolution could only be through freedom from that system. For those on the sidelines, not directly impacted, this story required not being a bystander. "I'm incredibly hopeful about what I'm seeing in this movement," affirmed celebrity-activist Alyssa Milano, who used her platform

Mainstreamization and the Movement

to support the FSA among other justice reforms, as she described the exodus story's reach: "People I've never seen have conversations about police brutality or criminal justice reform or the death penalty are having these conversations. White people are having these conversations in a way that makes me feel the message is being heard. And the message is *We deserve freedom from oppression*. . . . White people are educating other White people about the history of mass incarceration."[53]

The New Jim Crow became an unexpected cultural phenomenon through which the exodus story of the criminal justice system entered popular consciousness, sitting on *The New York Times* extended bestseller list for 285 weeks, close to five and a half years, and selling about 2 million copies in 2023.[54] It was adopted by 600 college and law school courses by 2014,[55] becoming a required reading staple in college classrooms, receiving widespread media coverage, and used as an organizing tool by left-leaning reform organizations, and by faith communities through study guides.[56] It was even used in judicial decisions, cited twice by Judge Shira Scheindlin in her ruling declaring the NYPD's stop-and-frisk practices unconstitutional.[57] It overlapped with, and provided an intellectual scaffolding for, Black Lives Matter, cited by many left-leaning participants as a critical factor in creating a receptiveness to criminal justice reform (or outright abolition) during a time when high-profile judicial, and extrajudicial, killings of Black men took the national stage. Troy Davis's 2011 execution despite large national and international protests and appeals from global leaders; the acquittal of George Zimmerman in the killing of Trayvon Martin in 2013 (which led to the hashtag #BlackLivesMatter); the 2014 killings of Mike Brown and Eric Garner by White police officers (leading to the "hands up, don't shoot!" and "I can't breathe" rallying cries): these killings could be well accounted for by the exodus narrative of Alexander and others.

Prior to *The New Jim Crow*, the phrase "mass incarceration" was both infrequently and inconsistently used. Only toward the 2010s did it refer consistently to US overincarceration and as a system of racialized social control. In fact, "mass incarceration" was used in the 1980s by journalists to refer to the internment of Japanese Americans. In the early to mid-2000s, some references to mass incarceration in the news media were made, almost always in coverage of critical sociologists like Bruce Western, who had begun using the term following one of the first academic conferences on "mass imprisonment," convened by David Garland at New York University in 2000.[58] It was only after Alexander, that the word and its linkage to racial justice and a history of slavery in the country became widely accepted. Embedded in the public mind, the story became even more powerful as an organizing tool, fueled by other popular successes in books and film. Bryan Stevenson's book *Just Mercy* was released in 2014, and in 2016 the Netflix documentary *13th* by director Ava Duvernay, which featured both Alexander and Stevenson, debuted. As noted by Baz Dreisinger of the Incarceration Nations Network, who herself appeared in *13th*,"having a Netflix film became everything [to the movement]."

The spread of the concept of mass incarceration can be tracked by charting its prevalence as a term. Figure 2.2 shows the number of unique news articles that use the "mass incarceration" in Nexis Uni. An academic database with over 17,000 news, business, and legal sources, Nexis Uni gives a good measure of general news coverage of the topic.[59] In 2010, there were 132 references in its news sources; in 2011, 254; in 2012—the year *The New Jim Crow* paperback was released and sold 175,000 copies in two months[60]— 469, and in 2016, 5,009. There was a rather remarkable decrease in references in 2017 to 3,675 (perhaps a sign of the media's singular obsession with Donald Trump), before rising in 2018 and especially in 2020, the year of sustained nationwide protests against the filmed police murder of the unarmed Black man George Floyd. The public linking of mass incarceration with racial injustice in criminal justice—not just in incarceration but in policing, the gateway to incarceration—is implied by the fact that after George Floyd, *Just Mercy* and *The New Jim Crow* soared back onto national bestseller lists.[61]

Journalists' use of "mass incarceration" speaks to dissemination of the term and a sense of the focus of their articles. But another way of exploring how the story and frames of mass incarceration infiltrated public consciousness is by analyzing patterns of searches on Google via Google Trends data, aggregated information taken from millions of searches from 2004 and used by social scientists to gauge public concern, interest, and attitudes while avoiding desirability biases.[62] Figure 2.3 presents the relative

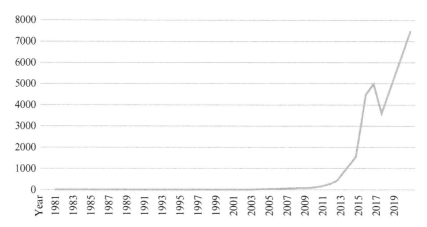

FIGURE 2.2. Nexis Uni articles using the phrase 'mass incarceration' 1981–2020

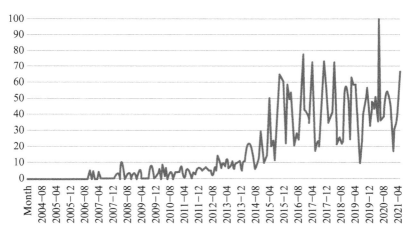

FIGURE 2.3. Google Trends: Searches for 'mass incarceration' 2004–2021

popularity of the search query "mass incarceration." Notable is not only that it was searched increasingly after 2010 but that the search reached its apex in the summer of 2020, after the George Floyd murder, again suggesting the term's association not only with criminal justice topics beyond incarceration (in this case policing) but with Black Americans' historical relationship with the criminal justice system. A final demonstration of this point is made in Figure 2.4, which shows the queries related to "mass

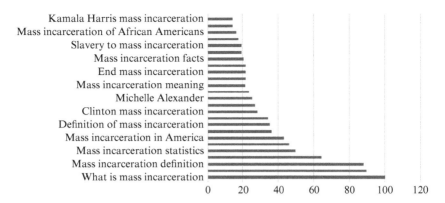

FIGURE 2.4. Google Trends: 'Mass incarceration' top related queries 2004–2021

incarceration" from 2004 to 2021. "Mass Incarceration of African Americans," "Slavery to Mass Incarceration," "Michelle Alexander" and "End Mass Incarceration" were the top related queries. Interestingly, two Democrats—"Clinton" (it is unclear which Clinton was being searched) and "Kamala Harris"—also were top related queries for mass incarceration but no Republicans.

THE REDEMPTION STORY AND CRIMINAL JUSTICE REFORM

The exodus story, with its linking of slavery to mass incarceration, and to an ongoing need to struggle for freedom, provided a narrative not exclusively resonant with the worldview of the left. For example, libertarians (a group that does not fit neatly into left or right but has a sizable presence in the reform space), could draw on some of this story: an oppressive government stripping citizens of freedom and overstepping into lives and livelihoods, especially for victimless crimes. Also, some conservatives adopted the language of "mass incarceration" in their opposition to it, focusing of the scale of the carceral state. "Mass incarceration is a bad thing that we've become exceptionally good at in the United States," began an article in *The American Conservative*.[63] Yet the connection to the origin story given by Alexander, Duvernay, and others in their use of "mass incarceration" is primarily found in left-leaning organizations.

Mainstreamization and the Movement   43

Because the exodus origin story was generally not adopted by right-leaning groups and libertarians, a different ideologically compelling story—one I call redemption—played this role from 2000 to 2020. The narrative fit well within a political demographic more likely to identify as Christian, read scripture, attend services, consider religion very important in their life, and look to religion for guidance on right and wrong.[64] According to this narrative, *over*-incarceration had its origin in a relatively recent error: an overreaction to the rise in crime and drugs in the 1970s, causing the system to be "broken" and causing fundamentally unfair, disproportionate harm by precluding the possibility for redemption among those incarcerated—the ability not only to have hope and be "saved" spiritually but to manifest that salvation through reintegration with family and community, contributing meaningfully to society through work. In this narrative, participation in the movement for criminal justice reform is to redeem the system by fixing it, bringing it more in line with an ethos that holds the possibility of redemption and forgiveness for individuals.

"The primary goal of the criminal justice system should be in most instances, redemption. That should be it. People shouldn't be defined by the worst mistake of their lives," said Jason Pye of FreedomWorks.[65] "Whether it's redemption, whatever you want to call it—it's a *second chance*." Though Pye himself did not describe himself as religious, he observed that some of the most ardent criminal justice reformers he had met came to the issue as a religious, moral imperative. He therefore explained to his activist community the biblical perspective of the reform mission and how to approach the work. The language of "second chances," and thus redemption, used in post-2000 legislation led by conservatives like George W. Bush and faith-focused conservative organizations such as Prison Fellowship, the largest Christian nonprofit dedicated to the incarcerated, captures the redemption story's emotional pull and connection to Judeo-Christian religion. George W. Bush, in signing the 2007 Second Chance Act, claimed that "the work of redemption reflects our values":

> The country was built on the belief that each human being has limitless potential and worth. We believe that even those who have struggled with a dark past can find brighter days ahead. One way we act on that belief

CHAPTER TWO

is by helping former prisoners who have paid for their crimes —we help them build new lives as productive members of our society.

Prison Fellowship, founded by Nixon White House counsel Chuck Colson, who spent time in federal prison for a Watergate-related crime and emerged repentant for his role in the War on Drugs, promoted a redemption-focused message through Second Chance initiatives. The annual "Second Chance Month" (a name it has trademarked), was founded in April 2017 partially to coincide with the Easter liturgical calendar, bringing attention to Christianity's message of Christ's resurrection and forgiveness. Craig DeRoche described the "lock 'em up" era and narratives that emerged during the 1970s as a fundamental moral and policy mistake that was being corrected: "Nixon changed the narrative from a Christian caring about someone's life and redemption and what they're worth to—discard the person," he related. "This mattered in the 1994 Crime Bill. It dehumanized people. With the First Step Act, President Trump said very loudly and clearly, 'I needed second, third, fourth, and maybe fifth chances on things in my life.' So it may not be the biggest policy bill, but it put America back on a different course from where we've been since the Rockefeller laws. Now you have the most conservative law and order guys saying this."

The stories of redemption and exodus led to a similar basic idea: that criminal justice in the United States has fundamental problems and there are moral and ethical reasons to be involved. Diagnosis and remedy, however, were predictably different, leading to tensions in the movement. The redemption narrative, in line with right-leaning ideology, sees the problems with criminal justice as emerging from a not-too-distant past and so "criminal justice *reform*" is emphasized rather than "ending mass incarceration." In my observations of the Prison Conservative Political Action Conference (CPAC), organized by the American Conservative Union in 2019, this difference in use was clear. Through a full day of panels, except for the few Democrats participating, no panelists or speakers used "mass incarceration."

Another look at how the mainstreaming of both overlapping yet conceptually different ideas played out in public discourse is found in Figures 2.5 and 2.6, this time investigating the presence of "criminal justice

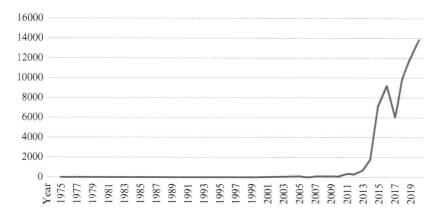

FIGURE 2.5. Nexis Uni articles using the phrase 'criminal justice reform' 1981–2020

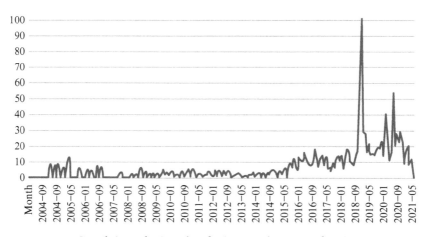

FIGURE 2.6. Google Trends: Searches for 'criminal justice reform' 2004–2021

reform" in the news and in Google Trends, which reveal that the term became widely used/searched after 2013, suggesting a reinforcing effect that benefited the movement as a whole. Notable about Figure 2.6 is that searches for "criminal justice reform" peaked during the FSA's signing. Figure 2.7 furthermore shows how the related queries' evidence for the term "criminal justice reform" is being connected to initiatives from "red" states and politicians. This does not necessarily mean that the right "owns"

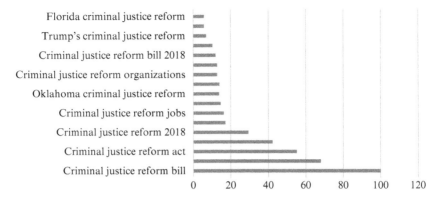

FIGURE 2.7. Google Trends: 'Criminal justice reform' top related queries 2004–2021

criminal justice reform or the left "owns" mass incarceration, but that together, the two stories that undergird their usage are pivotal in explaining mainstreamization in a public otherwise so polarized by ideology.

MAINSTREAMIZATION AND INFRASTRUCTURAL CHANGE: NATIONALIZATION AND THE WIDENING OF THE UMBRELLA

Mainstreamization was not only normative—that is, a matter of cultural replication and acceptance. It necessarily produced, and was the result of, structural changes in the organization of the reform movement. With acknowledgment and story, came an influx of resources. These resources drove a loosely organized yet nationalized movement, where connected individuals and advocacy groups were making criminal justice reform and/or ending mass incarceration a central part of their political portfolios, and new reform-focused organizations with national purviews sprouted in the more hospitable environment. Sue Ellen Allen, who founded Reinventing Reentry after her release from prison, noted, "[In the early 2000s] we were voices in the wilderness around the country. #cut50 didn't exist. The ACLU did, but they weren't really interested in prison."[56] Bill Cobb, former deputy director of the ACLU's Campaign for Smart Justice, remarked that prior to 2014, when George Soros's Open Society Foundation granted $50 million to the organization to wage a political campaign for criminal justice

Mainstreamization and the Movement

reform, the ACLU had been unknown for its work on criminal reform as such, and met with some derision by those already in that space. But with Soros's grant, the ACLU made its nationwide campaign one of the largest in its history.

Allen's sense of having been a "voice in the wilderness," without a coherent movement infrastructure, was shared among others who pointed out that national organizations' specific work on issues of reform was a phenomenon of 2000–2020, with an acceleration during the 2010s. Identity-focused civil rights organizations generally avoided criminal justice issues that did not fit into their civil rights framework and did not make criminal justice or mass incarceration a centerpiece of their work until the 2000s. The NAACP only started to work on criminal justice issues then with its careful foray into the space through its work on the collateral consequences of incarceration, with a focus on barriers to voting.[67] It broke its silence on mass incarceration when director Ben Jealous centered mass incarceration as one of the leading civil rights issues of the twentieth-first century and launched the "Safe and Smart Campaign,"[68] supported by both the Kochs and George Soros's Open Society Foundation.[69] LatinoJustice PRLDEF—an organization that has tried to bridge the immigration advocacy and criminal justice advocacy siloes—began its work on "what we would now call criminal justice reform" around 2005, according to president Juan Cartagena, when combating racial profiling of Latinos by police became a part of their work.

State-based criminal justice reform organizations at the same time were expanding their reach across the country. The successful state nonprofit Californians for Safety and Justice founded in 2012, launched its *national* organization, Alliance for Safety and Justice, in 2015, with the Tides Foundation as a "partner and fiscal sponsor."[70] In 2022 the Alliance announced that it was the nation's largest criminal justice reform organization, with a presence in 15 states. Other reform organizations, like JustLeadershipUSA founded in 2014 by formerly incarcerated leader Glenn Martin, conceived of themselves from the beginning as nationwide organizations. JLUSA by the 2020s had built a countrywide network of formerly incarcerated leaders and organizations, and expanded the scope of its advocacy to include a national platform to target federal legislation. This roadmap of reforms touted the power of change at that level and the institutional knowledge within the organization to make them.[71] And The Marshall Project, a major presence in online journalism focused exclusively on criminal justice from a reform-oriented perspective, was founded in 2014 with funding from former hedge fund manager Neil Barksy and other major high-networth players in the reform space, including the foundations of Laura and John Arnold, and Daniel Loeb. Like their more liberal counterparts, conservative nationally focused organizations were created or added criminal justice reform to their repertoire post-2000. Right on Crime, the national campaign of the Texas Public Policy Foundation, was founded in 2007; the American Conservative Union's Nolan Center for Criminal Justice Reform, in 2014.

The structural effects of the mainstreamization of reform meant nationalization but also that issues previously the focus of discrete, localized battles and or/self-identified movements were, willingly or not, pulled under that conceptual umbrella. In part, this was a function of the large national organizations from the right and left having newly homed in on mass/over incarceration with the capacity to fight on multiple fronts simultaneously and characterize those fronts as belonging to the same war. Right on Crime's "Conservative Criminal Justice Reforms" include nine initiatives, including law enforcement (e.g., police reforms to end militarization and civil asset forfeiture), overcriminalization, prisons, and juvenile justice. The ACLU's Criminal Law Reform Project focused on reforming police, public defense reform, and drug law reform. "Criminal justice reform," then, served as a kind of shorthand for the public to understand that an organization or initiative was focused on (1) decarceratory and (2) amelioratory objectives (e.g., reducing harms caused by criminal justice institutions and negative externalities). At least in the post-2000 period, the phrase would no longer be wielded by politicians as a goad for pro-carceratory agendas. "Criminal Justice Reformer" was even a title adopted by some in the movement on their LinkedIn and other social media pages,[72] and used in intragroup conversations in the 2010s and early 2020s.

Among the issues/movements subsumed under criminal justice reform were those for police reform or abolition—a critical issue in mainstreamization as, unlike prison-related abuses, problems with policing could be more publicly seen and documented, serving as front-facing evidence of internal criminal justice system dysfunction. Also crucial were the movements against the death penalty, against solitary confinement, drug/marijuana legalization or drug policy reform, reentry[73](which, as noted earlier, Jeremy Travis said, "didn't exist as a word" until about the year 2000), prisoners' rights, prison reform, prison abolition, sentencing reform, juvenile justice reform, victims/survivors, prosecutorial reform, restorative justice, collateral consequences, wrongful conviction, incarcerated women's rights, prison families, correctional education, parole and probation reform, the indigent defense/public defender movement, the movement to reform sex offender laws, bail reform, the rights of LGBT people in prison, and so-called "crimmigration."

These submovements were largely subsumed under the nationalized umbrella of criminal justice reform. That does not imply, though, that from the perspectives of political policy, public support, or social movement actors, there was equality of power or centrality among these groups/issues, or reciprocal endorsements of the groups' agendas as part of what it meant to be for reform collectively. Some have a long-standing history in the context of changes sought in the criminal justice system, whereas some are—necessarily—much younger. Some, like the movement to end capital punishment, have seen organizations embrace neutrality on other topics, avoiding conflict with important strategic partners, such as some victims' rights groups.[74] Where submovements and discrete issues exist under this larger umbrella—in the center or in the periphery; the density of connections and mutual support, also speaks to the ongoing process of mainstreamization—which stories are being told about which issue? Which submovements are given most resources, and see the most political action? Which are incorporated into a widening window of acceptability or, at the least—iterability—the *ability* to be named and articulated—to the public?

As with any issue becoming mainstreamed, lowest-hanging-fruit topics that, arguably, most easily gain political traction through transpartisan agreement, are in the criminal justice space also the most widely accepted as a common aim among submovements, and emphasized in outreach. (Although Udi Ofer of the ACLU would aptly argue: "I don't think anyone who is outside the academic space would categorize anything as 'easily achievable' in criminal justice advocacy work.") Very much centered in criminal justice reform, then, was sentencing reform for the most obviously sympathetic non-violent first time non-sexual offenses, especially drug offenses and decriminalization/legalization of marijuana, largely socially accepted but still a Schedule I drug. An already dramatic shift in public support for legalization of marijuana from 2000 to 2020 was punctuated by a large upward jump from 2012–2013 (from 50 to 58 percent supporting, also the same year that recreational legalization began),[75] perhaps again pointing to the influence of Alexander's *New Jim Crow* and its framing of the War on Drugs (support in 2020 stood at 68 percent in favor of legalization).

Other submovements/issues, however, are vying for a more prominent, normalized space under the reform umbrella, wanting to be part of the taken-for-granted changes required, such as LGBT concerns, death penalty abolition, crimmigration, and victim/survivors' issues. "It's hard to be representative in a movement that's not creating opportunities for you to even *be in* the movement," Dominique Morgan, executive director of Black and Pink, a prison abolitionist organization focused on supporting LGBT and HIV-positive people in prison, conferred.[76] She spoke of the sidelining of trans issues and people in criminal justice reform, and pressed for inclusion in that national conversation: "I've had some difficult conversations with a leader at #cut50 because I'm, like, I get it—First Step Act. But everybody I see walk out is cis. No one looks like me. I know a whole bunch of trans girls that was running dope for they men in the 90s that's doing a 20-year bid too. Why aren't they in on this? Reforms that are around gender aren't benefiting Black trans women because they're not expanding their work to those folks. Issues around fathers and men aren't looking at trans men."[77]

The anti-death penalty movement was similarly peripheral at the end of the 2010s. "[It] still operates quite independently of the wider penal reform movement to roll back the carceral state."[78] While none expressed support for the death penalty, several libertarian/conservative interviewees confirmed the view that, while they might be personally against it, it was possible for their organizations to maintain neutrality on this issue, even when Donald Trump showed enthusiasm for its more widespread use to deter drug trafficking.[79] Hannah Cox, a leader of Conservatives Concerned

About the Death Penalty, expressed, "We [in the anti-death penalty movement] have to fight sometimes to be at the table, I think for many years even as the criminal justice reform movement has really gotten its legs, the death penalty has been a bit siloed. The focus has been on nonviolent offenders, on reentry and workforce development. . . . Still, we're seeing more people welcome this into the fold in recent years." Laura Porter, a veteran anti-death penalty strategist and director of the 8th Amendment Project, noted: "There's a growing coalition in the wake of [California] Governor Newsome's moratorium on the death penalty that feels different from past coalitions, because people who are working on other reform issues are joining—it's more multifaceted, they're looking at [California's] Racial Justice Act—the analysis of the death penalty is broader, and it's less of that kind of siloing."[80]

"Crimmigration," or the nexus of immigration enforcement and police and the criminal justice system, at the national level remained mostly siloed, at the edge of the "reform" umbrella, at the beginning of the 2020s. Michael Mendoza, national director of #cut50, whose father had migrated to Mexico from California, stated, "I'm disappointed that we as a people haven't been invested enough in the conversation around immigration and criminal justice reform. There are strong connections we need to bring together and discuss."[81] Juan Cartagena described a two-way disconnect. On the one hand, the criminal justice reform movement has ignored crimmigration, and the specific ways in which Latinos encounter the criminal justice system: "Conversations about profiling, prison privatization, bail, are not centered around th[e] realities of Latino populations. They're still being talked about in primarily Black-White paradigms," he pointed out. "On the other hand, immigration/Latino rights groups excluded criminal justice reform in their own advocacy, not wanting to associate their immigrant constituents with criminality: "Latino national organizations [seemed] only interested in immigration abuse issues, immigration detention centers, which are really immigration prisons—border problems. The presumption is that Latino organizations are only interested in immigration issues and criminal justice issues are only of interest to African American communities. Which is BS on both sides. A lot of that is banked on the notion that in order for us to get immigration reform, we have to put our best foot forward. It's the premise of DACA.[82] But it belies the reality of our people." Cartagena had been a central figure in trying to convince major national Latino organizations to expand their purview, pointing to the inextricability of the concerns. "I started pushing [them] to understand you can't run an excellent youth development program for Latinos if you don't talk about the police officer that harasses them. You can't talk about a whole host of things including immigration without recognizing the intersection between criminal justice and immigration. I also started talking about marijuana legalization, but few national Latino organizations even talk about that . . . "

Victim/survivor issues, while having had, as Californians for Safety and Justice executive director Tinisch Hollins pointed out, "quite a big role in criminal justice conversations,"[83] have nevertheless had an uneasy relationship and space in the contemporary criminal justice reform movement. This has seen change from 2010 onward, spurred by reform leaders in California like Robert Rooks, who cofounded Californians for Safety and Justice, and later expanded its work nationally through the Alliance for Safety and Justice (LatinoJustice PRLDEF partnered with the Alliance for Safety and Justice on outreach to Latino victims of crime in Florida): "Until we brought forth a model of advancing justice reform with survivors' voices, experiences, and preferences at the center, there wasn't much attention paid to victims as part of the criminal justice reform agenda. That's starting to change. The reform community is now embracing the need to focus efforts on trauma and healing," Rooks noted.

Several reasons exist for this (gradually eroding) lack of attention and centering of these survivors/victims' issues as part of the reform umbrella. First, the victims' rights movement, despite the presence of groups like Murder Victims Family Members for Human Rights and other restorative-focused organizations, has served the political function, beginning in the late twentieth century, of reinforcing the carceral apparatus. Many well-funded victims' rights groups have received contributions from law enforcement or law enforcement-linked organizations,[84] and "law and order" has been the dominant ethos behind that push for rights,[85] resulting in tough on crime laws. Among many examples, the Justice for Victims of Trafficking Act of 2015, expanding federal mandatory minimum sentences, was signed into law by President Obama after being passed unanimously in the Senate. Second, the victims' movement was built around limited, often racialized and class-based notions of victimhood that created "legitimate/ good," "not legitimate/bad" victims, where the former were advocated for but the latter were deemed complicit in their own victimization. Tinisch Hollins, who lost both of her brothers to community violence, affirmed: "My victim experience wasn't reflected in a lot of the survivor policies that we have, that only name certain types of victim experiences."[86]

Given these factors, much of the focus of criminal justice reform on the left is centered on the harms of systems of punishment for those who have broken the law. Most rallies, conferences, and panels, while making sure to include the directly impacted by incarceration, do not include the discretely identified survivor perspective. Rebecca Weiker, program director at Re:Store Justice and a murder victim family member, said, "With criminal justice reform, you always kind start leaning toward the incarcerated side of things, away from survivor needs, though I see them as inextricably interlinked."[87] On the right, victims and survivors are often similarly left off of panels, spoken of through a kind a metonymy through the emphasis on public safety.

Most ostracized in the landscape of criminal justice reform—not taken up by right- or left-leaning national advocacy groups and unlikely to be processed through mainstreamization into public discourse—are those organizations and individuals pressing for reform of laws and policies impacting those convicted of sexual offenses, like Sex Offender Registration and Notification (SORN) laws. Sex offenses often serve as a convenient foil for offenses perceived as less egregious, and they provide justification for carceral regimes. For example, we don't need harsh punishment for drug offenses in the same way we do for those worst-of-the-worst monsters convicted of sex offenses; we need prisons for a few people and those few people include sexual offenders. This was particularly acute in an era of moral panic about sexual offenses against children fueled by QAnon conspiracies, and a public with overwhelmingly punitive and erroneous beliefs about those who commit sex offenses.[88] Some reform leaders described these issues as kryptonite threatening the forward momentum of the movement, however much they personally supported change. One reformer anonymously confided: "I would love nothing more than to be able to start working on the sex offender registry. But I don't think I can ever touch it. It is just radioactive. We're working to educate our activists, but there's some areas where they are saying: 'If you try to lead us there, we're not going to follow,'" hinting at an ongoing tension between where the reformers were on criminal justice issues, versus the general public, and the limits, even in a postdemocratic milieu of concentrated power, to decision-making without regard to mass opinion.

Mass opinion might not have been supportive of topics on the periphery of the reform umbrella, like SORN, when the registry was endorsed by almost three-quarters of Americans in 2017.[89] But criminal justice reform's mainstreamization post-2000—its ubiquity in political discourse and popular culture, its newfound shininess in philanthropy, and public support for its two basic tenets—was a remarkable phenomenon. It spoke not only to the power of a movement, nationalized by the start of the 2020s, and the resources and actions and influence that it was able to amass, but also to the fundamental scale of the problem with the carceral systems in the United States that made widespread acknowledgment almost ineluctable.

Such mainstreamization generated cynicism but was arguably much preferable to the "lock 'em up" ethos. It created a milieu where the submovements and issues had the oxygen to attempt to pry open the Overton window further. And certainly, other mainstreamed movements like that for marriage equality give evidence of the power of popular recognition, and the de-controversialization of what was once a divisive issue over time. Yet mainstreamization, and its necessary reductionism produced a mirage of consensus, a false sense of turnstile momentum where once one enters one cannot go back, of linear progress, and the newness of progress. It concealed the longer, messier history of the movement for more freedom and less immiseration. It hid fundamental rifts and tensions among movement players, and the actions of a new configuration of stakeholders necessary to achieve that national reevaluation. Departing from the story of the First Step Act and looking back at the critical period of change beginning in 2000, these stakeholders, their place in the movement, and the tensions between actors and objectives are the subject of the chapters to follow.

THREE

BILLIONAIRES, PHILANTHROPY, AND REFORM

FUELING THE FIRST STEP ACT

Doug Deason was still dealing with the aftermath of his home being narrowly missed by a tornado when our interview was scheduled in 2020, but he kept the appointment. He was fired up to talk about the First Step Act and criminal justice reform. The son of billionaire tech entrepreneur Darwin Deason and at one time a Dallas County Republican Party chair, he and his father had an outsized influence on what he described as the "Dallas Piggy Bank," where more money flows to Republicans than anywhere else in the country. He had donated close to a million dollars to the Trump campaign in 2016, while organizing fundraisers for Trump across the country and campaigning with Trump and Donald Trump, Jr. And, he had a prominent role in the First Step Act's passage, using his influence to prioritize the reform issue. Deason gave the story of his involvement with that bill and with criminal justice reform with an affable, conversational ease and candor about political inside ball. Unlike other high-networth activist-donors, he had not come to criminal justice reform through proximity to the harms of overincarceration via close family or friends, or proximity to the marginalized.[1] A brush with the possibility of incarceration as a teenager, and witnessing the double standard applied in his favor, had left him with a strong commitment to the narrative of "second chances."

As a teenager in Northwest Arkansas, Deason had entered a neighbor's house on the weekend using a key given to him by the neighbor's son and thrown a party so raucous that police were called. He was arrested and charged with felony burglary. His mother knew the people to call and reached out to city attorney Asa Hutchinson, coincidentally the future Governor of Arkansas, for whom Deason would fundraise. Hutchinson told her not to worry. The penalty could be reduced and Doug's record expunged if he stayed out of trouble. When Doug stood in front of the judge and Asa Hutchinson, they explained how bad a conviction could be for his life. He pled down to a misdemeanor and was put on probation: "I applied to the University of Arkansas that summer—I didn't have to check 'the box' because I was not convicted of a felony. It made me realize that if we hadn't had those connections, or we couldn't afford to pay a high-powered attorney to represent me, if I had been a person of color, I wouldn't have had the same opportunity. That's why I really started looking at second chances."[2]

Years later his commitment to working on reform was solidified listening to Charles Koch, billionaire founder of Koch Industries, during a 2012 Koch Seminar. He had been invited by a future Trump appointee[3] who was interested in reducing the prison population and had been bugging Deason to get more involved. As Koch spoke of reform and second chances to about 100 people, many wealthy, Deason said he was hooked: "It was like somebody told him my story! He's talking to me." After that day, he and his father started using their connections and capital to influence criminal justice reform, taking advantage of political opportunities such as having supported all Republican winners of statewide seats in 2014 and therefore having "every single person's cell number" to push legislation. With many Republican politicians as "good friends," he described the mechanisms of political influence such as bringing politicians to the Owners' Club suites during Dallas Cowboy games: "It's all billionaires and everybody is Republican and we're all politically active. Almost every game we have politicians with us and go from suite to suite. I call that the ATM of the Republican Party. Everybody comes through."

Billionaires, Philanthropy, and Reform　　57

Teaming up with the conservative Texas Public Policy Foundation (TPPF) and its national campaign Right on Crime, Deason would be involved in issues of clemency and pardons with Governors Ron DeSantis of Florida and Gregg Abbott of Texas, as well as sentencing reform, reentry, record expungement, and bail reform. In a 2016 fundraiser one-on-one with Donald Trump, one of the first questions Deason asked was for his position on criminal justice reform. Satisfied that Trump said he didn't think "a felon should wear an "F" on their forehead for the rest of their life," Deason committed right there to the campaign. Trump's election brought with it the offer of an ambassadorship abroad, which Deason turned down, asking instead to be an advisor on criminal justice reform however unacknowledged and behind the scenes that position would be. Told that the topic was not a "priority" for the White House, he pressed for a meeting with Trump's son-in-law Jared Kushner. Kushner, whose father Charles had been incarcerated for multiple counts of tax evasion, witness tampering, and lying to the Federal Election Commission,[4] had been given the position of senior advisor to the president. Describing his father's experience of incarceration as the "the most humbling, difficult, formative experience of [his] life," Kushner seemed like the ideal partner to get things done on reform with Deason. According to Deason, the two hit it off and planned a large summit on criminal justice in the White House, bringing together national advocates and political leaders to work on legislation.

Deason himself helped draft the invitation, specifying the conditions of the meeting—no asking for money—and sent it to a select group of Washington insiders, among them Republican senator John Cornyn of Texas, Democratic senator Sheldon Whitehouse of Rhode Island, Democratic congresswoman Sheila Jackson Lee of Texas, representatives from the DOJ, and leaders of large advocacy/policy organizations from the TPPF to the Urban League. The meeting, according to Deason, led to immediate discord, with Senator Whitehouse demanding that unless Republicans were willing to give up on demands for *mens rea* reforms, deals were going to be dead on arrival, with DOJ participants claiming that reform should really be a state issue, and with the Urban League pushing back against federal reform, making the case for its organization to receive $300 million to help tackle high rates of recidivism in the Black community. Deason fired back, criticizing the Urban League for asking for money against the rules of the invitation, the DOJ for not understanding the magnitude of the federal problem, and Senator Whitehouse, saying, "Your candidate Hillary Clinton would be in stripes right now if it weren't for mens rea." He and Kushner conferred after the meeting. Kushner agreed with Deason's reading of the situation: there was no point in involving "the left" at that point. "The left's expectations were going to be too far out to be able to accomplish, number one. Number two, we realized that the real challenge was not going to be winning over Democrats in the House and Senate [for potential reform legislation]. It was going to be [in winning over] Republicans," he said in explanation for their decision to leave out liberals from the inner circle—temporarily, except for trying to get the left to "sit on the chest of Democratic Senator Dick Durbin. And shut up Cory Booker. Shut up, quit talking about it, quit asking for the moon."

From then on, Deason and Kushner put together an advisory team of the right—conservative, libertarian, and faith-based. Subsequent off-the-record meetings would continue at the White House and through coalition calls in 2017 with Kushner and about a dozen participants—conservative Grover Norquist from Americans for Tax Reform, Adam Brandon from the libertarian FreedomWorks, Mark Holden from Koch Industries, a team from Right on Crime including Marc Levin, Craig DeRoche from Prison Fellowship, and representatives from the American Conservative Union, the Faith and Freedom Coalition, the Heritage Foundation, and the Due Process Institute. These would continue until, as Jason Pye of FreedomWorks said, by the end of 2017 "we knew we were going to make a run at it." Kushner would reach out to Van Jones and the #cut50 team in December 2017[5] to ask them to help with bipartisan buy-in for a draft bill that would become the First Step Act. The ideological contest around the content of the act would threaten to derail it in the months to come.

PHILANTHROCAPITALISM AND THE POST-2000 REFORM PHILANTHROPISTS

Besides Doug Deason, billionaire activists post-2000 would use their resources to advance the FSA as part of their philanthropic and political

Billionaires, Philanthropy, and Reform

focus on criminal justice reform, with varying degrees of involvement. The Kochs were "super-involved," while Third Point hedge fund manager and philanthropist Dan Loeb's head of public affairs, Jeff Cook-McCormac, spoke of their being supporting actors, using good relationships with the Republican conference, talking with individual senators who were sitting on the fence about the bill, and having multiple conversations with Republican leader Mitch McConnell.

"A lot of new philanthropists just really couldn't believe the injustice in the criminal justice system because they hadn't experienced it firsthand," Laura Arnold, cofounder of Arnold Ventures, one of the most influential philanthropic organizations in the criminal justice reform space, said in our interview. Limited direct experience (as we saw in Doug Deason's brush with the law) led some to the cause. Proximity led others. Michael Rubin, the billionaire cofounder of REFORM Alliance, received his education about the criminal justice system by witnessing the injustice experienced by his friend, rapper Meek Mill. Billionaire founder of Galaxy Gives, Michael Novogratz, said his daughter's internship at Bronx Defenders gave him a peek into the gross inadequacies of the system. Sir Richard Branson, billionaire founder of Virgin, met 150 people who had been freed from death row after having been found innocent.

Other philanthropists were drawn in through sheer incredulity and discomfort at the societal effects of incarceration. Dan Loeb was galvanized to enter the space after hearing statistics of the impact incarceration had on Black men at a 2015 American Enterprise Institute conference where, he said, "a light bulb went off," although his interest in criminal justice had begun earlier. In 2004, he followed the story of the harsh sentencing of a low-level energy-trading company employee to 24 years in prison, while others above him had pled out, getting no time. The unfairness struck a chord with Loeb, going contrary to his value system. And philanthropist and arts patron Agnes Gund, from one of the wealthiest families in the US, saw Ava DuVernay's *13th* in 2016 and was so disturbed by the racism it depicted that she promptly made a call and sold her prized Lichtenstein *Masterpiece* to hedge fund manager Steve Cohen for $165 million. The proceeds would be funneled to "Art for Justice," funding artists in prison and criminal justice reform organizations.[6]

The entry of billionaires and high-net-worth philanthropists and, relatedly, that of large philanthropic organizations (old and new) into the criminal justice reform space after 2000, of which the First Step Act's passage provides a snapshot, was a harbinger of, and a catalyst to, its mainstreamization, both normatively and structurally, as discussed in Chapter 2. It was a harbinger of mainstreamization in part because it demonstrated how the issue had become, at least in its broadest sense, uncontroversial and so unlikely to lead to a public relations nightmare, and it was one that resonated with individuals across the ideological spectrum. As Dan Loeb confirmed, after 2015 "criminal justice reform hit an inflection point and became more prominent and powerful. I think that's because it's a good cause. Education reform can get you in a lot of hot water. Like, nobody hates you because you are doing criminal justice reform, so there's not a lot of personal costs in doing it."[7]

Philanthropists' personal and institutional involvement in criminal justice reform, their use of social, political, and economic capital, is in itself nothing new. Much of the history of penal reform contains well-off, well-educated, and often sincere attempts at such elite interventions. In 1797 for example, Thomas Eddy, a wealthy Quaker businessman, used his power to steer reform in New York away from corporal and capital punishment. He worked with a state senator on legislation to construct the state's first prison, New Gate—where despite the stated humanitarian intention, there was forced labor for private contractors and frequent use of solitary confinement.[8] Eddy was among the first prominent Americans to call for separate cells for all incarcerated and to implement a classification system based on age, sex, and likelihood of improvement reminiscent of the algorithmic risk prediction systems of the current moment. He conducted evaluations of the incarcerated, concluding—200 years ago—that the causes of crime must be treated and that the vast majority of those in prison were kept there unnecessarily.[9]

Like philanthropists from the early days of penal reform, then, their criminal justice reform analogs of the 2000s–2020s used their position and capital to take advantage of opening political windows and to create new ones. They are *activist* philanthropists, not passive ones, and doers as well as givers. They work in their personal capacity to move legislation like the First Step Act. They intercede in sympathetic cases brought to their attention by close affiliates, often themselves prominent people from other sectors who could lend credibility to the asks. They also work through their foundations' support for, or indeed their own creation of, new criminal justice reform organizations. What was newer in the twenty-first century movement's philanthropist involvement in criminal justice was sociohistorical: it was taking place both during the era of philanthrocapitalism, which began in the late 1990s when wealthy private-sector actors were taking larger roles and infusing more money into addressing social problems, and concomitantly during an associated explosion in the nonprofit sector, mushrooming as more funding became available for professional work on reform and organizations absorbed, competed for, and deployed these resources toward various goals, with a range of strategies, messaging, and underlying ideological presuppositions.

The philanthrocapitalist movement in criminal justice reform could be discerned in the influx of unprecedented hundreds of millions of dollars into the space, in the number of billionaires and high-profile philanthropists signing their name to the cause (according to Galaxy Investment Partners CEO Michael Novogratz, around 15 to 20 such billionaires were involved in 2020),[10] and in the strategies pursued by foundations and the organizations supported. The scale of resources coming from the private sector was not unwanted—movement participants largely perceived that massive funding, and even more, would be needed to challenge the entrenched carceral system and implement new systems of harm reduction and community safety.[11]

The changed philanthropic landscape came with a shift to a nationalized movement, one that had prominent advocates with deep Rolodexes, was well-resourced compared to previous levels of funding and was professionalized (that is, led by salaried staff or policy experts, often with advanced degrees, who have careers "doing reform").[12]

This philanthropic moment revealed deep philosophical, ideological, and practical tensions within the movement, and created new debates it previously did not have to contend with because of a lack of funding. Many of these debates, for example about movement capture and co-optation, are perennial, faced by other large, complex movements, including the civil

CHAPTER THREE

rights.[13] How to achieve change—and who gets to decide what change looks like—in a political system nominally democratic but leaning toward a post-democratic landscape, where politics is largely in the hands of a small circle of government and corporate elites, political power is concentrated in the hands of a few in overlapping circles of business, politics, and entertainment, and media is decentralized? This is a particularly acute tension after *Citizens United v. FEC* (2010), which gave corporations, unions, and individuals the right to give voice to political preferences via unlimited independent expenditures. Their interests are much better represented in government accordingly.[14] Many at the grassroots level would argue that change has to be "bottom up." But without philanthropic firepower in this landscape, progress may be seriously hamstrung and individuals who could benefit from their intervention, left with little recourse.

THE LUCKY FEW: INTERVENTIONS IN INDIVIDUAL INJUSTICES

The impact of the entry of billionaires into the criminal justice space after 2000 and accelerating in the 2010s was at its largest scale and most systemic through their philanthropic donations and leadership within those organizations. However, several have demonstrated their leverage and capital in the political sphere through advocacy for individuals they consider blatant victims of injustice. "I think you try to save as many individuals as you can while you try to reform the system," Dan Loeb remarked in the Hudson Yards headquarters of his hedge fund, Third Point. Lava Records music executive Jason Flom, a board member of the Innocence Project and highly engaged in criminal justice reform, had been pressuring Loeb to get involved for years and was a key player in introducing him to cases like that of Bernard Noble, which immediately resonated with him[15]:

> I heard about this guy, sentenced to 13 years for two joints, riding the wrong way on a one-way street. I said, "This sounds really wrong." I've met with [Governor] Bobby Jindal. He solicited me a few times for his PAC. He's not a friend, but, you know, someone I can call up. I said, "Listen, Governor Jindal, there's been a terrible mistake, Bernard Noble is not a bad guy. Can you please commute his sentence?" He was polite, he sort

of wanted to help. There just wasn't the will to do it. So, we got Justice Action Network involved. I don't think we set out to spend two to three years on this and a couple hundred thousand dollars to get this guy I've never met out of jail. But [he added jokingly] we spent two to three years, and a couple hundred thousand.

In the Noble case, what originally began as a plea for clemency for an individual led to a change in policy that would assist others in obtaining executive relief. Justice Action Network subsequently lobbied for administrative changes to the clemency rules that had barred Jindal from granting Noble a reprieve.

Bernard Noble's case was one of several Loeb mentioned for which his intervention moved the proverbial needle. Jason Flom would also acquaint him with Tony Papa, Flom's friend who served 12 years of a 15-to-life sentence in New York for a first-time, nonviolent drug charge, and had a self-portrait displayed in the Whitney Museum. Papa was so burdened by the invisible punishment of his stigmatized status that he couldn't get a lease. So "we convinced Cuomo to pardon him," Loeb imparted. Additionally, formerly incarcerated activist Topeka Sam, who spoke at the signing of the FSA after her work with Van Jones and his #cut50 organization, was given a full presidential pardon by Trump after Loeb, Doug Deason, and others advocated for her. Loeb had made a call to Trump senior advisor Brooke Rollins. He said, "They were dealing with so many files—that might have made the difference." Loeb would later donate $1.5 million to Sam's nonprofit[16] and his team would tap her to help lead the new state coalition they were building, New Yorkers United for Justice, based on a successful similar coalitional model they used during their engagement with the marriage equality movement, New Yorkers United for Marriage.

Perhaps the most public of attempts by high-net-worth philanthropists to press for a more just outcome for an individual came from Philadelphia 76ers owner and CEO of Kynetic, Michael Rubin, in the case of his friend, rapper Meek Mill. Rubin had at first been incredulous at the Kafkaesque rules of probation and was astounded to see how the system was affecting Mill. Mill had been 19 in 2007 when he was arrested for gun and drug offenses, with a detective testifying that Mill had pointed a gun at him. He

64 CHAPTER THREE

was sentenced to county jail for up to 23 months, and 10 years' probation. The highly adversarial judge used Mill's minor probation violations—from traveling out of state for his own concerts to, most famously, popping a wheelie on his dirt bike on the streets of Manhattan—to restrict Mill's ability to make a living through touring, promoting brands, and recording. For Mill's 2017 probation hearing, Rubin wrote a letter to the judge mentioning his ownership of the 76ers and record of job creation, and attesting to Mill's character. He also attended and spoke at Mill's hearing, sitting alongside the CEO of Roc Nation, the entertainment company founded by rapper Jay-Z. Nevertheless, the judge sent Mill back to prison in 2017 for two to four years.[17]

Rubin marshalled his resources. On a call to the NBA commissioner, Rubin instructed him to "do whatever it takes to get Meek out." He recalled saying to Meek, "I will not stop until you're out of prison." He made donations to people hiring investigators to look into the judge's other cases for irregularities, then into the judge herself. With his own investigators, Rubin went back and interviewed all the police in Meek's case, finding a host of exculpatory evidence. The policing unit itself was dirty. He got an affidavit from a police officer attesting to Meek's never having pointed a gun, a key allegation in his conviction.[18] Mill—also backed by Rubin's billionaire friend and Patriots owner Robert Kraft and celebrities Kevin Hart and Jay-Z, whose Roc Nation would spearhead the #FREEMEEK campaign and related protests—would credit Rubin with getting Mill released on bail in 2018 and eventually having the conviction overturned after he was granted a new trial. Rubin picked him up in his helicopter from prison and brought him straight to the 76ers game to ring the opening bell. According to Rubin, he and Jay-Z had spent six months campaigning—and $6 million.

Meek Mill's story has obvious differences from that of, say, Bernard Noble—his own fame and wealth facilitated meeting Michael Rubin and celebrities who could use their combined resources to rally for his release. Yet both demonstrate how high-net-worth philanthropists have, through proximity, been led to acknowledge the failures of the criminal justice system, and become motivated to contribute to and publicly support reform via op-eds and radio and television appearances. Working on behalf of individuals was one such way—and one that in itself manifests some of the key tensions found in the movement. In the Noble and Mill cases, the advocacy was exclusively for highly "sympathetic" individuals whose legal incursions didn't carry much controversy and thus presented little reputational risk. From the philanthropists' perspective, this is perfectly reasonable. Despite their resources, they do not have infinite capacity to lobby for thousands of individuals, and the ones that hit a sympathetic nerve are more likely to move them. Also, a decision that backfires could stymie their ability to make future appeals to politicians. Still, advocacy for sympathetic individuals by philanthropists recreates the long-standing conundrum facing activists, to go for lower-hanging [read "safe"] fruit, although that limited action would do little to dent mass /overincarceration, or to take larger strides in addressing the root causes of overincarceration, including more felony prosecutions. Adding to the tensions of the reform movement, individuals were identified through personal networks. So, while the Bureau of Prisons (BOP) keeps over 96 percent of those who file appeals for clemency behind bars, and close to an estimated 12 percent of those in prison are actually innocent of certain types of violent crimes,[19] the success of those who have the serendipity of a philanthropist backing their release further emphasizes the legitimacy crisis where outcomes vary according to class, social capital, and race. At the same time, such cases demonstrate that, *even for billionaires*, the system is Kafkaesque and resilient to intervention, no matter how benevolent the intention and concerted the advocacy, and that (especially in Dan Loeb's support of Bernard Noble) not only the good of an individual's release from the system but also a systemic good may come of a private intervention.

A second, much more far-reaching way in which billionaires and high-net-worth philanthropists have entered the criminal justice reform space has been through establishing criminal justice reform as a goal of their foundations,[20] building a national organizational infrastructure to move on the issue, although not necessarily in concerted fashion. The changes to the movement this shift in philanthropy has brought have been massive, although their long-term impact on decarceration or on the conditions in prisons and for those returning from incarceration is still to be seen.

FOUNDATION SHIFTS

"The army has gotten really fucking big. I think we are a majority, not a minority. When you think of the rich guys, they're all getting on board. Not every one of them, but more and more," emphasized Michael Novogratz. His energetic zeal carried through pandemic-forced teleconferencing as he referred to the growing roster of prominent advocates of criminal justice reform. When we spoke, the billionaire founder of cryptocurrency investment firm Galaxy Digital had recently entered the criminal justice reform space, donating $36 million to the cause by 2019—the largest funding bucket of his Galaxy Gives foundation.[21] Among the knickknacks behind him on a bookshelf was the science fiction novel *Three Body Problem* by Cixin Liu, a ceramic mushroom (he was in 2020 one of the biggest investors in psychedelics in therapy), and a photo with "REFORM" in bold serving as a backdrop. In the photo, he stands with arms around Meek Mill and Michael Rubin, who had come to his office to make the pitch for joining their new organization, REFORM Alliance, to continue the momentum from the #FREEMEEK mobilizations. Also side by side on the stage of John Jay College of Criminal Justice in the photo was the CEO of REFORM Alliance, Van Jones, and founding partners Jay-Z and Dan Loeb. Fellow billionaires and new to the issue philanthropically were Vista Equity founder Robert Smith, Brooklyn Nets co-owner Clara Wu Tsai (spouse of Alibaba Group founder Joseph Tsai), and Robert Craft. Using the hashtags #reform and #fightdifferent, along with highly produced teaser trailers, REFORM began its work with $50 million in pledged funding with the objective to reform probation and parole.[22] Among its aims was to have a million people off probation in the US within five years.[23]

REFORM Alliance was one of the most self-conscious, manifest examples of the entry of "new money" philanthropic capital into organizations tasked with criminal justice reform, especially in the 2010s. Big philanthropy's footprint in reform was invoked consistently by interviewees as one of the most significant changes between 2000 and the early 2020s. Like the reason for mainstreamization of the issue, the most obvious change was in the scope of funding. "The millions of dollars being spent on criminal justice reform at large is stunning," Jeremy Travis of Arnold Ventures said in our interview. He described how, in the early 2000s while working at

FIGURE 3.1. REFORM Alliance launch, John Jay College of Criminal Justice, January 23, 2019, REUTERS/ Alamy Stock photo

the Urban Institute on reentry, "I started knocking on doors to try to raise money for this work and got turned down all over the place. No one cared about people in prison. A lot of foundations said their board wouldn't do this. My team and I got very clever about how to say, well, it's not *really* about people coming out of prison. This grant is really about health or really about unemployment, families, or children. The philanthropic community was just not there."

George Soros's Open Society Foundations were the first such major organizations to focus on prisons, beginning in 2001,[24] followed the same year by another significant left-leaning funder of criminal justice reform—Justice, Equity, Human Dignity and Tolerance (JEHT). Around 2005, the libertarian Koch brothers became involved with criminal justice reform and channeled large contributions to, for example, the National Association of Criminal Defense Lawyers to provide for indigent defense.[25] Even as reform funding began to gain momentum, said Laura Arnold about Arnold Ventures' 2011 expansion, "when we first entered the space, [there] were very few funders—very few. There were some very dedicated funders on juveniles, for example, there was the JEHT foundation—I'm not saying there was *nobody* but relative to something like the environment, climate, or education, certainly, to many of these larger issues, it was pretty lonely." That loneliness would only be amplified upon the JEHT foundation's shuttering in 2009 after its major funders' losses in the Bernie Madoff Ponzi scheme, a blow that *Prison Legal News* described as "a sad event for those interested in criminal justice reform, [one that] hurts criminal justice reform efforts."[26]

By March 2021, when asked about funds being channeled into the space, Galaxy Gives' Billy Watterson observed, "My guess is even in 2016, we were at like 200 million. And now we're around 600 million-plus coming from big institutional funders. And that's just the major funders. It's not counting the massive increase in mid-level donors or small donors." Beyond the major funders—Arnold Ventures, Koch Industries, Galaxy Gives, Open Society Foundations, the Open Philanthropy Project, the MacArthur Foundation, and the Ford Foundation—new funding came from a massive $350 million donation from Facebook CEO Mark Zuckerberg in 2021 for the Justice Accelerator Fund, a spinoff of his Chan Zuckerberg Initiative (CZI) to focus on criminal justice and immigration reform, in addition to a $100 million donation to its criminal justice advocacy organization, FWD.us.

The "civil rights piece of it really resonated," Laura Arnold posited [27] when asked to describe the individual motivations of philanthropists for reform. She had noticed that, after the death of Michael Brown and national protests against police brutality in Ferguson, Missouri, in 2014, there was "outrage at the injustice, disbelief that we are a nation that allows this." Similarly, Michael Novogratz observed that after the murder of George Floyd in the summer of 2020, money flowed into criminal justice reform from small and large donors alike, into organizations that were not linked to police reform, perceiving the linkage to be grounded in racial justice. The Bail Project, where he is a board member, received $25 million in donations just after the events of 2020. "Three different guys I knew called me up and each gave me a million," he imparted.

Still, as Novogratz would point out, criminal justice reform funding was dwarfed by spending on other issues. As we spoke, he pulled up data

Billionaires, Philanthropy, and Reform

on charter school funding, remarking on the long roster of prominent funders and wagering the funding to be a multiple of thirty times greater than that spent on criminal justice reform. According to Robert Rooks, Alliance for Safety and Justice cofounder, "We do not have a tenth of the resources needed to make real change happen. Even with the REFORM Alliance, Ford, Open Philanthropy . . . it's not close to being enough. . . . The way bureaucracies work is to protect themselves. We are dealing with an enormous, massive political force working to keep the criminal justice system the same as it is today. We need to make sure that we are strong at the local level, at the state level, that we're changing laws, that we're making sure the implementation of those laws is happening as intended. I can't find *one* state that's resourced enough to do that." Billy Watterson of Galaxy Gives agreed[28]: "[Even $600 million] is not fitting the scale of the problem. We've now built some strong infrastructure that can be scaled. If resources to do that don't come in fast enough . . . we're already seeing a backlash in 2021. Can society turn on criminal justice reform if crime rises? We need to invest more now, in implementing the wins that we're achieving, and fighting against the backlash."

Resources are critical to launch, grow, and sustain protracted campaigns, especially against such an institutionally embedded behemoth as the criminal justice system. Even with the perceived dearth of funding adequate to the task, the capital that was, and had the potential to be, mobilized through foundations changed the ecosystem of the movement. It led to a complex reality that defied simple moralistic "positive" versus "negative" evaluations, even when assessing a single funding entity. For example, Arnold Ventures alone had by 2021 made more than 450 criminal justice–related grants over 10 years. These ranged from general operating grants to the Innocence Project, grants to The Sentencing Project's efforts to prevent children being tried and sentenced as adults, to the much more controversial $3.7 million grant to Persistent Surveillance Systems' testing of the effect of its aerial surveillance program on violence reduction in conjunction with the Baltimore City Police Department. Arnold Ventures would later decline to make further investments in Persistent Surveillance Systems in other cities.[29]

Further complicating easy evaluations is the reality that, no matter size or political affiliation, conservative or avowedly abolitionist,[30] national advacacy and activist "grassroots" organizations take funding from individuals and foundations tied to wealthy philanthropists. In other words, there is no absolute distinction between organizations that are outside of the bounds of philanthrocapitalism and those that are within them. "Grassroots" may conjure an idea of self-driven funding and spontaneous civic engagement, but the reality is much messier, a matter of degree.

As such, the movement in its totality has been affected by characteristics of the philanthrocapitalistic shift in the criminal justice reform space over the past twenty years, a notable part of its mainstreamization. Among these characteristics, we will briefly look at four: the hedge fund approach, the corporatization of the movement through nonprofit professionalization, the subsequent competition for resources and "wins" in the space, and the often political, hierarchical driving of priorities.

PHILANTHROPY, RISK-TAKING, AND THE HEDGE FUND APPROACH

With such high-profile involvement of current and former hedge fund managers', financiers', and tech giants' philanthropic foundations in the criminal justice reform space—among them Dan Loeb, Michael Novogratz, John and Laura Arnold, George Soros, Mark Zuckerberg and his Facebook cofounder Dustin Moskovitz—the overlap between their views on what led to their success in business and what could lead to success in the criminal justice movement was to have far-reaching implications. In a sense, the age of philanthrocapitalism ushered in more of a hedge fund approach to funding the movement and therefore influenced the goals and strategies for it (indeed, the shift from some criminal justice–focused foundations like CZI and Arnold Ventures to LLCs, which can "function in part as a corporation and also as a business partnership," is one obvious sign of the change).[31] By hedge-fund approach, although of course the analogy doesn't hold perfectly for the philanthropic space, I mean characteristics of actual hedge funds that are adopted into a philanthropic entity. One, as Laura and John Arnold of Arnold Ventures described, is seeing grants and investments in criminal justice reform (and other social issues) as part of a portfolio. In that portfolio, riskier "bets" might produce greater "returns." For example, organizations in the criminal justice reform space that are

Billionaires, Philanthropy, and Reform

not large and well-established or have less conventional goals are "hedged" by investments in older, "mature," proven organizations. "We like to think of ourselves as producing big, bold ideas that will achieve transformative change. It's very important to have an investment portfolio that has a high degree of risk," Laura Arnold stated.[32]

A second, related characteristic is employing different strategies to produce returns on investment for shareholders, often by demonstrating "evidence-backed solutions'" success or failure through metrics—the kind of language that is abundant in the text of the First Step Act. The Open Philanthropy Project (OPP), among the top funders of criminal justice reform under program officer Chloe Cockburn, who self-described as an "aspiring movement nerd" on social media, is exemplary of this approach. Leaning heavily on quantitative assessments, OPP calculates grant amounts using the following equation: (number of prison years averted × $50,000)/100. OPP also has an equation for measuring expected returns on investment, where risks are taken if the potential financial savings are large enough.[33]

Arnold Ventures is perhaps the most front and center with what Laura Arnold described as "[a] really almost maniacal focus on data." She discussed the development of Arnold Ventures' algorithmic instrument for pretrial decisions about cash bail eligibility:

> When we started the pretrial work, we developed a risk assessment tool, which we have been validating and testing for years. We will continue to do that even as we've released it to more and more jurisdictions. I think one thing [we have done that] has been very meaningful to the space is that focus on empirical analysis. What do we know? What don't we know? Are we acting on intuition or on data? Do we not have enough data? Can we invest in gathering the data? There's lots of areas in criminal justice where there is a dearth of good data. So, part of what we're trying to do is build that data foundation so we can answer those questions and have a conversation that's not just based on [anecdotes, which] we don't think is the right way to think about policy. So there's lots and lots of funders who have come in and are much more visceral, who approach this differently, an emotional or ideological or a civil rights perspective. All of

which is very important. What we bring to the table is—we want to be in a position where we are sitting with a Republican, an Independent, a Democrat, a Libertarian, whoever wants to be in the room, and can have a conversation around the common denominator. That is the data.

Others are less focused on this type of model, taking a more qualitative approach. Dan Loeb, when I asked how he measured the success of a criminal justice reform investment, said, "We don't have economic models or quantitative metrics. I'd say all the organizations we've worked with, we feel we have quality content, like The Marshall Project or the Brennan Center, or we have real case studies [of successful outcomes]."

"Everyone has their own superpower," Michael Novogratz told me. "Macro traders [like me] think they can see the future—you recognize patterns and follow where the trends are going. I connect lots of little dots. I take pride in being three years early to this space, or having gotten into Bitcoin before everyone else did, or into psychedelics. So my investing regime is around systems change. What do I see happening and why? I was thinking this was a place where I could use my skills to help push the ball, which for thirty years they were pushing uphill. I got there, and I'm like—dudes! The ball is just cresting, and now it's gonna be more fun. That's why I'm telling my friends—get on the fucking bandwagon because the ball's going downhill. Get on the right side of history. If I can provide anything to this community, it's fresh eyes. You've been doing the same thing 30 years, no success. Sometimes you need some stupid, fresh eyes to say, why *that* number, why not *this* number?"

Dan Loeb, famous for his shareholder activism, reflected, "The similarity in social justice activism versus shareholder activism is that you have to understand the environment, the laws, rules, what the paths are forward, and you use whatever advantages, privileges, insights you have to try to change things. You work within the rules or change the rules to find—I won't say loopholes, but special cases."

Novogratz and Loeb captured another characteristic of the hedge fund mentality in philanthropy, which is the perceived advantage of reading large geopolitical, national, and economic shifts in the landscape to find opportune moments for intervention, as well as the managers' ability to

Billionaires, Philanthropy, and Reform

do so in a unique, insightful way. A part of this attentiveness to social and political patterns, as Laura Arnold said about Arnold Ventures' entrée into the space, is a "nose" for opening political windows, particularly ones where, due to mainstreamization, there is the opportunity for transpartisan buy-in to move the issue forward, decreasing the likelihood of stalemating. "We saw this political window very early on," she said. "There's lots and lots of things that we disagree with, on either side of the political spectrum. There's lots that we do agree with, and our work in criminal justice and everywhere else we focus on those areas of agreement, so in criminal justice we reached out to folks like the Koch Brothers, to the Ford Foundation, to MacArthur. Our first foray was this organization called the Coalition for Public Safety. The idea there was to just get in the room and to make a statement that this is not a partisan issue."

Last, the hedge fund philanthropic model views intractable social problems such as those associated with incarceration as market problems that require market-based solutions that are innovative and can be "scaled" in the same way other technologies are. Laura Arnold best captures this when describing Arnold Ventures: "We look to find market inefficiencies—by market I mean the nation, we typically work in the United States—we look for areas where the market has not achieved the optimal solution . . . we see severe inefficiencies due to imbalance of power and resources . . . [and so we work for] solutions that are workable and scalable."[34] Dan Loeb, in a *New York Times* interview, concurred: "Philanthropy is a lot more like hedge fund investing than you might think. You're thinking of ways to allocate capital and creating a scalable impact."[35]

What does the risk-based hedge fund mentality mean for philanthrocapitalism in criminal justice reform? In his critique of modern-day philanthropy, *Just Giving: Why Philanthropy Is Failing Democracy and How It Can Do Better*, Stanford political scientist Rob Reich provides a nuanced reading. On the one hand, he takes the entire system of philanthropy and nonprofits in the US to task because it allows the wealthy $50 billion a year in tax subsidies to be used in narrow, often self-serving ways. These wealthy donors have more money to give than ever, get bigger tax breaks for doing so, and influence policy, leading to a plutocratic/post-democratic system. On the other hand, he says, philanthropy *can* promote the aims of liberal democracy through a private/public partnership: "In the case of foundations, I argue that the goal is 'discovery,' an experimentalist approach to funding and assessing long-time-horizon policy innovations that, if successful, can be presented to a democratic public for the approval and incorporation into state policy or, alternatively, adopted into a market economy by corporate actors."[36] Thus, it is precisely the "risk-taking" that the foundations and LLCs of the ultra-wealthy can engage in by virtue of being *outside* of the public sphere, that can propel movements for change forward so long as such risks are not tied to short-term assessments. They are outside of massive government bureaucracies chugging along without appetite to reinvent themselves, and they don't have to live with the threat of losing elections. According to Jeremy Travis: "I'm all for risk-taking, in part because my view of progress is that it has been too slow. We need big ideas, breakthroughs, and maybe government will do it—that would be nice, but I think a lot of those breakthroughs will come from philanthropy. We're all impatient with the pace of change. How much longer can we wait? Will it be another 40 years? I've talked to my team here about taking more risks with ideas, people, and institutions. We have a big bet on prisons, gun violence, and national bail reform. Are those risks or smart investments? We have a goal of reducing unnecessary unjust pretrial detention nationally. We can do things that are hard for government to do."

Despite the ubiquitous language of risk-taking, some movement participants felt the risks being taken were too guarded, in some cases expanding the carceral system or diffusing more radical demands—for example, through algorithmic risk assessment, like the Public Safety Assessment (PSA) tool developed by Arnold Ventures, which provides data that informs judges' pretrial decisions based on prior encounters with police and courts. Furthermore, some interviewees believed that funders' risk *aversion* trickled down to grantees, limiting the potential of their work. As Adnan Khan, who cofounded Re:Store Justice while serving a 25-to-life sentence, emphasized in our interview, "*because* of funding, people are afraid to take risks."[37]

Jolene Forman, director of criminal justice policy for the Chan Zuckerberg Initiative, saw this dynamic firsthand: "It's hard to measure impact with criminal justice data, which is messy, and a lot of funders are focused

Billionaires, Philanthropy, and Reform

on that. . . . I think they prefer to invest in things that are safer and the problem with transforming our current legal system is you have to ensure that people are still safe." Forman's comment parsimoniously points to two other complications of "outcome"-focused funding interventions. There is a disjuncture between the premise that the problems of the criminal justice system can be technocratically solved and the reality that social issues are so overlapping and enmeshed that perfect double-blind experiments are impossible. And there is the ethical and political stickiness that comes with funding projects or policies that might backfire, creating harm.

DeAnna Hoskins of JustLeadershipUSA (JLUSA) pointed to other philanthrocapitalistic pitfalls. One is the potential conflict of interest between some philanthropists' investments and how they made their money and the cause to which they are contributing. Another is a general unwillingness to look at the more trenchant problems of racial inequality. "[Some funders] won't sit down with us because they know we're going to bring the pink elephant into the room—structural racism. If you are honest, you run the risk of not being funded." She added: "Funders say, 'We need more research.' Black people have been researched to death! But the research allows you to have control and have the voice."[38]

That Black people have been "researched to death," especially in the context of prison reform, without producing transformative, large-scale changes/solutions certainly has evidence in movement history. Prison reformers as early as the Progressive Era (1890–1950) would "gather statistics, analyze them through the methods of the social sciences, formulate resolutions, and seek public approval for their solutions. They turned to the government only when direct action was needed . . . these were part of an emerging group of professional experts who had chosen reform as a vocation . . . the idea of the expert or professional that emerged during the Progressive Period defined all future prison reform and rehabilitation efforts."[39] Probation and parole themselves came out of this period as part of a progressive ideal of rehabilitation and community improvement (in 1900 only six states had statutes governing probation). There was a "naive faith in scientific methods—progressives believed in successful parole predictions."[40] Meanwhile, the average sentence was longer under this "rehabilitative" regime than what had come before. Over 100 years after the start of the Progressive Era, Michael Mendoza, national director of #cut50 and a formerly incarcerated movement leader, diplomatically critiqued the continued reliance on that "naive faith": "There's still friction [between grantor and grantee].... Part of the friction comes [when] you have very intelligent people paying attention to data. Rightfully so, data is important. But they'd rather rely on that for direction versus helping support people who have lived expertise and trust in their work to make change."[41]

NONPROFIT PROFESSIONALIZATION, CORPORATIZATION, AND THE SCARCITY MINDSET

As just described, the emergence of "professional experts" who "chose reform as a vocation" has more than 100 years of history in criminal justice reform movements. However, as reform became less of a niche issue post-2000, it was de-risked and embraced by a contemporaneously emerging philanthrocapitalism. Correspondingly, there was an exponential expansion of the professionalized nonprofit sector built around and in reaction to overincarceration as well as in response to new funding opportunities allowing, among other things, "scaling up," hiring more staff, including those to handle grant-writing for more funding, in turn leading to a growing bureaucracy. A Johns Hopkins Center for Civil Society Studies report indicates the scale of proliferation generally: nonprofit work is now one of the most significant sectors in the US—the third largest workforce numerically—and better paying than its for-profit counterparts in most fields.[42] This phenomenon is pejoratively referred to as the "nonprofit industrial complex" or the "nonprofitization" of social movements among left-leaning critics who have pointed to some of its potentially deleterious consequences.[43]

As seen with other pressing social issues, criminal justice reform has, through nonprofitization, become heavily reliant on philanthropy-supported professional advocates and activists, an "elite class of nonprofit managers skilled at fundraising and formally educated."[44] There is a strong move toward making "reform" a career, with the corporatizing, business effect of this seen in the movement. Hierarchies of leadership and salary emerge; formal training and support-building is conducted by experts using tools and strategies replete with corporate buzzwords. There is an

Billionaires, Philanthropy, and Reform

emphasis on image and branding not just of organizations but also of the self *as* a movement actor, especially on social media, leading to cultivated "networked microcelebrity activism"[45] and the promotion of individuals' own names and "brands."

Assessing the impact of this extensive nonprofit sector again reveals movement tensions not easily resolved, as well as a need for nuance. When confronting overincarceration, having a dense network of nonprofits looking to alleviate harm, to fill in the gaps not filled in by government, or to remediate the harms *of* government, more resources—including more nonprofits with more professional leadership, training, collective action, and marketing and storytelling experts—seems like the minimum needed to tackle the Goliath of the criminal justice system. This is especially so given the rise in post-democratic civic disengagement in the US.[46] After all, as Robert Rooks from the Alliance for Safety and Justice pointed out, the criminal justice system *itself* is a massive, self-protecting, well-resourced bureaucracy with political teeth.

Yet, seminal social movement scholars Frances Fox Piven and Richard Cloward influentially argue that gains that marginalized people have made for their causes have come not in tidy fashion through leaders and organizers but through disruptive mass protests.[47] There is an inherent contradiction between the entrenchment of nonprofits devising carefully worded missions and cultivating stories to solve the problems of overincarceration and the immediacy of the need for change that would obviate their existence, between reform as a paid vocation and reform as a mass-based civic imperative. "The purpose of the work is to gain liberation, not to guarantee [an] organization's longevity," argues prison abolitionist Ruth Wilson Gilmore, cofounder (along with Angela Davis) of the organization Critical Resistance.[48]

At the Fortune Society in Queens, New York, one of the US's oldest nonprofits dedicated to the formerly incarcerated since its founding in 1967, Andre Ward, associate vice president of employment services and education, spoke to a central problem in the concomitant rise of the nonprofit sector in reform with the influx of foundation dollars born of philanthrocapitalist interest: "All of this element of competition [for money] hamstrings us from being able to move as a collective body," he stated. "It's just so nuanced. On the one hand you want to offer quality service provisions to people, yet the funders fund similar organizations to do the right thing. We are vying for pots of money to do the same work. This creates cleavages among people." Jessica Jackson, cofounder of #cut50, cited internal competition for funding as one of most surprising aspects of the movement she had encountered: "I've been disappointed to realize the role that the funding community and resources play in the movement. You're all fighting to get people out of prison, but what you don't realize is that you guys are going to fight each other because there's only so many resources and everyone has to get funding. I *hate* that. I hate that more than anything." Bill Cobb, former deputy director of the ACLU's Campaign for Smart Justice, viewed grant-makers in large philanthropic organizations enabling that fight and division. "New players like [the criminal justice program officer] from Open Philanthropy—too much money, too inexperienced. They have fractured that movement in the manner in which they've given out money, because they want to make kings and queens and have those individuals drive their outcomes. Very contentious, very formidable, very disruptive."

Movement participants consistently alluded to this unhealthy market of competition for resources and "wins" to show funders as corroding movement solidarity.[49] "The problem is at the grassroots level; we have this scarcity mindset. We don't stick together!" Bill Cobb lamented. But, as former Vera Institute of Justice president Michael Jacobson reflected, there is also "a lack of really specific unified strategies. Galaxy Gives does this, the Google guys do this, Microsoft does this. I'm sure they're all fine, but is it all sort of a cohesive strategy? If you really looked at it as a whole, you'd think . . . there must be a better way."[50] The perhaps inescapable model of vying for funding in the reform movement, where careers and organizational survival are on the line, is missing the mark.

WHO IS IN THE DRIVER'S SEAT? PHILANTHROCAPITALISM AND MOVEMENT PRIORITIES

Philanthrocapitalism began in the early 1990s, and its imprint on criminal justice reform is even more recent. Yet as social movement scholars have long observed, the funders of struggles have significant power in determining their content and direction. An analysis of funding's impact on

Billionaires, Philanthropy, and Reform

Black radicals and the civil rights movement shows that donations from foundations and corporations increased and flowed overwhelmingly into older, moderate organizations like the NAACP, away from young militant organizations.[51] Concerns about Black Lives Matter being co-opted have recently been voiced as the organization has accepted large donations from the Ford Foundation, one of the largest corporate foundations.[52] In his measured critique of philanthropy, Rob Reich writes: "Philanthropy is an exercise of power that reveals underlying social structures and hierarchies."[53] The power of foundations to determine the direction of a movement comes from their choice to fund organizations with whom they might be most ideologically aligned, but it also comes from methods they are willing to use to measure success and seek solutions and the priorities they establish for their grant-making. As Kevin Ring, president of Families Against Mandatory Minimums (FAMM), aptly observed, there is a kind of philanthropic Hawthorne effect in relation to criminal justice reform in the 2020s: "Donors getting in the field *themselves* shift the field. . . . When they decide to put millions of dollars into the Clean Slate Initiative, for example, all of a sudden that makes that a higher priority issue."[54]

Participants from across the political spectrum remarked on the top-down relationship of control—implicit or not—wielded by foundations and their ability to drive, and shift, priorities and to prioritize some movement leaders. DeAnna Hoskins of JustLeadershipUSA stated flatly: "Big money wants to control the movement, because they want to be at the top of the mountain with a white flag in the ground, saying they saved the Black people once again." Bill Cobb agreed: "They have the power. It's top down from philanthropy. . . . Money imposes that worldview upon all the institutions and all the players. I [might] want to do something in particular, but they want to give you money for what you *must* do. And so philanthropy influences criminal justice—they see shiny things that they can come and throw more funding at."

Michael Mendoza of #cut50 acknowledged the long history of control between foundation and grantee but presented evidence of positive changes in philanthropic culture he witnessed during the 2010s: "Now you have many foundations who are very vocal about their desire to fund organizations led by directly impacted, formerly incarcerated people." Still, this is a nascent development. Unseen is how transformative it will be or whether it will lead to what Bill Cobb implied are only new divisions, hierarchies, and "tokenizing," a problem raised by several interviewees that will be explored in Chapter 7.

AMMUNITION INTO THE GUNS WHILE AVOIDING A CIRCULAR FIRING SQUAD

The story of philanthropists' involvement in the FSA reflects the broader restructuring of the movement for reform as it transitioned into a mainstreamed, nationalized, well-funded, nonprofit-saturated cause. Occurring in an era of philanthrocapitalist desire to solve problems governments had been incapable of solving (or had created), philanthropists also seized on their ability to negotiate the close-knit power relationships of a post-democratic landscape to effectuate change. Given the scope of the social harms to be remedied, their artillery of economic and political capital created new possibilities for galvanizing public support through organized campaigns and media, influencing the messaging and policies of political leaders, even presidents, and building a more lasting infrastructure. As Herbert H. Haines notes in his study of the civil rights movement, "it has been rather firmly established that organized conflict cannot operate for long on shared discontent and moral commitment alone."[55] Thus, resources and capital are imperative. This chapter has imparted some of the enduring contradictions and questions raised for movement actors that come with this influx of resources. New relationships of power and influence are not easily resolved. At the heart of these questions is *who* gets to decide what changes and issues will be prioritized. And the key contradiction is that the better criminal justice reform is funded, the more such decisions are dependent on people in both philanthropy and the nonprofit sector who possess what the incarcerated generally lack: education, political power, wealth, and connections.

Marc Levin, founder of Right on Crime, pointed out that the shift toward foundations/grantors as "doers" was simultaneously a notable trend in the criminal justice philanthropic space—a characteristic of philanthrocapitalism.[56] This shift has influenced the answer to the question of who

Billionaires, Philanthropy, and Reform

decides what changes will take place and/or how, as those giving money are also interested in providing solutions, as well as having more direct access and lobbying heft with those in positions of political power. This shift conflicts with the simultaneous push on the movement's left to have formerly incarcerated and directly impacted people actively formulate the agenda for what is needed based on lived experience. Several advocates on the left supported a philanthropic model where there would be more trust in the leadership of the directly impacted and less tight control of how money is spent. "It's called 'funding the heat,'" DeAnna Hoskins explained. "Cut the check and get out the way." She described a divide between "old" and "new" funders in this strategy: "New money in this space [wants] to control how the money is being spent, to control the programming. They want white papers. Old money is starting to be at the point of—here's this money." Andre Ward of the Fortune Society, pointing to the advancement of many movements through subsidization by people of means, echoed Hoskins: "I think some funders are really understanding of the need to back up and allow those who are leading the work to lead it. Without attachments."[57] Michael Novogratz saw the philanthropist role along these lines. "You need Dan Loeb and me and others pouring ammunition into the guns of movement leaders," he stressed.

None of those interviewed from the nonprofit space suggested that "ammunition" from philanthropists or large philanthropies be eschewed wholesale. As mentioned, all were recipients of funding from the wealthy philanthropists. But some, like Taina Angeli Vargas, director of the California-based Initiate Justice, who like DeAnna Hoskins believed that "the role of funders is to fund us and get out of the way," suggested ways for the nonprofit sector to push back against charges of co-optation and movement capture[58]: "If I have a funder who is saying, we will fund you if you do X, and I firmly believe that this is not what we need to be prioritizing, I will not go after that money. Some money is too expensive." This conforms to the arguments of some critics of the nonprofit industrial complex, who say that foundations can be part of a strategy as long as they do not determine the direction of movement energy, divorce leaders from those most affected by criminal justice policies, or make grants a primary focus of organizational efforts.[59] This is something easier said than done with large amounts of money on the line. Yet even assuming that donors will cut checks and get out of the way, which leaders should receive those checks; who gets to speak for those affected by the criminal justice system; who is included in discussions of societal harm; which kinds of harm should be prioritized; what kinds of services, solutions, and organizations most deserve funding dollars; how are differences of opinion within the movement to be adjudicated—these questions exist not in a vacuum but in the context of extant relationships and connections, of formally arranged philanthropies and nonprofit institutions equipped to apply for and receive funds, capable of presenting compelling visions and evince their successes and alignment with the ideological priorities of the individual funder.

Individual philanthropists and large foundations are not themselves aligned, making possible conflicts horizontal as well as vertical. For all of the influence that Doug Deason had in pushing forward the processes that culminated in the FSA, and all the support of major philanthropies like Arnold Ventures and the Koch Foundation, more left-leaning foundations withheld support for the FSA, especially at the outset, linked as it was with the Trump administration. Van Jones and Jessica Jackson, as cofounders of #cut50, both noted the withdrawal of their liberal funders following their involvement with the Trump White House and the FSA. Van Jones was incredulous: "We *won* the First Step Act, and liberal funders refused to give #cut50 money that they had already promised to give. We won, and we've been punished for winning by the liberals." David Safavian of the American Conservative Union noted the fact that many philanthropic organizations are left-leaning: "You had folks in the nonprofit grant-making community that were hearing their friends on the left saying, 'Don't touch this.' They didn't tell us *not* to engage in it. But none of them were pursuing the First Step Act. It was only after it became absolutely clear that the bill was going to move that we were hearing more from grantors saying, 'Okay, tell him that we support it.'" He added sarcastically, "Profiles in courage!"[60]

Billionaire philanthropic leadership in criminal justice reform has been criticized by both the left and the right for being out of touch. On the left, critiques of philanthropy usually focus on it not being responsive enough to solutions from the ground in the direction of more radical/progressive reform (often focusing on the Kochs' or the Arnolds' involvement to show

Billionaires, Philanthropy, and Reform 83

how their solutions are regressive). On the right, the populist critique is that the elite are driving these reforms but that the involvement of left-leaning billionaires is the culprit. Tucker Carlson of Fox News railed: "Criminal justice reform has been one of the chief obsessions of our ruling class. . . . Normal people don't want criminal justice reform; they want criminal justice enforcement. They've always wanted that." He pointed to billionaire George Soros's funding of progressive prosecutors like Philadelphia district attorney Larry Krasner as a case in point.[61] The critiques from both sides imply a practical and moral bifurcation between the philanthropists and the "grassroots" or between the elites and the "masses," where the motives of the former are always pecuniary or intent on preserving their own privilege or narrow agenda, and the motives of the latter are more altruistic, purer, less tainted by monetary concerns. The reality, as always, is much more complex given human motivations that are themselves complex, the incentives that are offered, and the perceived paths available.

The contradiction of elite leadership in reform, whether billionaire philanthropists or the nonprofit sector, when those in prison are likely to be the most lacking in every kind of capital, is not easily resolved. Criminal justice policies in the US as described in Chapter 2 are highly responsive to shifts in public opinion. As we saw, punitive mass opinion was one of the primary drivers of overincarceration.[62] "More democracy," in the sense of a broad swath of Americans weighing in when it comes to criminal justice reform, may *not* equate to less incarceration or ameliorative outcomes, especially in the absence of viable, clearly articulated alternatives. Ultimately for criminal justice reform, the post-democratic tendency of elites to have an outsized influence over policy, where closed-door, invitation-only conversations among the connected can determine the direction of policy or reform, necessarily means that many voices are silenced. At the same time, democratic public opinion may be *more harsh* and resistant to decarceratory demands than what wealthy philanthropists envision. And nonprofits, themselves dedicated to reform, can become professionalized, bureaucratic, self-preserving echo chambers, upholding the status quo and lacking the uncompensated, sustained civic involvement and buy-in that would be necessary to make support for ending mass/overincarceration durable.

Philanthropy, as Rob Reich argues, might be enticed to dream a little bigger, present even bolder ideas and solutions, take more risks. This is one of the advantages of private giving and experimentation versus the public sector. Yet philanthropic dreams for the US criminal justice system still seem, for the most part, to involve cages. The focus on the tiny slice of "nonviolent, first-time drug offenders" still prevails. Dreaming a bigger dream and convincing the public to believe in its veracity, and having concrete alternatives in place at the local, state, and federal levels is essential, and will require a long-haul effort. Michael Jacobson expressed his worry: "My concern is 10 years, there will be some other issue they're into because this is not the thing where you can fund a huge legislative strategy nationally, and just three years from now declare victory. They are impatient because the want stuff to happen now. It's not like some stuff can't happen now, but it's a long-term commitment. To do really significant stuff here the politics are so complicated."

Connected to the philanthrocapitalist ethos of exerting its influence in criminal justice reform in the First Step Act and beyond are pop cultural figures and for-profit corporations entering the post-2000 space in force. They have applied their brands, lent their platforms to the cause, and in some instances changed their business practices to incorporate reform. "Just as celebrities are now an integral part of capitalism, due to their ability to touch and influence the mass market, so too they are becoming a key ingredient of philanthrocapitalism, particularly on issues for which mobilizing public opinion is crucial," according to Matthew Bishop and Michael Green, scholars of philanthrocapitalism.[63] In the following chapter, celebrity influence on the First Step Act—and the criminal justice reform movement of the past 20 years—is investigated.

FOUR

CELEBRITY ACTIVISM IN REFORM

THE FIRST STEP ACT(ORS AND ACTRESSES)

"It's amazing I'm not curled up in a fetal position on my bed." It was Fall 2020, and like many during the COVID pandemic, the interview with Alyssa Milano about her involvement in the First Step Act was prefaced by check-ins around health and family. Her 6- and 9-year-old were doing well after contracting the virus, but her bout with COVID-19 in the spring had been "just as awful as you can possibly imagine," with effects she shared with her more than 3 million social media followers to encourage taking the virus seriously. The actress, endeared to many for her performances as Samantha Micelli in *Who's the Boss* (1984–1992) and Jennifer Mancini in *Melrose Place* (1992–1999), maintained her active following. She had become what *The New York Times* termed a "celebrity activist for a celebrity presidential age." The liberal issues in which she had been involved since her teenage years were extensive. As a UNICEF ambassador, she had advocated, through direct lobbying, campaigning, knocking on doors, and using her personal platform, for immigrants' rights, children's rights, and women's rights. Her tweeting the hashtag #MeToo in 2017, sharing the story of her sexual abuse in Hollywood, propelled the viral discussion driving the feminist movement.[1] And in 2018, Milano added criminal justice reform to her roster.

Known for giving out her personal cell phone number to people she meets during her activist work, Milano began our discussion of the First Step Act and her activism around criminal justice reform saying, "I'm like an open book, so ask away!" She was one of more than 50 celebrities from television, movies, sports, and music who had tried to leverage their star power to move the First Step Act forward at a time when its passage was hanging in the balance in the fall of 2018. They had signed an open letter in November 2018 to Congressional leaders urging the passage of the bill before the mid-December congressional break, an initiative put forward through celebrity-activist Van Jones's #cut50. Earlier in the year, Artists & Athletes Alliance, an organization linking celebrities in sports and entertainment to Washington politics, had hosted a dinner where #cut50 educated guests about and galvanized support for the FSA. "As a result, more than 60 celebrities signed a letter urging President Trump to endorse the bill. The president announced his support during a press conference just a few days later," according to the Artists & Athletes Alliance in 2019, implying some causality, as they celebrated the FSA's passage at the Four Seasons Hotel in Beverly Hills with Milano, Danny Trejo, David Arquette, Brie Larson, and, of course, Van Jones.[2]

Among the signees of the letter to Congress besides Milano was reality TV star and daughter of OJ Simpson defense attorney Robert Kardashian, Kim Kardashian. She had taken a central role in the drama of the FSA's passage in 2018 after being moved by a viral video about Alice Marie Johnson produced for *Mic* in partnership with Google and with the collaboration of Topeka Sam, formerly incarcerated activist and director of the DIGNITY Campaign for Incarcerated Women at #cut50. Johnson, a 63-year-old great-grandmother from Mississippi, serving life in federal prison for a first-time nonviolent drug offense, had been denied clemency under President Obama. Kardashian hired Johnson a legal team. Around the time her husband, rapper Kanye West, was taking selfies wearing a "Make America Great Again" hat and expressing his support for Trump, Kardashian began communicating with the White House, determined to get clemency for Johnson. She called Trump's daughter Ivanka, whom she'd previously met informally at social functions like the Met Gala.[3] Ivanka then introduced Kardashian to her husband Jared Kushner, who was working on the prison

Celebrity Activism in Reform

reform efforts that would culminate in the FSA.[4] With Kushner's pressure, Kardashian was able to get a meeting with President Trump to discuss Johnson in May 2018. Following the meeting, Trump tweeted a photo with her in the Oval Office, writing, "Great meeting with @KimKardashian, talked about prison reform and sentencing." By June, he had commuted Johnson's sentence. A few months later, having been drawn into the wider prison reform discussion at the White House with Kushner, Van Jones and Jessica Jackson of #cut50 invited Kardashian to a meeting with Kushner, Ivanka Trump, and the bipartisan advocates working on prison reform.[5] From that point on, she was all in, organizing influencers and celebrities to use their platforms to push for the First Step Act.[6]

Like Kim Kardashian, who was friends with the #cut50 team's Jessica Jackson by way of Van Jones' introduction, Alyssa Milano said that Van Jones, Jessica Jackson, and #cut50 had been influential in her engagement with criminal justice reform and with the FSA specifically. "I had worked with Van on the Dignity for Incarcerated Women Act [in 2018]," she recalled. "News was coming out that pregnant women were being forced to give birth in shackles. Most women in prison are sexual assault survivors. They are denied any sort of hygiene items in prison, they have to purchase them, putting money back into the system, which I thought was horrible. So the DIGNITY Campaign was led by previously incarcerated women and changed policies in ten states, which I thought was pretty spectacular." Given her focus on women's rights, this seemed to Milano like a natural extension of that work.

Having been drawn into #cut50's DIGNITY Campaign when that team was working on the First Step Act's passage, Milano confirmed she would be supporting the FSA. "I was willing to do whatever, whenever I could, and it looked like Trump was going to pass it. I thought, well, this certainly doesn't hurt the cause. In my experience with Van and Jessica and the different organizers that were on the ground working towards some kind of solution, it seemed as though this was the right move." She expressed how sensitive and fraught decisions to endorse any cause are for celebrities and the manner in which they do so. She acknowledged that many criminal justice reform and civil rights groups felt the FSA didn't go far enough and were not in support of it. She also pointed out that Van

Jones's statements supportive of President Donald Trump during the push for the First Step Act had led more left-leaning activists to mistrust him. But, she concluded, "Something needed to be done. It's like that great Cory Booker quote: 'Don't let your inability to do everything prevent you from doing something.'" So she didn't confine her reform advocacy to the FSA. She threw her weight behind opposing what she perceived to be racially biased bail reforms in California and, through platforms like her podcast, promoted the voices of formerly incarcerated activists, including those working for prison abolition like Initiate Justice cofounder Richie Reseda.

CELEBRITY AND SOCIAL MOVEMENTS

Milano and other celebrities' endorsement of the FSA; Kardashian's direct lobbying of President Trump, himself a former reality TV icon; the involvement of John Legend, Jay-Z, Danny Trejo, Charles Dutton, Meek Mill, Kevin Hart, Nipsey Hussle, Susan Sarandon, and Danny Glover, among others: this celebrity activism by those with and without personal experience in promoting decarceratory, less punitive policies, and the *extent* seen in the criminal justice reform space post-2000 specifically was new. The star power attention celebrities drove to the issue was yet another indication of the reform movement's mainstreamization and changing composition over 20 years at the start of the 2020s. This shift, as we saw with the entry of billionaire philanthropists (Chapter 3), reflected a movement that had gained national acknowledgment because of the scope of the problem, and one whose resonant stories impelled more resource acquisition and action.

The new shift also reflected the movement's taking place in the era of philanthrocapitalism and the expansion of the nonprofit sector, with which celebrities had been intertwined as spokespeople, supporters, and fundraising magnets. It reflected post-democratic political transformations in the United States. In such a milieu—marked by low levels of trust toward the political establishment, political consumerism, concentration of political power in the hands of elites,[7] and competition for attention as media fractured—celebrities' entrance into criminal justice reform can be read as a rational, congruent way to build attention and advance movement objectives. They are "outside" the political establishment and yet have access to it; they hold a kind of moral authority with their fan base; their personal "brands" are well suited for consumer-based politics. Their platforms and direct reach to their fans hold as much, if not more, power than that of politicians or other social movement actors. Celebrities' ability to catalyze the political behavior of large numbers of people through modern media has been convincingly demonstrated by case studies and correlational evidence.[8]

But however new celebrity saturation in the reform movement may be in the post-2000s, celebrity politics and activism is not a new development of twenty-first century movements generally. Some scholars contend that fame as such has been embroiled with politics for millennia.[9] And it is not new for certain topics that are now lumped under the reform umbrella described in Chapter 2, such as opposition to the death penalty, which saw celebrity activism like Joan Baez's much earlier (though framed as a human rights concern rather than one of mass/overincarceration).[10] The blurring of boundaries between politics and celebrity in the US began as early as the nineteenth century and was used by all political parties as it became inextricably intertwined with the rise of mass communication in the early twentieth century.[11] By the 1930s, Franklin Roosevelt was wielding celebrity for political gain, tapping into endorsements from Bing Crosby and Humphrey Bogart.[12] Frank Sinatra and Marilyn Monroe were major supporters of John F. Kennedy, while comedian Jackie Gleason was Richard Nixon's golfing buddy and public endorser.[13]

Beyond endorsing politicians, in the twentieth century, celebrities became linked to issues, movements, and international diplomacy. U2's Bono is emblematic of this phenomenon,[14] with an intensification of advocacy beginning in the late 1980s.[15] As film stars were liberated from Hollywood studio publicity control in the 1960s and 1970s, they could be found in activism across a range of issues and were strategically used by movement leaders. Martin Luther King, Jr., drew on Joan Baez, Bob Dylan, Harry Belafonte, and Marlon Brando.[16] Actor Sidney Poitier, called a "soul brother" by King, gave the keynote at the 10th annual convention of the Southern Christian Leadership Conference.[17] These celebrities would become "key members of the campaign to end racial segregation in the South."[18] And perhaps there is no more famous twentieth-century example of a celebrity athlete becoming integrally connected with social justice causes and politics than charismatic world-champion boxer Muhammad Ali.[19]

Celebrity activism in social movements has brought division and scholarly debate over its utility in achieving goals. Critics have pointed to its potential corrosive effects on representative democratic processes and its cheapening of political discourse, as well as its usurping of grassroots organizing to bring about change.[20] The full-scale use of stars in criminal justice reform has reprised many of the same controversies. Several years removed from the passage of the First Step Act in 2020, Holly Harris of Justice Action Network mused on the reform movement's changes since the mid-2010s: "The landscape is driven so much now by money and celebrity. And, look. Anytime you can bring a celebrity to the table, if it's done strategically, it can be helpful. We've used and employed those strategies. But," she added reflectively, "celebrity for the sake of celebrity can be counterproductive. . . . I worry about the optics of a movement that is designed to help disadvantaged people and give a voice to the voiceless that is really predicated on money and sparkle and celebrity."

Harris captured a central paradox that was predictable for a movement becoming mainstreamed in a post-democratic era where access to political power is concentrated in the hands of a few in overlapping circles of business, politics, and entertainment, and where media is decentralized, no longer reliant on a limited number of broadcasts. Mainstreamization *by definition* implies that an issue is popularized. It is a movement phase in which celebrities, as widely recognized cultural symbols, play a quintessential role. They serve as shorthand for that process and contribute to it. They legitimize the movement as nonfringe and trendy, throw issues, especially for low-information voters, into public discourse and consumption, mobilize participation, draw media and money, and create a sense of shared community around an issue.[21] They allow entrée to political leaders who otherwise might be resistant to meeting with grassroots organizations. And yet, like the dynamic seen with philanthropists, celebrities taking the stage and influencing the direction of reform initiatives, assuming the

Celebrity Activism in Reform

mantle of support for arguably the most disempowered—after decades of criminal justice reform being all but ignored—has led to divisions about direction and tactics.

Movement participants' appraisal of celebrity involvement in criminal justice reform centers on four overlapping issues: the attention celebrities bring; the elite levels of access they generate; the identity- and experience-based considerations of stars as advocates for the cause, and their messaging and motives. While some movement participants interviewed for this project expressed a firm "pro" or "anti" stance on celebrity involvement, most held nuanced or ambivalent positions, often caught in paradoxes not easily resolved and in need of active negotiation and reconciliation. Philosophical questions central to this book about the direction of the movement arise: To whom, for whom, and by what means is change made? What is the significance of this for democratic processes?

ATTENTION: THE DOUBLE-EDGE SWORD OF CELEBRITY CAPITAL

"Any time Jay-Z squeaks, a billion people pay attention. Once you get Jay-Z, you could call the Pope and he'll join you," quipped philanthropist Michael Novogratz. He was talking about the power of the REFORM Alliance, formed in 2019 to tackle probation and parole. Its founders include Jay-Z, Meek Mill, and Van Jones.[22] Novogratz's comment points to a general characteristic of celebrities' "capital" of value to social movements: they have an unparalleled capacity to command the crucial but limited resource of mass attention. One scholar of celebrity goes so far as to define celebrities as the *embodiment* of that abstract capital,[23] born of their easy recognition by large numbers of people. Indeed, a 2019 nationally representative survey conducted for *The New York Times* showed that Kim Kardashian was recognizable by 67 percent of the US population, well ahead of politicians like House Speaker Mitch McConnell (35 percent) and Senator Cory Booker (28 percent).[24] Celebrities can bring attention directly through social media platforms and indirectly through mainstream media drawn to cover their appearances and actions.

This celebrity capital is a unique form of power in that it is distinctly fungible.[25] It can be monetized into economic capital, which is why stars are so eagerly sought for fundraising events or as spokespeople. Gala fundraisers featuring celebrities and often mimicking the Oscars in their use of red carpets and luxury venues, have been in the playbook of nonprofits since the 1970s, borrowing from the splashy Met Gala's groundbreaking incorporation of celebrity in 1972, which only accelerated around the year 2000.[26] Criminal justice reform organizations, since their mainstreamization and acquisition of more resources, have followed suit. The Doe Fund, a nonprofit working for forty years in employment, housing, and education of the formerly incarcerated, has used red carpet, "star-studded" gala fundraisers at the high-end Cipriani's in Manhattan since at least 2009, raising millions. In 2016, it brought in over $1.5 million in a highly produced evening featuring actor Ethan Hawke, who would be a financial patron of future galas, and fashion designer Steve Madden in attendance.[27] Formerly incarcerated activist Susan Burton's prominent nonprofit A New Way of Life, which provides housing and reentry support for women nationally, has harnessed star power for its annual gala fundraisers since 2009. On a red carpet in front of the Los Angles Omni Hotel in 2012, English actor Jason Isaacs of the *Harry Potter* franchise, hosted the nonprofit's fourth gala event; he answered questions for reporters, giving his pitch for donating to a New Way of Life and supporting incarcerated women.[28] His wife, a documentary film maker, became drawn to the cause, producing the film *Susan: A Documentary* about Burton and her organization. Well past 2012, the galas continued with celebrities headlining. During the 2020 pandemic, a virtual gala for a New Way of Life featured celebrities from film and journalism, including Natalie Portman, Soledad O'Brien, and Felicity Huffman, who had recently served 11 days in federal prison for her part in a college admissions scandal.

Celebrity capital is malleable not only into economic capital but also into political, social and symbolic capital,[29] more reason for social movement leaders, including those in criminal justice reform, to seek celebrity backing. Congressional hearings with celebrity witnesses, for instance, are three times as likely to have *New York Times* coverage. Political endorsements can be broadcast to large fan bases. With such power, celebrities have gravitas with politicians. They influence elections, sometimes decisively. Oprah's endorsement of Barack Obama had an estimated impact

Celebrity Activism in Reform

of 1 million votes in his favor.[30] They can mobilize political action, as seen when, in 2019, Susan Sarandon, who played anti-death-penalty activist Sister Helen Prejean in the film *Dead Man Walking*, joined fellow celebrities Rhianna, Beyoncé, LL Cool J, Meek Mill, and Kim Kardashian to pressure the Texas governor to stay the execution of Rodney Reed, who had strong claims to innocence in a racially charged homicide. Their intervention brought major news coverage to the case, and a petition online produced hundreds of thousands of signatures.[31] Reed's execution was stayed by the Texas Court of Criminal Appeals and he was granted an evidentiary hearing.

The elite status of celebrities born of their attention-as-capital brings them even more money, connections, and status, which grants them personal access to the highest levels of governmental power, allowing them through doors that would be steadfastly closed to others. We saw this with Kim Kardashian's meetings in the White House with Trump, arguably helping with the FSA's passage. Jeffrey Deskovic, who was wrongfully convicted as a teenager and spent 16 years in prison, and who is heavily involved in state-based coalitional work for changes through his own nonprofit, said he welcomed celebrity intervention for just this social capital: "They have a louder megaphone than we do, they can access people we can't," he explained. "I couldn't get a meeting with Obama, the closest I got was a senior staffer. The access fame gives—that's a responsible use of their platform." In examining the influence of celebrity on international development, Dan Brockington notes: "Within post-democratic environments celebrity advocates are most welcome allies for nonprofits, for they will give to the organizations they support welcome access to otherwise inaccessible places."[32]

Van Jones showed his exasperation with critiques of celebrity involvement in criminal justice reform in our interview. It was a tactic he enthusiastically embraced for at least 20 years as part of his larger vision for progressive movements becoming "a lot bigger and a lot stronger."[33] Far from rejecting a capitalistic embrace of reform, he has been trying to scale that embrace. Even before the start of the reform movement's mainstreamization in 2000, he had been a major player in activist groups in California. He had enlisted the support of rappers Mos Def and MC Hammer in trying, but ultimately failing, to prevent California's regressive Proposition 21,[34] getting MTV coverage of the artists' rallies for the cause. Jones argued for celebrities' integration in the movement on the basis of just that ability that Novogratz ascribed to Jay-Z: to get a billion people to pay attention with a squeak. He referenced a successful use of celebrity in the South African anti-apartheid movement as the playbook from which he and his organizations, REFORM Alliance and #cut50, were borrowing in integrating celebrity heavily into their advocacy, as most clearly seen in the celebrity letter to Congress endorsing the First Step Act. For Jones a case in point was the 70th birthday concert for Nelson Mandela staged in London's Wembley Stadium in 1988—a pop cultural, commercialized fusion with movement politics that brought massive attention to Mandela's incarceration and the South African apartheid system. Six hundred million TV viewers tuned in to watch a global all-star list of celebrity musicians perform.[35] This concert, like others in the 1980s that blended the commercial with the political, showed the "marketability of social consciousness" to businesses,[36] and refreshed the coffers of anti-apartheid organizations, increased membership, and, while difficult to quantify, had an impact on Mandela's release.

Events, social media messaging, and political actions by #cut50 and REFORM Alliance clearly displayed their leaning into this strategy to gather attention to and participation in events. During #cut50's national "Day of Empathy," first launched in 2017—"a day of action to generate empathy on a massive scale for millions of Americans impacted by the criminal justice system"—celebrities participated in mediated discussions and political actions with activists, politicians, and those who had signed on to their "empathy network."[37] Alyssa Milano gave a teaser introduction to the virtual Day of Empathy in 2020, pointing to the "hopeless" condition of people behind bars during the pandemic and imploring: "I encourage every state to take immediate action to support recommendations and reforms that protect people behind bars from the Coronavirus."[38] As predicted by research on the press attention granted to political events with celebrities, mainstream media outlets CNN, MSNBC, Associated Press, and Fox News have covered the Day of Empathy, most using the name of an affiliated celebrity in the headline.

The REFORM Alliance's tactic of even more heavily relying on celebrity capital (its board exclusively comprising celebrities and billionaire

Celebrity Activism in Reform   95

FIGURE 4.1. REFORM Alliance social media

influencers) can be visually appreciated by the social media image reproduced in Figure 4.1, where actors Robert Downey Jr. and Sean Penn, both of whom had been incarcerated, are depicted alongside formerly incarcerated activists Louis Reed (#cut50) and Susan Burton who through a graphic design effect are symbolically "celebritized."

In 2019, REFORM's advocacy of a Pennsylvania probation bill, SB14, one that had been considerably narrowed from an earlier, more ambitious rendition which caused internal controversy among more progressive allies, was led by cofounder Meek Mill.[39] The organization would use its celebrity capital and star power to put pressure on Mississippi governor Tate Reeve's veto of prison reform bill SB2123 in 2020, involving a radio campaign by rapper Yo Gotti.[40] In 2021 Mill traveled with fellow REFORM board member and billionaire Michael Rubin to sign HB 2038 with Virginia governor Ralph Northam. At the signing, Mill said, "I'm a rapper . . . that's how I got in a position to be here . . . I have the resources and I'm in a position to do better," articulating an unspoken consensus around celebrities and corporations as it relates to politics in the twenty-first century, that from those to whom much is given much is expected, that they were morally responsible to use their platform, to advance mainstreamed issues, particularly around gender and racial justice in the 2010s.

It was fitting, given Van Jones's invocation of both Mandela and the anti-apartheid movement as the model from which he was borrowing, that Meek Mill received the Nelson Mandela Changemaker Award in 2021 for his work with REFORM Alliance. He dropped the track, "Mandela Freestyle" in the weeks to follow, the lyrics directly discussing his use of his fame, platform, and wealth to bring together billionaires to support those, unlike him, not in a position to do so. The music video, gaining over 4.5 million views on YouTube in six months, included a montage of him with the REFORM Alliance cofounders flying in Michael Rubin's helicopter, with New England Patriot's owner Robert Kraft, and at his mansion with a pool behind him. There was also archival footage of Mandela, leading to a straightforward artistic endorsement of the kind of movement strategies that REFORM Alliance, #cut50, and others have championed: an unironic, fluid merging of capitalist ideals of success, philanthrocapitalist ideals of change, acknowledgment of inequality, pop culture, and a push for reform.

For Van Jones, celebrity involvement, and the attention it commanded, was not evidence of the movement's being usurped by a removed, disconnected elite—a frequent critique leveled at #cut50 and REFORM's celebrity leadership in the movement and at the celebrities themselves—but the opposite. He saw it as removing reform discourse from the realm of

Celebrity Activism in Reform

academic conferences, insular discussions, and incomprehensibility. For him, this was taking reform out of the hands of a group of activists who had been toiling in relative obscurity without much success. Perplexed, he asked: "People who have tens of millions of followers, products that tens of millions of people use—they can't be part of *populist* movements? If you take a public bus and ask *them*—normal people—would they rather have a movement that has the backing of celebrities, or a movement that has to fight without them. Ordinary people will say . . . 'No! We need help!'" From the perspective of having worked on criminal justice reform before entering into fame, he described internal movement opposition to celebrities as growing pains, an inability to accept the nonmarginalization of reform, the upsetting of its internal equilibrium, relationships, and status quo, as it entered the mainstream. "The reform movement was a smaller pond in the 1990s. We were always marginal. We were always small. We had the benefits of grassroots purity. . . . It was the main coin of the realm because there were no other coins to have. We were always righteous. And—we were always losing."

Serena Liguori, involved in state reforms since returning home from prison in the mid-2000s and executive director of New Hour for Women and Children, alluded to the movement dynamics Jones had described. She at first had been resistant to celebrity involvement, seeing celebrities as separate from the "real" work that those "on the ground" had been toiling to push through without any sparkle and glamor. But she had come to recognize celebrities' value to the movement, speaking of the difficulty she had in getting media attention for the work she was doing for thousands of women. "There's a reason why influencers are called influencers," she argued, adding "This has elevated issues we [in the reform movement] have been struggling to elevate for years, and now the general public is able to consume. It's bittersweet for those of us who have been doing the work."

Like Liguori, other movement leaders expressed their ambivalence about celebrities in the movement, with some steadfastly opposed to any pretense of their leadership. The most common concern centered on the very thing that makes up celebrity capital—which is attention. The attention they inevitably attract, as Holly Harris noted, can "take the oxygen out of the room," overshadowing those who have been long-time advocates and/or those directly impacted by the criminal justice system, from those without capital and glamour or from those who are simply more authoritative on the issues by way of expertise. This subverts the ideal of representative processes. Celebrity involvement can reify and replicate the same inequalities premised on financial status and connections that are mirrored in how the criminal justice system processes those with financial status and connections versus those without, especially in an environment of intense competition for funding dollars. Being connected with celebrity as an activist/nonprofit professional confers a vicarious fame and attention, opening doors to higher compensation in leadership positions, or sometimes financial support that can become an end in itself. "[Celebrity involvement] has turned the movement into a very ego-driven thing," according to Baz Dreisinger of the Incarceration Nations Network.[41] Jason Pye of FreedomWorks expressed, "People attach themselves to the celebrity, define their working in criminal justice by their association with a celebrity, or their ability to get celebrities to come out and do something." And Harris concurred: "We've got to be very careful we're not getting sucked into something that makes us *feel* like celebrities, that we're using this to benefit ourselves and our organizations. I do see the movement becoming a bit like the Hunger Games, everyone jockeying for position. It turns the narrative on its head about what we're trying to do, which is to help underserved communities, the people who have been most impacted by our broken justice system."

Scholars investigating celebrity in social movements have noted the conflict born of the double-edged sword of attention across issues. According to sociologist Zeynep Tufekci, "Social movements are attracted to celebrities for their ability to command attention; however, just like aiming for mass media coverage to acquire attention, this strategy comes with trade-offs." Among the trade-offs is that "they may drown out other movement actors and may dilute the message to make it conform to the needs of the celebrity persona."[42]

Identity-linked concerns about *which* celebrities—if any—can or should be a messenger for criminal justice reform; how representative they are of those impacted by the criminal justice system; how *much* presence celebrities should give; what their message should be, and for what

Celebrity Activism in Reform   99

objectives they should advocate are questions the movement grappled with at the start of the 2020s. After all, who speaks for a newly nationalized yet generally disaggregated movement battling for federal, state, and local change in multiple institutions and actors having varying political ideologies leading to very different end objectives?

CELEBRITY MESSENGERS . . . AND MESSAGING

In an interview with actress Whoopi Goldberg on *The View* about her documentary "Kim Kardashian West: The Justice Project," Kardashian described her motivation to tell the stories of incarcerated people deserving of second chances, that she wished "to be that voice for them and let people know there are two sides to every story."[43] Kardashian was not the only celebrity to use this phrase to describe their advocacy for reform. Actor David Arquette, a repeat #cut50 Day of Empathy participant and producer of a critical documentary, *The Survivors' Guide to Prison*, concluded his appearance in 2020 saying, "Let's give a voice to people that are locked up who are suffering right now."[44]

Adnan Khan, who founded the nonprofit Re:Store Justice while in San Quentin State Prison, was having none of this construction of the celebrity's role: "We're tired of celebrities trying to be our quote-unquote voice. . . . We don't need you to be our voice. *We're* out here. We need a presence, we need a platform. All the celebs are not centering or learning from the leadership of people who are formerly incarcerated."[45] The demand for celebrities, as for philanthropists, to use their resources to provide a platform for advocates and then promptly retreat to the backstage was echoed by participants on the left concerned about encroaching celebrity dominance of the reform movement, particularly those celebrities without the "authenticity" of direct connection to the impact of the criminal justice system. "You can't celebritize the movement," Andre Ward of the Fortune Society argued. "Celebrities are larger than life, they diminish the voice and power of those most impacted. Celebrities, give your presence, and then back off." DeAnna Hoskins of JustLeadershipUSA similarly posited, "I do believe there is a place for celebrities. They should utilize their platform, and then get out the way. Let the advocates run the show. Kim

Kardashian hasn't lived this life." Van Jones in his interview rebutted this view: "I believe that Kim Kardashian, the mother of four Black kids can be as much a part of this movement as somebody sitting in a prison cell right now. . . . They have no problem with each other. It's the other people who have this problem." The divide about movement building and strategy was clear, with both camps claiming moral authority for their tactics on the same basis—to speak on behalf of the people for whom they were advocating, with both claiming that representativeness and inclusivity were being denied by the other side.

The perils of celebrity advocacy that came without depth of knowledge or working in the movement in a substantive way—a kind of privileging of style, appearance, and puffery over substance—was pointed to by others. FAMM president Kevin Ring described the appetite for celebrity endorsements and activism in reform as producing a "carnival atmosphere, where it's like—please, Kim Kardashian, tweet *this*!" Jason Pye, stating his lack of interest in the celebrity dimension of reform (he had to ask his wife what Kim Kardashian was famous for), asserted that the celebrity dominance of the late 2010s and early 2020s diverted attention from activists or political figures deserving of the spotlight. For him these included libertarian-leaning figures who had advocated for the First Step Act, like Senator Mike Lee, who would resonate more with his target audience of right-leaning activists rather than delegitimize the issue in their eyes. The celebrities were, in fact, a distraction from the issues or an impediment to gaining support. For example, if a celebrity is very liberal, and becomes a "face" of criminal justice reform, does this signal to conservatives that the space is not for them? Pye, speaking of the celebrity letter endorsing the FSA, said, "[Other advocates] were like, can you promote it? I'm like . . . to who? Do you think our activists *like* any of these people?"

Involved as she was in a variety of left-leaning causes, Alyssa Milano was keenly aware of the contested nature of celebrity involvement in reform. This was especially acute as she had not been affected directly by the system when, at that moment, direct experience was being valorized. She was also a newcomer to the issue, wading in through the First Step Act. "We have to be aware of the fact that there are people that have been fighting for a really long time," she imparted. "To give them their kudos

Celebrity Activism in Reform

is really important. I try to be very, very aware of what's happening." She spoke of the imperative that she felt, because of her status as a public figure, to educate herself as much as possible on the issue, to "share my platform, hand over my mic, and highlight the work in support of what our Black leaders are doing throughout the country."

Given her stated willingness to share her platform and hand over the mic to the advocates, I asked how she decides which criminal justice initiatives or advocates to highlight or support through her platform. She acknowledged the complications and said, "For me, I look at the team of people that's behind it, but I also need to try to listen to the voices that are closest to the pain." She emphasized that as an independent activist who was not being compensated for her work, she did not have allegiance to one organization or group but would reach out to organizations with a racial justice focus, such as Black Lives Matter (BLM), White People for Black Lives, and personal contacts with experience of incarceration, like Richie Reseda. As for the messaging she put out on her platform, she indicated she tried to follow the lead of the advocates: "A message is usually created and distributed by the creators of the movement. . . . So, they'll send toolkits, where you will have the opportunity to make suggested tweets your own. Normally the organizers have put in the work of actually testing and working through messaging. By the time that I get involved, that is usually already in place."

Milano offered the example of her publicly pressing voters to reject California's Proposition 25 in 2020, which would have replaced the money bail system with one based on an algorithmic, computer-generated risk determination system to assess public safety and flight risk. Advocating against eliminating cash bail at first seemed counterintuitive. "I was so confused by the wording that I called a few of the leaders in the Black Lives Matter Movement. I asked—what are you doing with 25? They said, 'It's no, and here's why.' I tweeted out: 'California, it's no to 25 no matter how confusing that language is.'" Yet even if celebrities like Milano express willingness to turn over their platforms, following the lead of activists as she did in reaching out to BLM leaders for guidance on Proposition 25, a lack of alignment of goals, including among those with direct experiences of incarceration, can lead to very publicly played out rifts in the movement projected onto a wider stage, with higher stakes.

The issue of who has the authority to speak for a nationalized movement is that it comes with a range of ideological vantage points which, of course, means that even if a celebrity wishes to defer to messages from, say, a grassroots leader—there is the problem of *which* leader. Such divides pit celebrities and their attention-based capital against each other on behalf of reform organizations, sometimes with the same rationales and frames for why divergent policies should be pursued. "There's a lot of different organizations," Milano said in discussing some of the concerns around messaging. "A lot of them are doing really good work. But a lot of them are not communicating with each other. And that pisses a lot of people off." Unlike Milano, Danny Trejo, a formerly incarcerated celebrity/actor and a reform activist, argued *for* Prop 25. He appeared in social media ads as part of a campaign supported by labor unions, reform organizations like the Alliance for Safety and Justice, and Arnold Ventures, and funded by John Arnold and billionaire Stephen Ballmer, former CEO of Microsoft. Milano, BLM, and some civil rights groups were ironically aligned with the bail bonds industry and law enforcement, which fought against the bill—of course having completely different motivations for doing so. Both sides with their celebrity advocates presented the opposing stance as classist and racist. For those against Prop 25, algorithmic risk assessments had racism "baked in," whereas for those in support, cash bail was a marker of racism and classism. In his ad, Trejo said, "Why am I voting yes on Proposition 25? The money bail system is totally messed up. Long ago I was in that system for real. Under money bail poor people stay in jail, even for minor offenses. The wealthy—they get out, they've got the money to pay. That's discriminatory and unfair. Because the size of your wallet shouldn't determine whether or not you're in jail, vote yes on Proposition 25 to end the money bail system."[46]

The movement schisms over yes or no to Prop 25 and to endorse or not endorse the FSA demonstrate that the question of whether celebrities can be messengers for criminal justice reform, and in what capacity, is further complicated by the widespread impact of the criminal justice system. Robert Downey Jr., who featured in REFORM Alliance social media, had spent a year in prison. Meek Mill, as noted, followed his experience of incarceration by cofounding the billionaire-led REFORM Alliance. Jay-Z, also of REFORM Alliance, had been on three years' probation after stabbing a record producer in 1999. Rapper Nipsey Hustle, murdered in March 2019, had announced that criminal justice reform was a priority for him at the February 2019 Grammys and that he had joined the advisory board of the nonprofit WordsUncaged. The neat dichotomy between elite stars who engage in social causes from their penthouses and those who have been affected by the system they are advocating about and so have stronger claims to authenticity may therefore not exist. If a celebrity does have direct experience of the criminal justice system, are they automatically positioned to be vocal advocates for reform? Do they need to have certain types of incarceration experience, for certain crimes, with certain experiences of probation? Do they need to have given a certain amount of time to the movement before wading into the issues? Are all viewpoints tolerated? After all, being caught up in the criminal justice system does not imply monolithic thinking about causes or solutions, as Prop 25 exemplified. What if the advocates on the ground *themselves* disagree, each has celebrities backing their organization in campaigns, some of whom may be directly impacted, and each is funded by wealthy philanthropists? Or what if a nonimpacted celebrity, like Alyssa Milano, takes what some advocates consider a "better" stance, say on Prop 25, than the impacted Danny Trejo? It becomes apparent that tensions about celebrity advocacy go beyond surface concerns about identity and experience. The disagreements may be a means of projecting internal movement divisions onto a more public screen. And as in other movement conflicts, celebrity became a more abundant resource to compete for among organizations and leaders in the post-2000s in the bid to advance a particular vision forward.

SKIN, AND MONEY, IN THE GAME: MOTIVE PURITY AND CELEBRITY

Beyond the question of the legitimacy of the celebrity to speak for the reform movement on the basis of experience/identity, "skin in the game," and purity of motives was also a matter of importance raised by movement actors, celebrities, and others. Alyssa Milano reflected on some perceived opportunism among celebrities dabbling in the activist space: "I have a lot of resentment when I see a celeb that just shows up for the photo-op, where

I'm like—oh, really? Where have you been the last four years?" Unlike Mohammad Ali, who faced prison time and was banned from competitive boxing for his political stances, most celebrity activism for an issue like criminal justice, which had been de-risked, could be performative. It might even be financially advantageous. DeAnna Hoskins, in speaking about Kim Kardashian, observed, "She feels sorry and has sympathy. But she also did a damn reality show off of it. It's kind of like if you buy a hungry person a meal—don't call the cameras to let them know you bought the meal."

The multimillion-dollar investment of Jay-Z, through his entertainment management company Roc Nation, in a new "decarceration start up" smartphone app called Promise was cited by left-leaning interviewees as demonstrating the ulterior financial motives of celebrities. Cofounded by the former manager of the musician Prince, also the former CEO of Van Jones's Green For All organization, Promise was paid for by fees from government agencies[47] and develops care plans for people released from custody pretrial and postconviction which "monitor and support participants by helping them know when they're supposed to appear in court and remind them of obligations like drug testing and substance abuse treatment."[48] It provides "real-time location tracking and immediate notification of violations" to government agencies. Jay-Z, in arguing for the benefit of Promise, said, "Money, time and lives are wasted with the current policies. It's time for an innovative and progressive technology that offers sustainable solutions to tough problems. Promise's team is building an app that can help provide 'liberty and justice for all' to millions."[49] While supporters commended Promise's technological solution to barriers faced by those on probation and parole, it was firmly opposed by The Black Youth Project and other progressive organizations. The expressed concern was its impact in widening the reach of government surveillance, its failure to tackle the root causes of incarceration, and its lack of understanding of criminal justice data systems.[50]

The Promise app and its financial backing from Roc Nation, headed as it is by a former celebrity-entrepreneur who is also leading a nonprofit that promotes criminal justice legislation potentially affected by such technology, regardless of *actual* primacy of motivations, illustrates some of the

Celebrity Activism in Reform 105

complexities inherent in a mainstreamed movement unfolding in a socio-historical context of philanthrocapitalism and post-democracy in the US. The injection of celebrity capital into the reform movement in the 2000s and accelerating in the 2010s was both a consequence and a driver of its mainstreamization, intersecting logically with the entry of ultra-wealthy philanthropists from other fields into the space as it became a nationally acknowledged problem. The same cultural impulse and even a demand for those with the resources—money, platform/attention, or both—to advocate for social justice change, to "not be silent" and, if not taking the lead overtly, to actively amplify or accelerate change, drives both celebrities and philanthropy. And yet the fact that celebrities, like businesses and corporations, have "brands" raises the question of ulterior motives. Their advocacy could be seen as a handmaiden to their wealth acquisition, only carried out if it does not threaten their class position in society.

With the expansion of career-based advocacy for reform, including well-compensated positions in the nonprofit sector, and the "celebritizing" of advocacy, questioning individual motivations may turn out to be a circular firing squad. Purity of intent is impossible given the complexity of human motivations. In assessing the role of celebrity in reform, objective outcomes may be of greater utility, even if they must be measured using different yardsticks according to political orientations and goals. If celebrity is producing a hyper-consumerist simulacrum of a movement, as the ill-conceived 2021 CBS reality television show *The Activist* almost satirically portrayed,[51] where attention exists, great marketing and buzzwords, but there is no increased, sustained civic engagement by individuals and groups that are not on the payroll, then a reevaluation is warranted. If the end goal is to *become* celebritized rather than celebrity being used as a tool; if possibilities for action are being constrained because the circle is being drawn so tightly among overlapping networks of cultural, financial, and political elites that don't allow unfunded and underfunded "voices from below"—the plot has been lost. Reform participants from left and right and libertarians are raising flags about celebrity's centrality, its going from opportunity-creating to opportunistic.

The FSA brought tactical and conspicuous use of celebrity in the reform movement into the spotlight, allowing analysis of one instance of how its dynamics have played out post-2000 as reform became mainstreamed. Also involved in the FSA, and intertwined with celebrity entry into the space as hinted at in Jay-Z and Roc Nation's funding of the Promise app, were corporations, which beginning in the 1980s were being shown the "marketability of social consciousness,"[52] an ethos that gained traction in the 2000s. The capital that corporations offered the movement mirrored many of the attributes of celebrity capital, such as the ability to command attention through media platforms, brand recognition, the conferring of legitimacy on an issue by making it appear "normal" and de-risked, and political heft through lobbying to influence legislation and regulations. They also mirrored the resources of big philanthropy in their ability to provide large amounts of funding directly to nonprofit initiatives. However, corporations brought an additional form of power—the ability as employers to change internal, industry policies and practices that affect the lives of people with a criminal record. Predictably, as with the other interconnected groups of stakeholders, the entry of corporations into reform created its own divisions and controversies, reprising many of the fundamental questions about the movement's ends and whom they were for, what change meant, and who was able to best steer that vision.

FIVE

REFORM®: CORPORATE SOCIAL ACTIVISM

THE FIRST STEP AND SECOND CHANCES

Jenny Kim, who led Koch Companies Public Sector, LLC's criminal justice portfolio as its deputy general counsel and vice president for public policy, was in her 10th year advocating for criminal justice reform when we spoke in 2020 about Koch's 16-year involvement in that space and in the passage of the First Step Act. Having grown up in the 1990s in a lower-middle-class apartment complex in Queens, the daughter of South Korean immigrants, she had encountered boys in the complex who cycled in and out of Rikers Island, New York's infamous jail. Bucking her parents' advice to avoid their eyes in the elevator, she would try to find out their aspirations. After time in the G. W. Bush White House as a fellow, and joining Koch to do political law compliance, she ended up enmeshed in the company's criminal justice work, becoming, as one article would describe her, a "force of nature for second chance hiring."[1] With a lawyerly matter-of-fact enthusiasm, she punctuated her descriptions of the reform process with colorful analogies to dieting and sports. "You can certainly try Beyoncé's vinegar and lemon juice diet and in eight weeks lose all the weight, right? That's not a long term, sustainable solution," she described about businesses' entry into second chance hiring.[2]

CHAPTER FIVE

Under its libertarian CEO Charles Koch, more than any single corporation, the Koch Industries conglomerate, the second-largest private corporation in the US and liberal bogeyman had put its political capital behind the FSA. "Koch played a huge role," Kim stated. "We had been working on some version of the First Step Act for the last four years, and in 2018, it took a lot of meetings at the White House and on the Hill, galvanizing as many contacts as possible. To an outsider it may have seemed like it happened overnight, but the relationships and touch points—it's no different than a campaign running for office. It really was a bill over 10 years in the making."

Koch had indeed been an insider. Activist-philanthropist Doug Deason, whose involvement in the FSA was described in Chapter 3, was a good friend of Koch Industries senior vice president Mark Holden. A former jailer turned lawyer, during his 25-year tenure at Koch, Holden had involved the company in criminal justice reform for about 12 years.[3] Deason, by his own account, had brought Mark Holden into the inner circle of those discussing prison reform at the White House. Holden was present at the September 2017 White House Office of American Innovation listening session on criminal justice reform, focused on reentry. He would stay with the process through its stages, with conversations among conservative groups and then later with the liberal #cut50 as an advocate until the FSA's passage, when he stood behind Van Jones at the signing in the White House in December 2018.

As noted in Chapter 1, the FSA contained provisions directly related to business. It mandated prerelease planning to ensure that those being released from prison had the documentation necessary to be employed. It also reauthorized the Second Chance Act of 2007 that improved transitions to employment. However, besides Koch Industries, few corporations gave their official imprimatur to the act. The #cut50 list of supporters of the FSA did not include a section for businesses and corporations, though some foundations linked to businesses appeared. Dave's Killer Bread Foundation, for instance, endorsed the FSA. Tied to the largest organic bread company in North America, it was co-founded in 2005 by a formerly incarcerated businessperson whose willingness to hire others with criminal records became exemplary of second chance hiring. Telecommunications

Reform: *Corporate Social Activism* 109

giant Verizon and tech giant Google were among the exceptions, giving public endorsement of the FSA. Verizon, with 135,000 employees and a market cap of $225 billion, weighed in at the final hour using hashtags #CJReform and #FirstStepAct on its social media account to "[urge] Congress to move quickly to pass the First Step Act and to continue progress on other criminal justice reform legislation." The company simultaneously released a statement: "Verizon Supports Criminal Justice Reform." Notable about this was the emphasis on bipartisanship, on the bill's focus on people who had committed nonviolent offenses, curbing recidivism, and the shared economic and social interests that should motivate "every American" to support the bill. There were no appeals to identity-based concerns over disparate impact but only to civil rights generally. This would change dramatically after 2018. Google, having partnered with *Mic* to produce the digital op-ed about Alice Marie Johnson that sparked Kim Kardashian's interest in her case, also released a statement in the days following the FSA's passage. The company's senior vice president for global affairs used Johnson's case as a jumping-off point to describe its support for the bill as a first step of more to be taken for reform. He noted its "long" endorsement of giving "second chances," for example by banning the box on employment applications asking whether the applicant had a criminal history, efforts aimed at "improv[ing] our criminal justice system," and "end[ing] mass incarceration."[4]

Other exceptions where individual companies made statements about the FSA were CoreCivic and its competitor Geo Group. CoreCivic, formerly Corrections Corporation of America, a private prison company, in 2018 owned and managed 77 correctional, detention, and residential reentry facilities, with 78,000 beds. Damon Hininger, its CEO, submitted a strong letter of support for the FSA, indicating CoreCivic had lobbied for the bill. He pointed to efforts to "diversify" the company and focus on reentry services to reduce recidivism—hundreds of millions in national reentry centers and reentry programs in the company's facilities[5] followed the leveling off and decrease in the US prison population in 2010—which were seen as the future of the industry.[6] Geo Group, "specializ[ing] in the ownership, leasing and management of correctional, detention and reentry facilities and the provision of community-based services and youth services" likewise applauded the bill upon its passage. Criminal justice reform meant decarceration, and Geo Group would not fight against that, especially as private prisons only housed 8 percent of the federal and state incarcerated population in 2019. Instead, it would position itself to be a formidable part of the "treatment industrial complex," including e-carceration, making it eligible for the $375 million authorized for post-prison services by the FSA.[7]

CoreCivic and Geo Group were predictable FSA supporters based on their direct material interest. More unexpected was the entry of corporations only tangentially impacted by mass/overincarceration into the reform space in their collective endorsements through some of the most influential business organizations in the US. The nation's biggest business lobby and the world's largest federation of businesses, albeit criticized for representing a narrow group of interests (e.g., banking and fossil fuels[8]), the US Chamber of Commerce (USCOC) championed the FSA. On November 20, 2018, the hundred-year-old organization made a statement before the US Senate praising the FSA and pressing for its enactment.[9] The statement's language closely mirrored Verizon's, lauding the act's bipartisanship, invoking its need to reduce recidivism, and pointing out its facilitation of "gainful employment upon return" through job training: "These individuals will be better prepared for the millions of job openings that exist," the USCOC stated.

A Business Roundtable (BRT) statement in support of the FSA would follow a week after that of the Chamber of Commerce. At the time an almost 50-year-old organization comprising 200 CEOs from the leading companies in the US with a collective 20 million employees and $9 trillion in annual revenue, the BRT was another heavyweight of political influence. An additional letter, directed to Senate leaders "in strong support of the First Step Act and meaningful criminal justice reform," would come on the eve of the Act's passage, when the spectre of Congress adjourning without passage looked like a possibility. Jamie Dimon, CEO of JPMorgan Chase, and Wes Bush, then CEO of defense contractor Northrup Grumman, as leaders of the BRT, signed the letter, which succinctly pointed out, with the preferred language of corporations in 2018, the benefits of the "bipartisan" bill: the "pathways to a career" it would make available, its reduction of recidivism, and its benefits to society at large.[10]

Reform®: Corporate Social Activism

This high-profile corporate backing of the FSA in 2018 was reflective of what Jenny Kim emphasized in our interview as "the biggest shift over the past ten years in the criminal justice reform space: businesses' willingness to hire and retain people with criminal records and consider them part of the likely workforce, and to be able to share those successes. That's a big cultural change." The shift was also remarkable because, as Executive Director of the Stanford Criminal Justice Center, Debbie Mukamal, described: "there were employers who hired formerly incarcerated people before 2000, but they absolutely did not want to be recognized for it. When we would try to say, 'Let us give you an award for doing the right thing!' they'd say, 'No thanks!'"[11]

Corporate social activism (CSA) itself (e.g., companies taking stands on social issues to create change by influencing the attitudes and behaviors of actors in their institutional environment[12]) didn't include, for the most part, criminal justice reform issues as such prior to 2000. But CSA began long before then. It is a hallmark of post-democracy, a merging of consumerism, politics, and social movements. After World War II, most significant US-based social movements, including civil rights, women's rights, gay rights, and anti–Vietnam War, incorporated CSA, even as some businesses were passive bystanders or actively resisted demands.[13] This CSA accelerated in the 1980s because in the anti-apartheid movement businesses saw the commercial potential of politicized pop culture and felt pressure to take a stand amid changing sensibilities that posited *as* activism individual lifestyle choices and symbolic action, especially in media.[14] As Van Jones argued in our interview, "the anti-apartheid struggle succeeded because it was able to bring in big corporate brands that were at first sitting on the sidelines."[15]

US societal demands shifted too after the 1980s, with consumers and employees expecting businesses and their leadership to engage issues of the day, the same drive motivating philanthrocapitalism. Sitting it out had become less of an option, even as, in a politically polarized environment, taking a position on almost anything could lead to loss of some consumer loyalty. By 2020, 60 percent of Americans wanted the companies they buy products from to have a position about issues such as racial discrimination, police brutality, and social justice. Fifty percent said they often do online research to see how a brand reacts to social issues. [16] Following the demand, after the George Floyd murder in the summer of 2020, "corporate executives called out rogue [police] officers and excessive use of force in Black communities and committed to addressing disparities in the criminal justice system."[17]

The FSA's passage again provides an anecdote and a microcosm through which we can step back and investigate the criminal justice reform movement's stakeholders and dynamics, in this case corporations, businesses, and CSA in this space since 2000.

SECOND CHANCES AND OVERINCARCERATION

As Jenny Kim of Koch Industries noted, the strong business interest in criminal justice reform measures to reduce barriers for the formerly incarcerated to employment was a development of the 2000s, accelerating in the 2010s as social pressures and corporate interest converged. This first led to large-scale endorsements of "second chance" initiatives premised on overincarceration, but later expanded in more limited fashion to initiatives premised on *mass* incarceration linked to racial and economic injustice.

Jeff Korzenik of the Council of Criminal Justice and a chief investment strategist at Fifth Third Bank, describes Koch as an outlier for being "long involved" in criminal justice policy, noting in his 2020 book *Untapped Talent*, a "past lack of widespread engagement by the business community that resulted in policies that serve neither our economy nor our communities nor the principle of justice," which he sees as changing.[18] Certainly, private business has deep roots in the history of American criminal justice institutions, as not only could companies profit from the labor of incarcerated people but the capitalist ethic of hard work as a way to redemption provided a quasi-religious ideological justification for the practice. This attitude could be seen in the founding of the republic with the Quakers' eighteenth-century introduction of hard labor as a replacement for physical punishment. Businesses in the nineteenth century were profiting from the labor of the incarcerated, a phenomenon described in activist and academic discourse as the prison industrial complex, most egregiously through convict leasing of overwhelmingly Black men in the post–Civil War South:

Reform®: Corporate Social Activism

"The construction of prisons and the expansion of prison industries became the hallmark of corrections. . . . The notion of inmate labor on a 'for profit' basis was perceived not only as a reform measure (inmates being productively busy), but as economically sound," prison scholars note.[19] However, the notion was challenged by other private businesses, unions, and the public and not necessarily for noble reasons; rather, cheap prison labor hindered competitiveness.

Prison industries gradually fell out of favor under a more rehabilitative penal model up to the 1950s. But after costs of incarceration rose and crime increased, private-sector prisons and prison partnerships made a resurgence. President Jimmy Carter signed the Justice System Improvement Act in 1979, lifting a ban on interstate commerce in goods made with prison labor.[20] Still, the "second chance" or "fair chance" hiring of the twenty-first century was something different from that type of business intervention in criminal justice, however much a similar work-*as*-redemption ethos and economic motive might undergird the two initiatives. It was not about cheap labor contracts from *within* the prison, rationalized as a means of making the incarcerated "job ready."[21]

Second chance hiring, coherently linked to industry-wide efforts such as would be seen in the late 2010s followed as a logical extension of the reentry movement, which began in the late 1990s.[22] Around that time, in 1996, work opportunity tax credits (WOTCs) were offered to incentivize hiring those having been convicted of a felony under state or federal law within one year of the individual's conviction or his or her release from prison.[23] Dramatic change was not immediately apparent, though. WOTCs were not very effective in enticing employers, while other incentives, like the welfare-to-work tax credit, gave employers a much larger tax break.[24] And some of the first references in news sources to offering "second chances" in employment in the late 1990s were to the "same-old same-old" of private companies hiring *currently* incarcerated people through cheap contract labor, not to post-incarceration employment. In fact, even in the aftermath of the September 11 terrorist attacks, security fears put a damper on hiring the formerly incarcerated.[25]

The earnest wading of corporations into criminal justice reform, centering first and most logically on the socioeconomic impact of the

CHAPTER FIVE

slow-moving disaster of mass/overincarceration on the American labor market, was a forced acknowledgment of a major problem that could no longer be considered in isolation. It was a social variable that was not independent of production and consumption. President George W. Bush's 2004 State of the Union speech and the Second Chance Act he championed in 2007 were FSA-like canaries in the coal mine, testing the more rapid changes to come in business, where the "redemption" narrative so compelling to right-leaning ideologies would intersect with the practical need for an affordable, skilled workforce. Bush declared in 2004:

> [This year] 600,000 inmates will be released from prison back into society. . . . I propose a 4-year, $300 million prisoner reentry initiative to expand job training and placement services, to provide transitional housing, and to help newly released prisoners get mentoring, including from faith-based groups. America is the land of second chance, and when the gates of the prison open, the path ahead should lead to a better life.[26]

The noting by Bush of the number of those affected by a criminal record before going on to talk about job training and placement was apposite. By 2009, a "severe labor and talent shortage" and lowered productivity were leading businesses large and small to report that employee cost, availability, and retainment were among their biggest concerns, persisting at the start of the 2020s. Lagging fertility rates, baby boomer retirement, and a "missing labor force" had led to a labor gap of about 1 million workers per year. That missing force was partially attributable to the large-scale impact of the "incarceration and recidivism cycle" of 19 million people (about the population of New York State) in the US, including one in three Black men with felony convictions; tens of millions more with misdemeanor convictions,[27] and up to 100 million people having some criminal record.[28] The Brookings Institution documented the high incarceration rates and low employment rates among the formerly incarcerated, with one-third of all nonworking 30-year-old men either incarcerated or formerly incarcerated and unemployed.[29] Jeff Korzenik captures the interest convergence impelling corporate sector involvement in reform: "Second chance hiring done right is business, not charity." Without thoughtfully incorporating

Reform®: Corporate Social Activism

formerly incarcerated people into the workforce to address a shortage projected to last for decades, he warns of drags on productivity, and a cost of failure in terms of forsaken economic growth in the trillions: "It's big money, it's not a tiny sector. All of our prosperity benefits when we can have a more inclusive economy."

Some of the largest, most recognizable corporations and business associations in the US from banking to big tech—Business Roundtable, Chamber of Commerce, JPMorgan Chase, Home Depot, Bank of America, Walmart, Capital One, Butterball, Prudential, Puma, Koch Industries, Microsoft, Google, Verizon, CVS, Visa, Virgin, PepsiCo, Ben & Jerry's—had by 2021 committed to advocating for criminal justice reform internally and externally, primarily centering on second chance and fair chance hiring. More than that, as Jenny Kim pointed out in our interview, after 2015 these companies were more willing to openly talk about these practices. They waded deeper into their commitment, and formed organizations to more effectively communicate and strategize as sectors around reforms. While many corporate efforts in this space could be investigated, two brief case studies illustrate the move toward redemption narrative–driven second chance initiatives of the post 2000s—JPMorgan Chase, a large global bank, and Nehemiah Manufacturing, a much smaller company of less than 200 employees. The limitations, obstacles, and controversies surrounding *how* these and other companies go about implementing their second chance initiatives, and for whom, point to some of the larger conflicts in the movement.

FAIR CHANCE DAVIDS AND GOLIATHS: NEHEMIAH MANUFACTURING AND JPMORGAN

The Wall Street Journal dubbed it "The Company of Second Chances."[30] Even the name, Nehemiah Manufacturing, is evocative of the redemption narrative of the early 2000s to late 2010s motivating most private business wading into criminal justice reform. Rayshun Holt, formerly incarcerated and the manager of new product development at the Cincinnati-based company, founded in 2009, explained to me: "[The Book of] Nehemiah is a Biblical story about a broken city that was going through a lot of difficult times and turmoil. And the goal of the prophet Nehemiah was to rebuild the city. You can kind of tell where the minds and hearts of the founders of the company were at."[31] In fact, their Christian beliefs were cited by *The Wall Street Journal* as having been a key motivator, coupled with struggles the family of one of the founders was having with substance abuse, which led them to see the issue of second chances as personal.

At first Nehemiah's founders' socially linked business goal was to bring manufacturing back into the city. But in 2011, they started a concerted effort to hire people with a record, like Holt, who had been tried as an adult and convicted of homicide at 15, spending 21 years in prison before being paroled. "We're described as a second chance company. But for me it was my first chance," Holt imparted. His story of reentry in 2016 as a 36-year-old with a violent felony record highlights the insufficiency of in-prison work readiness programs. He had taken advantage of whatever educational opportunities had come to him in prison, certifications and apprenticeships, but he had discovered that all of this was insufficient as he tried to navigate his way into the workforce. He would disclose his record to interviewers, was several times offered jobs, but then saw the offers rescinded: "I was hired and rejected simultaneously," he conferred. Having heard about Nehemiah through the outreach and mentoring programs he participated in, he applied and was hired as a shift supervisor before moving on to a more senior role.

With his newborn daughter crying and tended to by his wife in the background during our online interview during the COVID shutdowns Holt warmly described his employer and the Nehemiah culture as loving, supportive, and nonstigmatizing. Indeed, by 2020, 80 percent of Nehemiah's employees had a criminal record, reducing the likelihood of internal stigmatization based on an incarceration record, and there was much lower turnover than in comparable companies. Holt noted that second chance initiatives had been "trending" since he had come home. "It's humbling because we know the more this business model takes hold, the more good that'll be done . . . so many lives are changed when you hire just one person."

Nehemiah Manufacturing is by most accounts a successful second chance "experiment" from a business perspective. *The Wall Street Journal* made sure to point out, as noted earlier, that the 2010s were one of the

Reform: Corporate Social Activism

"tightest labor markets in decades," and so second chance hiring was not merely a moral imperative but a practical one. Nehemiah made $60 million in revenue in 2021, placing it in the top 20 manufacturing companies in the US by earnings,[32] even as it paid its workers the national average for similar work and offered a benefits package including retirement savings, health insurance, and a 7 percent year-end bonus.[33]

Yet this is not an uncomplicated feel-good story. Nehemiah encountered early problems with retaining employees due to their unique needs coming from prison: many were not "job ready" or were still struggling with substance abuse. The business was able to solve many such concerns through a more rigorous screening process, but, most innovatively from a private-sector perspective, it created dense wraparound services that anticipate the demographic-specific struggles: 70 percent of Nehemiah's employees had been incarcerated for drug-related crimes or had substance abuse disorders. Nehemiah brought a social service team on board at a cost of $120,000 and hired a lawyer to help employees work through their legal barriers to employment. According to Holt, "Nehemiah connected individuals with GED courses or even college tuition reimbursement programs. They helped people get provided with day care services and financial counseling, legal assistance, housing (the company rents apartment units out to employees at half the market rate) and transportation services. The list is almost endless."

As Jenny Kim had noted about changes she had witnessed over the past 10 years in the reform space, Nehemiah was willing not only to focus on second chance hiring but to evangelize and demystify it. In 2015, the company launched a nonprofit organization, the Beacon of Hope Business Alliance, sharing the second chance business model with other interested business leaders, who, according to Katie Schad, a former social worker at Nehemiah, were interested primarily due to staffing shortages, but also due to CEO-to-CEO conversations, and what she called "CEO ego," a kind of fear of missing out on what other prominent CEOs and their companies were doing. "Dan Meyers, Nehemiah's CEO, was instrumental in Beacon of Hope," she said, and "[Nehemiah cofounder] Tom Williams, a principal owners of the Cincinnati Reds, had been very influential. And then the CEO of [retail giant] Kroger, Rodney McMullin, visited Nehemiah and started this at Kroger. When Kroger joined, interest from other companies took off. Like, if Kroger's doing it, we'll all do it." The model has since been adopted by more than 50 organizations, and Kroger, with almost half a million employees, brought it nationwide.[34]

While Rayshun Holt argued that Nehemiah was "the gold standard" for other companies to emulate, as someone with a violent felony record he was aware of one of the elephants in the room occupied by corporate activism in criminal justice reform: a general skittishness about the hiring of individuals other than nonviolent, nonsexual first-time offenders, and a lack of understanding of their distinct struggles and the resources it would take to bring them into the working population: "Whatever opportunities that were supposed to be available to individuals to accommodate the prison reform agenda has completely circumvented violent offenders, who are likely to serve more time," he argued. "Take me. I came home 21 years later. I didn't know how to use a telephone; I didn't know how to navigate public transportation. I didn't know how to use the self-checkout at Kroger's. . . . You got to reach back and try to touch them individuals and connect them with the proper resources. They needed a job the day before they got released, not to be out in the matrix scratching and clawing their way to find employment after burdens are starting to build in real time."[35]

Nehemiah was willing to hire Holt, who had a violent record, and it had an ecosystem with services to ensure that employees like him would be supported. Yet, as *The Wall Street Journal* pointed out, "more employers are comfortable overlooking minor drug offenses, but not violent crimes, or sexual offenses."[36] Employees, too, are less comfortable working alongside coworkers with violent offense records versus those with nonviolent offense records—47 versus 78 percent, respectively.[37] As Chapter 1 made clear, the language of politicians endorsing the FSA homed in on second chances for the least controversial, most sympathetic category of minor nonviolent drug offenses, however much they comprise a tiny minority of offenses for which people are incarcerated. Only about 1 percent of those incarcerated in state prisons, and two percent in federal prison, are there for low-level, nonviolent drug offenses.[38]

Nehemiah's Katie Schad, in her work as a social worker with Beacon of Hope, saw how sexual offense records in particular were a third rail in the

Reform®: Corporate Social Activism 119

willingness of businesses to expand reform policies, as they were for other stakeholder groups in the movement: "We've never had a ton of success placing sexual offenders," she reflected. "It's kind of nuts. We've successfully placed people who've committed manslaughter and more violent crimes than those who have committed sexual offenses."[39] Indeed, only 10 percent of managers and HR employees in 2018 reported knowledge of their company hiring people with sexual offense records. In some cases, even if the business was comfortable with a certain criminal record profile, regulations could prohibit it from hiring, a factor cited by approximately one-third of managers and employees across the US as a reason for concern in hiring people with criminal records.[40] For example, Nehemiah's location near a school means that it cannot hire someone with a sexual offense record.

Jenny Kim reflected on the conundrum of limited hiring according to offense category, and on the likelihood of corporations expanding the scope of offenses they would permit for employees. "Small and medium-sized businesses like Nehemiah have been doing it for a long time so they feel more comfortable expanding their [second chance hiring]. . . . It's more of a risk-based approach." She described the dilemma for most employers looking for simple employee reliability and ability to pass drug tests, which means they default to what they perceive of as the least risky offense categories, until "their minds and hearts are expanded to something else."

In banking, a much different, highly regulated sector, JPMorgan Chase, the largest bank in the US with 250,000 more employees than Nehemiah, began its high-profile entry into reform with a push for second chance hiring, experiencing some of the same basic tensions and fundamental questions about who would be embraced by newfound corporate support of reform. Heather Higginbottom, Deputy Secretary of State for Management and Resources under Obama, was at JPMorgan Chase as head of its new Policy Center when we discussed the bank's role in the reform space in 2020. On the recentness of JPMorgan's outspoken interest in the issue, she indicated that it had been a phenomenon of fewer than five years. The long-tenured CEO, billionaire Jamie Dimon, she pointed out, had been using his political capital to highlight the issue in Washington and making supportive statements only since 2017. Coincidentally, this was the same year he became chair of the Business Roundtable. When asked why she thought criminal justice had become an issue championed by JPMorgan, she pointed to the scale of overincarceration: "It impacts so many people: one in two people has a criminal background, and this has a ripple effect into communities and families."[41] Describing herself as a lifelong progressive Democrat and admitting how incongruent it was for someone with her political orientation to give a shout-out to Koch Industries, she said she gave the Kochs "a ton of credit" for having "really moved the needle on the bipartisan landscape," making more industry movement possible.

In 2018 Dimon took several unlikely steps for the CEO of the largest bank in the US. In his annual letter to shareholders, he described the *responsibility* of JPMorgan to hire those with "minor" records who had been incarcerated. He supported a proposal to amend Section 19 of the Federal Deposit Insurance Act, approved in 2020, to allow banks to more easily hire people convicted of minor criminal offenses by removing the requirement to seek FDIC permission.[42] He couched his argument as a matter of public safety, linking employment to reduced recidivism.[43] That same year, he and an Obama-era secretary of education co-authored an op-ed for the *Chicago Tribune*, "Hiring Returning Citizens Is Good For Business."[44] While referring to the higher toll of a criminal record on Black and Latino communities, the two primarily leaned into the standard narrative of second chances and redemption, which has been polled as among the most resonant messages for the public.[45] Describing jobs as providing "dignity" and the possibility of "[achieving] the American Dream," they wrote: "It is morally and economically bad for our country if we do not start removing barriers that prevent returning citizens from a shot at a better life after they have paid their debt to society. . . . Business should be at the forefront of solving this challenge. Frankly, it's in our best interest to do so," and pointed out successful partnerships between nonprofits and businesses preparing "productive" and "high-performing" employees.

In 2019, the year that the Policy Center was created and Higginbottom was hired, JPMorgan took a few more steps in second chance hiring reform. In October the company announced that it had "banned the box" on its employment applications, removing questions about criminal history, as part of its "fair chance" hiring practices. Only after

Reform: Corporate Social Activism

a conditional offer of employment was made would the company run a background check. If a criminal conviction existed, it would be assessed internally if the individual presented an "undue" risk to other employees, clients, and the public. In an attempt to quell fears about how far the bank would take this initiative, or to point out how it really was allowing applicants to take a first step toward the American dream, JPMorgan emphasized that of the 10 percent of its hirees with criminal histories, many were in entry-level positions and had an arrest or conviction for a low-level offense like drug possession or driving while intoxicated.[46] Information was not given about how this percentage changed over time. Ten percent appears low given the company's own statistic that one in two people in the US has a criminal "background." In addition to the regulatory constraints in hiring that exist for banks ("We probably wouldn't want to hire someone who has robbed a bank or committed a financial crime," Higginbottom remarked jokingly), other obstacles would exist for those with convictions, even if the hiring process was free of bias against a criminal record. Barriers already exist in the form of work experience and education (typically a minimum of a bachelor's degree) requirements for white-collar, professional jobs. Most of the formerly incarcerated are dramatically behind the general population in educational attainment, with almost 25 percent lacking a high school diploma, 20 percent with a only high school diploma, 33 percent with a standard or in-prison GED, and about 5 percent with a college degree.[47]

Like Nehemiah Manufacturing, JPMorgan's pursuit of second chance employees in a tight labor market, and the revision of its internal policies, demonstrates Jenny Kim's larger point about the shift toward businesses publicly discussing the hiring of those with a criminal history and organizing other US companies to do so. Higginbottom said that at the moment in 2020, "no table really exists for employers to learn from one another and experts how to do [second chance and fair chance hiring], how to overcome the challenges for business to doing this. We've had success at JPMorgan in the Veterans' Jobs Mission [business coalition]. We were one of the founders of this. We're taking lessons learned from that and working with the Society for Human Resource Management and Koch to assemble a large coalition to translate statements into actual policy."

CHAPTER FIVE

By 2021, the Second Chance Business Coalition (SCBC), had been launched. In partnership with the Business Roundtable, with Jamie Dimon as cochair, and 30 blue chip companies representing almost $10 trillion in market cap, the SCBC's goals were to bring together large businesses to share best practices for recruiting and retaining successful second chance employees, and to test and assess new approaches to hiring, often in coordination with community-based nonprofits.[48] That it was doing this was a clear sign of the scope of the problem of criminal history in employment in the US during a tight labor market, as noted. It was also a sign of confidence that a public relations disaster would not ensue—the movement had become mainstreamed enough for such a large company not to experience a significant backlash from customers. JPMorgan's several-minutes-long paid advertisement in *The New York Times* (online) featuring Heather Higginbottom (Figure 5.1), as well as formerly incarcerated employees, proclaimed its commitment to "inclusive hiring."

"If you're struggling to find work because you're an ex-con, try hitting up Jamie Dimon," was the *New York Post*'s sardonic response to the launch,[49] but otherwise there was little negative press. And Heather Higginbottom noted that, although there had been internal complaints from a few employees "who would say, 'Why are we giving someone a *second* chance? We should be promoting and investing in the people who are already here!'" Largely the response from clients, employees and leadership has been very, very positive. The comments on our company home page when we make the announcements is 'This makes me proud to work here.'" This anecdotal account was partially backed up by a 2021 nationally representative survey that showed two-thirds of Americans would be proud to work for an organization that offered training and mentorship to people with criminal records. An increasing number of consumers said they would feel comfortable patronizing an establishment known to do second chance hiring, even of employees who had spent more than five years in prison.[50] Still, only about half said they would feel proud to work for an employer that actually *hired* people with criminal records. And although almost 80 percent said they would be comfortable with coworkers who had nonviolent offense records, this percentage dropped by almost a third when queried about working with those with violent offense records.[51]

Reform: *Corporate Social Activism*

FIGURE 5.1. JPMorgan Chase second chance hiring advertisement, 2021

FROM REDEMPTION TO EXODUS NARRATIVES IN CORPORATE REFORM

A few months after the SCBC launched, *The New York Times* gave Jamie Dimon space on its Op-Ed page to make the case that "if you paid your debt to society, you should be allowed to work."[52] As evidenced in that op-ed, by

CHAPTER FIVE

2021 the rationale and scope of advocacy by JPMorgan, companies like Verizon and AT&T, and business organizations had shifted noticeably from what we read, for example, in their support of the FSA in 2018. "A history of systemic racism in our criminal justice system disproportionately impact[s] communities of color, especially Black people," wrote Dimon, who laid out his argument for a range of policy reforms like automatic expungement of certain criminal records, which were part of the "Second Chance Agenda," of JPMorgan's Policy Center, including federal Pell Grant restoration[53] for incarcerated students, reforming laws to end debt-based drivers' license suspensions, and expanding entrepreneurial training programs for the formerly incarcerated.[54]

In the early 2020s, corporate activism was still fueled by the ideologically resonant narrative of redemption and second chances that took hold in the early 2000s, which emphasized work as dignity/salvation and as a way to avoid recidivism, but it had shifted perceptibly. It was becoming more impelled by the exodus narrative—for example, the tying of criminal justice reform to racial justice and therefore opposing *mass* incarceration rather than overincarceration. While this shift among large corporations began in the 2010s, it accelerated dramatically after 2015, and especially in the wake of the 2020 racial justice protests and sustained activism around the murder of George Floyd by police officer Derek Chauvin.

Large companies and business organizations have since made statements about the harms of the criminal justice system: in addition to being a societal issue of second chances for everyone, it was becoming an issue of racial justice and racial equity specifically. They actively encouraged employee "advocacy" and "calls to action" in workplace forums dedicated to the topic, sometimes sponsored by newly expanded diversity, equity, and inclusion offices. Verizon, for instance, pledged millions to large nonprofits working against racism, like the NAACP, in 2020. It launched a YouTube series called #Next20, the first episode of which focused on criminal justice reform, hosting activists who discussed two-tiered systems, systemic racism, the need for fewer police, and diversion of funds into the community. For this, the company was criticized for its support of "defunding" the police.[55]

Even more telling of the shift is the discourse and the expansion of focus in the reform space among large business organizations, as they have more collective power, the ability to speak with a unified voice across sectors, and members who influence each other. The USCOC in June 2020 launched a national initiative to address race-based inequality of opportunity through, among other approaches, criminal justice reform. Citing the George Floyd murder, the president of the USCOC said, "We stand in solidarity against racism and advocate for diversity, equity and inclusion in our society and economy," noting that the initiative would build on the chamber's recent support for the First Step Act.[56] In August, the chamber sent a letter to Congress endorsing bills that would help "close long-standing opportunity gaps that exist for Black Americans and people of color." Among these criminal justice–focused bills were the REAL Act, which would reinstate Pell grants for incarcerated students, and the Driving for Opportunity Act, which would allow the federal government to make grants to states that do not use failure to pay civil/criminal fines and fees as a rationale for suspending drivers' licenses.[57] The Business Roundtable, in addition to the SCBS it helped to coordinate, included justice reforms in its policy portfolio under the umbrella of "Racial Equity and Justice," underscoring first and foremost racial inequalities in the justice system.[58] The subcommittee working on policies under this umbrella, headed up by AT&T CEO Randall Stephenson, released principles calling for congressional reform of policing, principles "representing the collective views of America's top business leaders," in 2020. Stephenson had for several years spoken publicly in support of the BLM movement, encouraging employee activism rather than "tolerance," which he labeled cowardly.[59] AT&T also deployed its employees and lobbyists to meet with legislators in 21 states where policing reforms were on the table.[60] AT&T announced this engagement as public relations fodder for themselves, tying it to previous social movements for racial equality: "Since the 1960s, our company has been at the forefront of civil rights advocacy and the fight for equality."[61]

After 2015, and even more so after 2020, driven by the exodus narrative and its demands for racial justice, but still linked to the redemption narrative that provided a bulwark for the mainstreaming of the reform movement, and fueled by the tight labor market and by the moment of safety in limiting their positions, large corporations and business organizations became more involved in these reforms. In a kind of mission creep, the range of initiatives they were backing, and the modes of doing so—investing more political and economic capital in issues not directly related to their core business function—expanded, whether on stage or behind the scenes.[62] Verizon took a position against extreme sentences for juveniles. Walmart, via its newly founded Center for Racial Equity, gave money to nonprofits to "reimagine" policing and criminal justice.[63] Facebook Vice President of Civil Rights Roy Austin Jr. was quoted by the Vera Institute as saying, "Bail is the stupidest thing in the criminal justice system." And a large symbolic[64] victory was achieved in 2019, when JPMorgan, Bank of America, Wells Fargo, and five other banks that had underwritten loans for CoreCivic and Geo Group, said they would stop financing these private prison companies in response to activist pressure.[65]

At Koch Industries, Jenny Kim remarked that her 2010 portfolio focused just on overcriminalization and the mass proliferation of laws, at federal, state, and local levels, but by 2020 it had "five buckets, big components we care about, because the criminal justice system is an interconnected holistic system. You have how the laws are made, then how they are implemented and processed at the grand jury level, and the prosecutorial level. There's the courts, and the right to counsel. The fourth element is sentencing reform—what is the right level of punishment for things. The last piece is trying to eliminate or reduce as many of the collateral consequences for those returning back to society." Signaling this widened focus, Charles Koch put up $70 million between 2019 and 2021 in support of more criminal justice reform and specifically marijuana legalization, even though he admitted to having consumed marijuana, accidentally in a brownie, only once in his lifetime.[66]

Still, in the 2020s, large US companies for the most part veered away from taking direct stances on more controversial criminal justice issues. Policy statements against capital punishment are few, for instance, even as European corporate leaders and businesses have been exerting their influence to abolish the death penalty in the US and even as some US leaders have endorsed its abolition. To be sure, a few mid-sized companies that have championed deeper rosters of liberal-leaning causes and self-identify as having progressive values, like LUSH Cosmetics and the Vermont-based Ben & Jerry's, have gone far beyond tenuously dipping their toes into

Reform®: Corporate Social Activism

criminal justice reform and are advocating for more systemic and polarizing changes. They have also demonstrated how reform can itself be a commercialized product, part of a company's brand. In 2019 Ben & Jerry's unveiled its Justice ReMix'd flavor ("cinnamon and chocolate ice cream with gobs of cinnamon bun dough and spicy fudge brownie chunks"). The company got behind "cannabis justice," using its platform to point out inequities in drug enforcement and partnering with the ACLU on a related petition. Rooting its discussion of the criminal justice system in Michelle Alexander's *New Jim Crow*, the company also dedicated space on its platform to a petition advocating for, and explaining, the movement to defund the police and how it was "the best opportunity in generations to completely transform our model of policing and create stronger, safer communities where Black Americans and people of color can finally experience and celebrate true freedom."[67]

PUMA launched their 2019 Meek Mill collection of Clyde and Clyde Court #REFORM sneakers. With #REFORM as part of the design on the tongue and outsole, the inscription on the shoe read "We had to be seen because we could not be heard" (Figure 5.2). All proceeds from the collection would go to Meek Mill's #REFORM Alliance, which according to its website is "working to radically reform criminal justice in America,"[68] demonstrating neatly the linkage among wealthy philanthropists, celebrity, and corporations in the post-2000 reform movement.

When evaluating the mainstreamization of the reform movement and its embrace by the business community, looking to corporations that have been historically disconnected from social causes might be most instructive of the changes of the past 20 years, rather than looking to Ben & Jerry's. Still, the engagement of these brands, from LUSH to JPMorgan to Koch to PUMA, is reflective of the philanthrocapitalist and post-democratic era characterized by consumer politics. It is a manifestation of a broader trend affecting all movements that makes corporate activism a central feature of the landscape.

Whether the change in the past 20 years in corporate activism and internal business policies and practice, which we can place under the "criminal justice reform" umbrella, is evidence of the nationalization and mainstreamization of that movement, and whether it will have a substantial

FIGURE 5.2. PUMA Meek Mill Collection Clyde shoes advertisement, 2019

impact on decarceration or ameliorating the harms of the carceral system, will be assessed in the decades to come.

There is already some evidence that, despite the well-meaning intentions of reform advocates and organizations that introduced and championed such measures, policies like "banning the box" may do more harm than good to the populations of young Black and Latino men they are intended to help.[69] And despite the strong statements made after high-profile police killings of Black men from Mike Brown to George Floyd, corporations have dedicated relatively small amounts to criminal justice reform organizations. "The issue of criminal justice reform, governed by the public sector, with less clear paths for results, may simply be too new or divisive for

Reform*: Corporate Social Activism

corporate America ... too far a reach for some companies."[70] Only 2 percent of corporate commitments to racial justice in the year after the 2020 George Floyd protests went to criminal justice reform. Most of them went to major organizations that do types of criminal justice work as part of their mission like the NAACP's Legal Defense Fund. Ultimately, the majority went to more redemption/second chance/protestant work ethic causes traditionally associated with corporations, devoted to upward economic progress through homeownership in the form of mortgages, entrepreneurship, and education. This is not to say that these things are disconnected from criminal justice, given that predictors of criminal justice system involvement are linked not only to racial but to class and educational disparities; nevertheless, they demonstrate that the business community has not stepped too far out if its wheelhouse and comfort zone.

There are reasons for cautious optimism: businesses and corporations, especially large ones, can have an enormous normative and legislative impact. Van Jones, in describing his evolution as an activist, said, "I realized there are a lot of people who are capitalists—shudder shudder—who are really committed to fairly significant change in the economy, and were having bigger impacts than me and a lot of my friends with our protest signs."[71] Like celebrities or like in-group members of a political organization vouching for a policy, businesses can lend credibility to a cause. "A well-known CEO may lend legitimacy when delivering information."[72] Also, analogous to celebrities, corporations have recognizability, fan loyalty, and command attention from both the public and elites with targeted ads, savvy marketing, and the resources to be highly influential in their lobbying efforts. They can coerce government to respond to changes that they internally adopt well in advance of slower moving legislative change from the outside. They can lend their brands, and media platforms, political heft, and staff to the cause, enabled to go beyond where celebrities can go by changing industry norms and internal policy. And, of course, they can be powerful bankrollers of nonprofits linked to criminal justice reform.

A further reason for cautious optimism is that the corporations getting behind reform, in an environment of intensifying political binaries, were differentially associated with right- and left-leaning political causes and polarized consumer bases. This was not a narrowly delimited push. It hinted at the "strange bedfellow" consensus about the need for ameliorative and decarceratory changes post-2000 (even if intense battle lines were drawn about what that looked like) that formed between right- and left-leaning politicians and national advocacy groups, which was a large factor in the passage of the First Step Act, constituting a major feature of the movement landscape.

SIX

STRANGE BEDFELLOWS

An oversized book with a black-and-white photo of Nelson Mandela was prominently seen behind #cut50's Van Jones as the backdrop to his 2020 pandemic interview. As he reflected on his participation in the First Step Act and criminal justice reform, he spoke to the deeply felt moral pull of action and his belief in an ideologically and racially diverse movement. "You want to understand why this beautiful flower emerged in the middle of war. It wasn't just a political strategy, or 'interest group convergence,'" he insisted with a sense of urgency. He positioned himself in the "Mandela Path" tradition, which he constructed as a spiritual place premised on obtaining human freedom: "There were two movements in South Africa against apartheid. One was the ANC, which was open to everyone. They wanted one person, one vote. The other was the PAC, open only to Blacks. They wanted one White settler, one bullet. There's a lot of that thinking on the left—figuratively. They want revenge. . . . Mandela—his great power over everyone was that he felt like he needed the best of everybody to have the South Africa he wanted to build. That's how I feel. If we build a movement that says from the beginning, if you're a straight White male, you're the devil, if you're a conservative, you're my enemy, you're an ignorant racist—vote for me! That's not very inviting, it's not very smart. As

CHAPTER SIX

I've gotten older, I've realized how many potential allies there are who are different from me. I've tried to be the most visible person refusing to bow down to either side. If they want me to dehumanize anybody, I won't do it."

This role, of perhaps the most recognizable advocate for bipartisan reform on the left and the most ardent liberal proponent from a national advocacy organization for the First Step Act, would have seemed unlikely for Jones in his early activism. His roots were in the radical left. In the early 1990s, driven by the racial inequalities he saw in criminal justice, such as the acquittal in the vicious beating of Rodney King, he went from a self-described rowdy Black nationalist to a communist. He formed STORM, a socialist collective steeped in Marxist-Leninist ideology. During this period, he joined a national mobilization to convince President Clinton to dismantle an HIV-positive prison camp in Guantanamo holding Haitian asylum seekers. And in 1995, he formed the Ella Baker Center for Human Rights, which launched campaigns like Bay Area Police Watch and Books Not Bars that successfully closed five California youth prisons.[1]

Jones's spearheading of bipartisanship from the left in the FSA would have seemed further impossible as of 2009. When tapped by the Obama White House to be a green jobs czar, he resigned after criticism from Republicans for calling them assholes and for his advocacy of former Black Panther Mumia Abdul Jamal, who had been convicted and sent to death row for the killing a police officer.[2] #cut50, the nonprofit he cofounded in 2014 with Jessica Jackson, advocated for the decidedly nonconservative goal of slashing the nation's incarcerated population in half within 10 years.

Van Jones's becoming an "unlikely" proponent of working with Republicans and libertarian and conservative organizations on reform was an individual example of a key dynamic of the post-2000s mainstreamed and nationalized movement: its "strange bedfellow" characteristic, which he was participant in creating.[3] Starting in the 2010s, he developed relationships with right advocacy organizations and leaders through former Republican House Speaker Newt Gingrich, whom he met while cohosting "Crossfire" on CNN in 2013. By March 2015, Gingrich's multimedia company and Van Jones' #cut50 were coproducing the Bipartisan Criminal Justice Reform Summit in Washington DC. Many of the key players and stakeholders in the movement, who were later central to the FSA and endorsed its passage, were at the summit—business and large advocacy group leaders, some of whom were formerly incarcerated, celebrities and philanthropists, Republican governors, and President Obama, who presented. According to Van Jones, Koch had made a "quiet truce with the Obama White House" as a byproduct of the bipartisan alliance and the friendship of Jones and Gingrich. Following the 2015 Bipartisan Summit, "[Obama] wasn't criticized by a single right winger [on reform] because we worked behind the scenes to create an understanding—[we wanted] the country to be able to get to a better place on criminal justice."

A few months later, in July 2015, criminal justice reform was centered by Obama. He had just become the first sitting president to visit a federal prison, had commuted 46 sentences, and was outlining his proposals for reform. At the NAACP annual conference in Philadelphia, he proclaimed to the audience: "This is a cause that's bringing people in both houses of Congress together. It's created some unlikely bedfellows. You've got Van Jones and Newt Gingrich." He paused for the audience's laughter. "You've got Americans for Tax Reform and the ACLU. . . . You have the NAACP and the *Koch brothers*," pausing again as more laughter filled the room at the perceived outrageousness of the combination, although outrageousness could only be perceived with a historical amnesia, as mass/overincarceration had long been a bipartisan political creation.[4]

That year, *Time* magazine ran an article, "Criminal Justice Reform Is Becoming Washington's Bipartisan Cause," noting that "the need to reform the broken US criminal-justice system is fast becoming the rare cause for which Washington's warring factions will lay down their weapons and work together."[5] The tenor of the article would be echoed in countless media accounts, expressive of a shock, during a time of such political polarization, at the existence of bipartisanship. The year 2015 was also the year the largest national bipartisan organization dedicated to criminal justice reform, the Coalition for Public Safety, was brought together and funded by the Arnold Foundation, Koch Industries, and the MacArthur and Ford Foundations, under the leadership of Holly Harris, a major figure in the FSA story. The year furthermore saw the SAFE Justice Act, presented as "bipartisan legislation that puts lessons learned from states to work at the federal level"[6] to reduce incarceration, reinvest money in antirecidivism programs, and other reforms, supported by large national advocacy groups on the right (FreedomWorks, American Conservative Union, R Street Institute) and left (NAACP, Urban League).[7]

The passage of the FSA three years later, for conceptual, symbolic, and narrative purposes, is a useful lens through which we can see a slice of the mainstreamed, national reform movement, its key stakeholders and dynamics, which included "strange bedfellow" bipartisanship and controversies among national advocacy groups. Its passage, though, was made possible by earlier "steps" in the preceding 15–20 years, in state and federal reforms promoted by many of the same leaders in the national advocacy groups.

One of the signs of bipartisan movement and developing consensus away from the "throw away the key" penal attitude was the 2007 Second Chance Act (SCA), signed by George W. Bush. Its signing was made possible by the redemption story–focused, faith-oriented Prison Fellowship, also a major player in the FSA, which "unit[ed] a broad coalition of right and left support for the SCA."[8]

As more national organizations were created or expanded due to the infusion of funding post-2000, efforts were made by these groups to cultivate bipartisanship (in the sense of working together, finding and expanding commonality, even if messaging to respective bases was different) largely behind the scenes at first but later more publicly.[9] Robert Rooks, a veteran in the reform space as cofounder of the Alliance for Safety and Justice, and former criminal justice director of the NAACP, reflected: "Around 2010, we at the NAACP wanted to work across the aisle to help get the message of overincarceration out. This was around the time Right on Crime was being created. We thought that was the best way forward, [given] the composition of Congress. Ben Jealous was president of the NAACP, it was something he wanted to make sure was part of our strategy." He added, "and I definitely do believe bipartisanship is important."

"You have tea party activists and NAACP activists pushing the same [incarceration reform] bills," Ben Jealous observed during that period Rooks was describing.[10] The NAACP under his leadership would partner with Right on Crime and with advocates/advocacy groups joining the "usual list of suspects" for national coalitional work. For example, in 2011 the NAACP launched its national "Smart and Safe Campaign" to reduce prison spending and increase education budgets. At the press conference to announce the campaign were leaders from Prison Fellowship, Right on Crime, and the American Conservative Union.[11] The NAACP report "Misplaced Priorities: Over Incarcerate, Under Educate" was endorsed by those groups, as well as by Americans for Tax Reform's Grover Norquist, who, as we saw, also had a seat at the White House discussions leading to the First Step Act.

Conservative/right-leaning and left-leaning individuals and advocacy groups working specifically and independently for ameliorative or decarceratory policies and practices predate the post 2000s-era mainstreaming of reform, of course, with "ideological true believers who worked for years against near-hopeless odds. . . . Trans-partisan agreement on criminal justice reform was a long time in the making, and not merely a hasty gambit to attract votes for a specific piece of legislation."[12] But few reform-dedicated groups had national scope and infrastructure such as would be seen after 2000,[13] and few were actively seeking bipartisan alliances. Criminal justice reform in the sense described in this book, as an ameliorative, decarceratory impulse, did appear to be witnessing, post-2000, some of the new, extraordinary bipartisan convergence that Van Jones proclaimed in 2015 among national, elite advocacy groups, which found its apex at the federal level in the passage of the FSA. And it was remarkable. Michael Jacobson, former corrections commissioner of NYC and former president of the Vera Institute of Justice, observed: "It's the only example I can think of, where even if it's vague or a little ephemeral, there's an intersection between those groups." This was possible because newly created national advocacy groups, as well as established groups newly focused on criminal justice reform from the right and left, actively sought partnerships at the federal and state level, recognizing the limitations of large-scale work premised on ideological narrowness.

Yet this narrative of unlikely alliances in popular coverage concealed the deep national movement rifts over that bipartisan direction among advocacy groups, especially from the left. By 2018, in the lead-up to the passage of the FSA, Van Jones was a controversial figure, being called a "sellout, coon, an Uncle Tom" and a "Black token,"[14] distrusted by some community members and organizational leaders on the *left*[15] for his relationships with the right. *The Root*, a Black-oriented magazine, which had made Jones an honoree in 2013, now was publishing acerbic pieces calling him two-faced and a traitor.[16] He appeared in photos with President Donald Trump, Ivanka Trump, and Jared Kushner, one of the main drivers of the bill inside the White House. He praised Trump in the lead-up to passage as a "uniter-in-chief." He stood behind the Oval Office desk during the Act's signing and would declare at the 2019 CPAC that conservatives were now the leaders in criminal justice reform. For some on the left, praise for Trump, and working with him and his allies on the FSA, was not a bridge. It was a bridge too far.[17]

The internal movement dynamics surrounding Van Jones and his alliances with conservatives and their advocacy groups were at the individual level, and those seen in the FSA concerned a single bill impacting only the federal system. Yet they were reflective of how the mainstreamization and nationalization of the criminal justice reform movement brought intergroup and intragroup unity, but also bitter clashes in ideology and strategy.

THE FIRST STEP ACT AS "BIPARTISAN" . . . AND A FLASHPOINT

"Trump gets elected and everybody's like, criminal justice reform is never going to happen," Jason Pye, associate director of justice reform for FreedomWorks, recalled. The rhetoric Trump had campaigned on was one of Nixon-esque "law and order," with his overtly labeling of himself as the law and order candidate in the 2016 presidential election. He emphasized a racialized specter of crime and drugs from immigrants from South America and the Middle East[18] and violence in "inner cities" as a looming threat. Even during the years of an ostensibly more justice reform–friendly Obama administration (although the 2010 Fair Sentencing Act became the first Congressional repeal of a mandatory minimum since Nixon),[19] another attempt at bipartisan federal criminal justice reform, the Sentencing Reform and Corrections Act, failed. Though this legislation had been similar to the FSA, with many of the same groups and actors involved, according to Pye, "Republican staffers and Republican members [of Congress] themselves specifically told me they didn't want to vote for criminal justice reform because they didn't want to give Obama a win. [When Trump came in], the dynamic had shifted. Republicans were interested, but there were Democrats who didn't want to hand Trump a win."

Given the first-blush hostility of the Trump administration to *any* gesture toward criminal justice reform as defined here—as decarcerative and ameliorative—and given the political climate where party polarization, already high under Presidents Obama and George W. Bush, reached an apex,[20] the FSA's eventual passage was anything but a given. Still, some of the social conditions were ripe: despite Trump's rhetoric, crime was at historic lows, the labor market continued to be tight, and the right-leaning base was supportive. As David Safavian, the American Conservative Union's director of the Nolan Center for Justice, told me, "In [2018] we did a Conservative Political Action Conference (CPAC) straw poll. We asked, 'Should conservatives be involved in the criminal justice reform movement?' And the numbers worked out to be 82 or 88 percent." The issue had also lost salience among voters and the conservative leadership: The CPAC 2017 straw poll showed that the most important issues for Republican voters were the economy (46 percent) and national security (29 percent). Crime as such was not even offered as a choice.[21] So when Texas Republican activist-donor and self-described criminal justice reformer Doug Deason (Chapter 3) partnered with Jared Kushner, whose father's incarceration had made the issue personal, on federal criminal justice reform, it set in motion an unexpected chain of events. A major explanation of the First Step Act "puzzle"—*how* it succeeded in passing but also the *form* it took, as described in Chapter 1, encompassing prison reform *and* sentencing reform—can be teased out by looking at the place of national interest/advocacy groups: those that became a part of Deason and Kushner's initiative, from the right and left, as well as those that used their weight from the outside to exert pressure on the bill's provisions.

The mainstreamization and nationalization of the movement since 2000, seen in the entrenchment of elite, well-established advocacy organizations with divergent ideological underpinnings for reform referred to reductively as bipartisan, was obvious from the first informal steps taken to pursue reform legislation by Deason and Kushner. Those first steps, after all, were a literal invitation-only affair. Among those invited to the first

White House summit in 2017, and those who constituted the "advisory group" that was to continue working on the bill, though all were prominent, most (with the exception of Prison Fellowship) had not had a strong focus on criminal justice reform before 2000 or simply had not existed at all.

On the left, for instance, the National Urban League, invited to that White House summit, was representative of elite identity-based organizations that "in the 1990s . . . became more outspoken about criminal justice issues [but in those years] criminal justice was not a top priority. Neither was mass incarceration."[22] Indeed, even post-2000 there was criticism of the lack of attention the Urban League gave to mass incarceration's impact on the Black community.[23] Bill Cobb, former deputy director of the ACLU Campaign for Smart Justice would jest that prior to the 2010s the ACLU was the "ACL—who?" on issues of mass incarceration. The $50 million grant from George Soros's Open Society Foundations for the ACLU to "end mass incarceration" meant a major shift in 2014. The ACLU had been criticized for accepting the grant, Cobb noted, given that it was "not rooted in criminal justice work at all. It was Bigfoot—liberal, big, disconnected. But they weren't going to give the money back. They had the opportunity to conduct the largest campaign in their 150-year history that would position them as leaders in the criminal justice space." The NAACP's national agenda calling for a reduction in mass incarceration, according to Robert Rooks, the first criminal justice director in its history, was established in 2009 and "released a national report that positioned the NAACP as a national leader on justice reform." Prior to this, "the NAACP would weigh in on criminal justice issues only when they more clearly overlapped with a violation of someone's civil rights such as a police shooting." On the right, invitees included Right on Crime. Marc Levin and his colleagues at the think tank Texas Public Policy Foundation launched this national conservative criminal justice reform initiative only in 2010.[24] And the libertarian-right FreedomWorks, though founded in 2004, began its criminal justice reform projects in 2014.[25]

Characteristic of post-democracy and the philanthrocapitalist turn in the twenty-first century, the sheer primacy of these limited key national advocacy organizations was enabled because of funding capacity,

Strange Bedfellows

recognizability, perceived legitimacy both within and beyond ideological "team" affiliations, and social networks among leadership. This meant they had an outsized role in determining what the parameters of bipartisanship looked like for legislative efforts, and which groups had the bona fides to influence them. Mainstreamization and conducive economic and social conditions and outside pressure to reform created a hospitable environment for this legislation. But ultimately, the First Step Act was hammered out, contested, and then shepherded to passage by a relatively small set of these advocacy group leaders, who leveraged their political,[26] social, and cultural capital.

Of the national advocacy groups, those on the right[27] were predictably the most dominant in the early internal conversations at the Trump White House. As Doug Deason noted about the initial, listening session–style meeting, he perceived the expectations and demands from those invited from the left—like the leader of the Urban League who Deason said asked for $300 million over five years to reduce recidivism among Black male youth—to be contrary to his aims in that early stage. "The problem with the Democrats," Deason opined, "[is that] they have this myopic mentality. They want it all. They want to eat the whole apple. If you want consensus, if you want to get a bipartisan bill passed, you can't try to bite off the whole thing." He argued that "the left" was not excluded after the meeting but neither was it part of the nucleus for a time.

Deason's reasoning for "working on it from the right," was as strategic as it was ideological: "The real challenge was not going to be winning over the House and Senate, it was going to be Republican," he conferred. "And then the challenge was going to be getting the President on board." Having the figurative right messenger and messaging was therefore paramount. And for this, the team he and Kushner assembled had an already robust record of experience. Right on Crime, hugely influential in those White House discussions, had been "revolutionary in helping conservative messaging," according to libertarian Hannah Cox of Conservatives Concerned About the Death Penalty. As David Dagan and Steven Teles identified in *Prison Break: Why Conservatives Turned Against Mass Incarceration*, a key reason for the successes of the right-leaning movement post-2000 is identity vouching.[28] To reach constituents and decision makers on the right, the "asks" not only have to be couched in authentic messaging that appeals to their sensibilities and "ideologically resonance stories," as described in the Chapter 2, but also must be delivered by someone with credentials as a part of that tribe, conferring another layer of authenticity. This provides "cover" and space for other leaders to follow their lead. And so, they say, "much of the initial work of changing minds and forming low-profile coalitions of elite actors began [in the early to mid-2000s] before it was clear that the macro-politics of the issue changed[29] . . . a very small core group of movement leaders [decided] their group's position needed to change . . . they then [sought] to change the positions of the larger group of highly visible, ideologically unassailable movement leaders."[30]

Though it was this right-leaning cadre of advocacy groups first involved in the "coalition" that had weekly calls and regular meetings at the White House, disagreement on what the bill should do emerged between some of the advocates and Jared Kushner. According to Jason Pye of Freedom-Works, in the months before the First Step Act was to go up for a vote in the House, he confronted Kushner about the limitations of the bill, which at the time only focused on prison (corrections) reform: "I looked directly at Jared and said, 'You need sentencing reform in this bill; 924c,[31] Fair Sentencing Act retroactivity—those are the lowest-hanging fruit. It's stuff there's bipartisan support for, and I don't think you can pass this in the Senate without sentencing reform.' Kushner said, 'We want a 'clean prison reform bill.' Grover Norquist from Americans for Tax Reform[32] spoke up. He told Jared, 'Jason has a point. At the very least we should outline what you are willing to live with on sentencing reform.' Kushner responded: 'We want a clean prison bill.'" Kushner's attitude was shared by some Republican political leaders, who "believed that [sentencing reform provisions] made it a nonstarter among conservatives"[33] But without Democrats' support, the bill would have been dead on arrival. Liberal political and national liberal advocacy group support was needed to dial up the pressure. For that, Kushner turned to Van Jones.

Jessica Jackson, cofounder of #cut50 with Jones, said Kushner's ask came about after he had spoken to CNN's president, who told Kushner about the work Jones and Newt Gingrich had done in hosting the Bipartisan Criminal Justice Reform Summit of 2015. She said, "Jared called. He said he wanted to pull together a bipartisan meeting at the White House. Right off the bat, the first thing he talked about was the impact on him from his dad's incarceration. I felt like I had a lot in common with him because I had been through something similar, from the same loved ones' perspective." From then, #cut50 attempted to bring in left advocacy groups, especially established large national advocacy groups, to the preexisting right coalition to coalesce around the push for the federal criminal justice reform bill. In February of 2018, they were asked to put together bipartisan roundtables, along with Marc Levin of Right on Crime, to this end.[34] The clashes that ensued among the leadership of the advocacy groups were as deeply revelatory of intraleft ideological and tactical divisions as they were of the ability of national advocacy groups to use their weight to influence federal policy and political actors.

"We asked everybody," Jackson said. "The criminal justice director at the Brennan Center, Inimai Chettiar, was there. But [other than Chettiar] nobody would [come]. We didn't have a lot of DC insider groups. The ACLU wouldn't come. The DC insider groups were [saying], 'They're just full of shit, it's stupid.' I decided to pull together a bunch of groups on the left in #cut50's Empathy Network that were in direct services. Because I knew they would show up. We had Kevin Gay from Operation New Hope in Florida. We had Sue Ellen Allen from Reinventing ReEntry. So it was us." The general aversion of national liberal advocacy groups toward working on the bill could also be seen in large liberal funders' decisions at this time, as pointed out in Chapter 3. They either did not prioritize the FSA, withholding support in response to feedback from left-leaning non-profits,[35] or cut funding FSA advocates, as was the case with #cut50.[36]

Though #cut50 agreed to bring in representative advocacy groups from the left, the organization itself had reservations about what Kushner and the right coalition members were presenting. "Let me be very clear with you," Jackson asserted, "The draft bill that existed the day Jared talked to us was a piece of shit. Basically, it said, 'As an incentive, we'll give people extra phone time *if* they do . . . boom, boom, boom, boom, boom.' And it was like—yeah, no. There's a lot more common ground in reform. We need to do those too. At that point, the line I took with everybody was: we support the process, but we were not yet in support of the bill." #cut50 held that line for three drafts of the bill while conferring on them via email threads with the leaders of national liberal advocacy groups, like the Leadership Conference on Civil and Human Rights, the ACLU, and the centrist FAMM.[37] Even with the limited scope of a bipartisan bill on prison reform, it looked like it would be doomed to fail among Democrats at several points. The Department of Justice, led by "law and order" Attorney General Jeff Sessions, handed down a draft that "had multiple poison pills in it," including new mandatory minimums, according to Jackson.

"They put bird poop in the Kool-Aid" was Van Jones' blunt response to reporters about the DOJ draft. He and Jackson felt that the DOJ was acting in bad faith, and that it would end up costing the team the bill's passage.[38] #cut50 pushed back against the draft with Kushner. Trump's special assistant for domestic policy, Ja'ron Smith, called the DOJ, drawing a line in the sand: the administration would not accept the DOJ's "poison pill" suggestions. The DOJ acquiesced. According to Jackson, "we were able to pull together a decent bill that was just prison reform and reentry. At that point it was called the Prison Reform and Redemption Act,"[39] a name that spoke to its rootedness in the right's redemption story as the primary driving narrative of their engagement with reform. With some minor improvements, the Prison Reform and Redemption Act became the First Step Act.[40] Before the bill was voted on in the House in May 2018, the White House hosted a Prison Reform Summit, where President Trump praised several Republican governors for their criminal justice reforms, as well as Van Jones and Jared Kushner. About the now familiar themes of returning the formerly incarcerated to their communities where they could restore their dignity and contribute as workers, Trump discussed the stigma of incarceration for employment, mental health challenges, and drug treatment post-incarceration. "My administration strongly supports efforts [to reform the federal prison system]. Get a bill to my desk and I'll sign it. . . . We want the finest prison reform that you have anywhere." Looking at Kushner and Van Jones, he added, "Van . . . it's just as hard to go through the process and get a good bill as it is to get a bad bill, so let's get it right, will you please make sure, okay? If you see something you don't like . . . call me, we'll get it changed before we sign it and have to go through the whole process again."[41] With Trump's imprimatur, a few days later, the House voted.

In the vote and during its lead-up, the divisions among the liberal national advocacy organizations about this Trump-endorsed and Republican cosponsored bill were evident, as was their influence on Democratic members of Congress. Prior to the vote, a Dear Colleague letter[42] went out on May 17 from Democratic Senators Kamala Harris, Cory Booker, Dick Durbin, Sheila Jackson Lee, and civil rights icon John Lewis. It stated that they had heard from stakeholders[43] that their colleagues should oppose the bill. These stakeholders included the largest national liberal advocacy groups described by Jackson as "DC insiders" like the NAACP, the ACLU, the Southern Poverty Law Center, Human Rights Watch, the Drug Policy Alliance, and others, including JustLeadershipUSA and LatinoJustice PRLDEF, all members of the Leadership Council on Civil and Human Rights (LCCHR). Attached to the letter was an LCCHR letter entitled "Vote No on the FIRST STEP Act."[44] In bold in the first paragraph, the sentence "The Leadership Conference on Civil and Human Rights plans to include your position on the FIRST STEP Act in our voting scorecard for the 115th Congress" made clear the political consequences of a yes vote.[45] The final 2018 record released by the LCCHR did in fact score a vote *against* the First Step Act as a "pro-civil rights" vote.[46] Yet other large national advocacy groups, notably the National Urban League from the left and the centrist FAMM, urged a yes vote. And the bill's progressive Democrat cosponsor, Representative Hakeem Jeffries of New York, shot off a rejoinder Dear Colleague Letter with attachments from national advocacy organizations criticizing the points raised by the opposition letter submitted a day earlier, saying it was riddled with inaccuracies threatening to derail the reform effort.[47]

Among national right-leaning advocacy groups for criminal justice reform, such "deal breaker" differences were not as apparent as they were on the left, although ideological divisions certainly existed, say between libertarians and faith-based conservative groups. Division from the right came rather from an antireform contingent of the Republican Party, led by Senator Tom Cotton and from right-wing pundits like Tucker Carlson, who decried the bill as led by "elites." But at the center of the debate among left advocacy groups, as articulated in their letters of opposition and support, were two primary areas of contention that were to shape the progress and process of the final bill.

First, and perhaps most important, those on the left opposing the bill argued that it did not go far enough. The prison population potentially affected was too narrow and the bill did not take meaningful steps towards racial equity in the criminal justice system or toward "reduc[ing] rates of mass incarceration." Key to the left's opposition: the bill included "front-end" prison reforms but none on the "back end"—that is, sentencing reforms, such as those in the Sentencing Reform and Corrections Act (SRCA), which was at that moment held up in the Senate by majority leader Mitch McConnell in spite of a high probability of having the votes to pass.[48] The LCCHR wrote: "Without changes to sentencing laws that eliminate mandatory minimums, restore judicial discretion, reduce the national prison population, and mitigate disparate impacts on communities of color, the First Step Act would have little impact."[49] The Brennan Center, under the leadership of Inimai Chettiar, was not on the LCCHR letter as a signatory but urged a no vote on the "Trump prison bill" in a separate letter to Congress.[50] However, it was reported that "Chettiar said she would support the legislation on the merits if it was paired with a sentencing reform bill. 'No one's opposing anything in the First Step Act itself,' Chettiar [expressed]. 'It's more that it's not part of this broader package.'"[51]

DeAnna Hoskins, president of JustLeadershipUSA (JLUSA), which had an organizational goal of cutting the prison population in half by 2030, signed the LCCHR opposition letter. She attributed part of its narrow focus to what she described as an exclusionary process by which the bill had been drafted. "How the sausage was made was *unethical*," she emphasized. "The Leadership Council said they had never seen bills and negotiations happen behind back doors like that." Distinguishing JLUSA's strategy from that demonstrated in the First Step Act's development, she explained: "We sit and do community listening sessions and say, 'if this policy happens, how many of you in this room will it impact?'"

The second issue oppositional national groups focused on, which they saw as actually committing harm beyond the harm of omission, was that the FSA required a then-undeveloped algorithmic risk assessment tool that could "amplify racial disparities and perpetuate other injustices in the criminal justice system."[52] Hoskins, in speaking about the assessment tool, contended that the bill "locked Black people out of recidivism reduction programs such as education and programming, because we are simply high risk based on the color of our skin, the zip codes we come from. It was a structurally racist policy that got support from certain African Americans who don't understand policy and how it impacts marginalized communities. You just created *another* bill that blocked out people of color inside the correctional system from getting access to the services and resources they need."

The liberal and centrist advocacy groups who urged a yes vote disagreed. They saw opposition as an instance of letting the perfect be the enemy of the good during a time of Republican dominance in all branches of government, when some reform to ameliorate conditions of confinement and provide opportunities for early release was better than nothing. Holly Harris pointed out that endorsement was painful for FAMM without sentencing reform, "but it did have the expansion of the good time credit that was going to take a significant amount of time off of the sentences. They work so closely with these families who are so desperate to get their loved ones back that they really felt this is something we need to do."

Joshua Hoe, a formerly incarcerated activist who had consulted for #cut50, pushed back on the argument that the risk assessment system to be used was worse than what was already in place and therefore should be a deal breaker for the bill: "Risk assessments are inherently biased. But the question is, are they more or less biased than judicial discretion or prison discretion or warden discretion alone? People who make that decision absent a risk assessment tool are arguably worse. And probably more than any other piece of legislation that had been put out to date, there were more checks on algorithmic bias than I'd ever seen before: The methodology had to be posted. It had to be openly debated every year."[53]

Other leaders thought that the opposition was more directly based in politics than in good-faith opposition to the measures of the FSA. David Safavian, among others who had worked on the bill, told me that "It didn't go far enough" was the "public" reason, but the "private reason was they didn't want to give Trump and the Republicans a win," just as the Republicans had prevented reform under Obama.[54] Van Jones described hearing from "institutional liberals with big organizations to run" that they were afraid to work with the Trump White House because of a related dynamic:

progressive peer disapproval within the advocacy space of helping Trump achieve a "win," disapproval that could have monetary consequences because "they'll lose all their invitations to progressive conferences, just as we [at #cut50] lost our invitations. They'll lose their funding just as we lost our funding."

The voices from national advocacy groups opposing the First Step Act had an impact. The bill cleared the House 360–59, but 96 percent of the no votes came from Democrats.[55] While some saw this opposition to a sentencing reform–free First Step Act launched by liberal advocacy groups, as stymying reform efforts, others in the movement, like Holly Harris, saw a different motive: "I thought their opposition was strategic, they are principled," she stated. "Some might say shame on them, they only piled onto the bill when the sentencing piece got in there. You know, man—I think one of the mistakes we made in the beginning, was in thinking bipartisanship meant everybody in lockstep: if we issue a statement, everybody signs onto it. When we weren't trying to control the groups, when we finally cut the groups loose to speak in their own voice, to their own constituencies, to impact the relationships that they had, and to run their own strategy, even though we were coordinating that, it worked so much better."

By withholding support, some of the national liberal advocacy groups amenable to backing a bill that also included sentencing reforms may have gambled on the seemingly slim chance of being able to press for a more ambitious bill in the Senate. The gamble was large in that it would have to be supported by right-leaning advocacy groups, President Trump, and congressional leaders—especially the vocal antireform contingency led by Senator Tom Cotton. While I do not suggest that national advocacy groups have *more* power to determine legislative outcomes than "institutional" actors, like politicians, or that they single-handedly determined the outcome of the bill, certainly their strong influence was discernible in the FSA story. FAMM vice president Molly Gill had written that the Act splintered the reform advocacy community: "The future passage of federal criminal justice reform may not depend on who lives in the White House. Instead, it may depend on whether the criminal justice reform community—and its allies in Congress—are willing to accept an incremental bill like the First Step Act without sentencing reforms."[56]

Ultimately, sentencing reforms were on the table when the First Step Act moved over to the Senate, with pressure from national advocates. This was aided by President Trump's stated willingness to sign a bill with sentencing reforms, which several attributed to his meeting, brokered by Kim Kardashian, with Alice Johnson, the grandmother sentenced to life for a first-time drug offense.[57] Holly Harris pointed to Inimai Chettiar from the Brennan Center, who had withheld her support for a prison reform–only bill but, when provisions from the SRCA were added, now leveraged her support *for* the bill as an example of strategic liberal advocacy. This advocacy may have been partially attributable to the tight networks that formed among some national advocates that allowed close discussion and persuasion: Jessica Jackson of #cut50 told me of going on a mountain hike with Chettiar while she was still considering endorsing the bill. "We were talking through the whole thing and she was saying—if they actually added [sentencing] stuff, it would be a step in the right direction." The Brennan Center wasn't the only organizational opponent to flip, adding its name to the list of 200 advocacy organizations endorsing the FSA *with* sentencing reform. The ACLU and the NAACP likewise added their heavily qualified support. Bill Cobb pointed to "multiple clandestine meetings at the White House with [the executive director of the ACLU] and Trump. [The ACLU] finally did acquiesce to the First Step Act." He added emphatically, "It is a piece of shit legislation that don't mean nothing." Other national left advocacy groups like JustLeadershipUSA withheld support throughout.

With sentencing now on the table to win over more of the left/Democrats, the national advocacy groups (and, as described in previous chapters, philanthropists, business groups, and celebrities) launched their social and political capital to urge passage, lobbying aggressively using their strong preestablished relationships on the Hill. A key element of their eventual success was that, though the bill was bipartisan, it relied on ideologically tailored framing and language adopted by advocates in appealing to their constituencies. Trusted messengers with tribal credentials and resonant messaging were chosen depending on the target.

On the right, Holly Harris, playfully dubbed the McConnell whisperer,[58] was a former general counsel and finance chair for the Republican

Party of Kentucky. She had "every editorial board in Kentucky writing pieces about this, keeping the pressure on [McConnell]." Harris spoke of her strategy in reaching the majority leader, who would be responsible for bringing the bill to a vote and had the power to bury it: "You gotta take the folks that are gonna have the most impact [with McConnell]. The Faith and Freedom Coalition were critical in helping him get judges confirmed. So I took that group. McConnell just loved a former US attorney from Utah. I took him." McConnell also showed respect for Harris herself, inviting her to take a literal and figurative place of prominence next to him during a key meeting on the First Step Act. Because some Republican senators were more skeptical of sentencing reform than Democrats, in spite of Trump's support for it, framing some of the reforms as congruous with bread-and-butter Republican concerns for second amendment rights, for example, was utilized. According to Jessica Jackson, who also lobbied Republicans, "what was helpful was really working with the conservatives and finding the language that they would get onboard with. I walked into conservatives' offices with 924c [sentencing enhancement] cases: we had one guy who had been caught selling crack at his grandfather's house. His grandfather had been in the war and had a service weapon that had been through a fire and didn't work anymore up on the mantle, and he got a 924c. Like, 924c is the government coming for your gun rights! At that point, we were able to really build out our Republicans."

Between May and December 2018, the national advocacy groups most centrally involved counteracted and removed numerous roadblocks to the bill's progress, challenging incorrect whip counts that belied the extent of support for the bill and convincing sponsors not to back out. With only a few days to spare, and not without some last-ditch attempts to put a wrench in the works by antireform Republicans, on December 18 the FSA passed the Senate with a commanding bipartisan majority, 87 to 12. One hundred percent of the opposition votes this time came from Republicans. Senator Kamala Harris, who had coauthored the Dear Colleague letter of opposition to the earlier version, voted for it. The bill passed quickly and decisively in the House as well, 358 to 36, with 100 percent of the opposition votes, also in a flip from the summer, coming from Republicans.

SIMILAR TEAM, LOCAL GAMES: BIPARTISANSHIP AT THE STATE LEVEL

The bipartisan "formula" and many of the same national advocacy organizations and players seen in the FSA passage banked putatively more impactful though less visible results at the state level. The ACLU's Justice Division director, Udi Ofer, in an interview at a downtown New York café before the 2020 pandemic, said that he thought the successes in some red states were a much bigger story than the FSA itself, demonstrative of bipartisan victories with more aggressive reforms: "The last 15 years some of those same groups on the right [who were involved with the First Step Act] supported [major reforms at the state level]." He pointed to a recent Louisiana reform package, termed in the press as "an ambitious revamp."[59] "Until a few years ago [Louisiana] had the highest incarceration rate in the country," Ofer said. "And in 2017, a red legislature passed ten criminal justice reform bills that are expected to reduce the prison population by 10 percent over the next decade. It took on everything from habitual offender laws to mandatory minimums. I mean, it was really audacious, and this was in *Louisiana*!" he noted enthusiastically. "It happened in a red state with a red legislature, but a Democratic governor. Right-wing organizations like Right on Crime supported it, left-wing organizations supported it, grassroots organizations like VOTE [Voice of the Experienced, founded by formerly incarcerated activist Norris Henderson, a former Soros fellow] supported it." The "bipartisan" Louisiana suite of criminal justice bills was indeed sweeping. In addition to what Ofer mentioned, those incarcerated for first-time violent offenses (predictably excluding sexual offenses) were eligible for parole with less time served; there was a medical furlough program, an overhaul of drug sentencing, and expanded prison alternatives and reentry initiatives. The story of Louisiana also bore the marks of the acrimonious debates around the FSA's inclusion of sentencing reform: the original bills included more sentencing changes for violent offenses and a proposal to reclassify felonies, which were ultimately chopped.

Numerous examples of right and left national advocacy groups pushing criminal justice reform at the state level exist. In 2015 Holly Harris announced that her Justice Action Network (JAN) would be descending on the state of Michigan to actively lobby for decarceratory/ameliorative criminal justice reforms over a range of issues. Similar pushes by JAN would begin in Pennsylvania and Ohio that same year. "Hell freezes over—GOP and ACLU push prison reform," a headline announced,[60] as the move had the backing of the left-leaning ACLU and LCCHR (which, as we saw, opposed the FSA) and the right-leaning Faith & Freedom Coalition, the Center for American Progress, Right on Crime, and FreedomWorks. By 2020 a slate of what the Pew Research Center described as landmark criminal justice reform bills—20 of them—had passed in Michigan. These centered on, per usual, less violent offenses, providing arrest alternatives like citations, alternatives to jail like community service, community supervision reforms like lowering the amount of time on probation, and less punitive responses to traffic violations.[61] Some press coverage noted the parallel in movement dynamics with that seen at the federal level: "The coalition that has advanced criminal justice reform in Michigan spanned the progressive ACLU to the right-wing, Koch-funded Americans for Prosperity. A similar alliance of strange bedfellows was also instrumental in passing national legislation signed by President Donald Trump in 2018."[62]

There was also shared collaboration among advocacy groups on national initiatives aimed at reinforcing public understanding of a less carceral punitive framework. Craig DeRoche, President of Justice Fellowship, who was in the Oval Office for the FSA signing, helped establish April as national Second Chance Month in 2017, created with a Christian theological focus on resurrection—as DeRoche explained: "Second chances is what the cross is about, that's what spring is about, and that's what America is about." He wanted it to signal a broader cultural shift that would be nonpartisan. "The prosecutors and defense lawyers, the ACLU, the Tea Party—you name it, they all do Second Chance Month, and they all do their own events for their own organizations. And that was a strategic decision, because we wanted it to be durable."

"You've had this left-and-right Kumbaya moment on criminal justice reform for the past couple years," said former Texas Public Policy Foundation director of public affairs David Guenthner about the 2020 Michigan reforms.[63] Indeed, as we have seen, so much of the discourse surrounding criminal justice "bipartisanship" post-2000 between the right and left focused on and implied a "strange bedfellows" Kumbaya. Though the

Strange Bedfellows

discourse of bipartisanship/strange bedfellows/unlikely alliances suggests a fetishized coming together of two sides in reconciliation, compromise, and shared interest, which was partially true for reforms like the FSA, it hides a messier truth, as demonstrated in the Act's passage: although the commitment to reform is shared, what that means and how to get there *is* partisan. Differences and divisions by ideology among national advocacy groups were expressed by leaders of these groups. Some were superficial, but some were so fundamental that success for one group would instantly signal failure for the other.

FRICTIONS, FRACTURES, AND COMPLEMENTS

"I really love the Frederick Douglass quote, 'I would unite with anybody to do right and with nobody to do wrong,'" said Hannah Cox of Conservatives Concerned About the Death Penalty in response to my question about groups with whom she would not work. As a conservative libertarian, she had been criticized for an article against the death penalty for the ACLU because of the organization's firm pro-choice stance. She countered the critics, saying, "I'm not talking about abortion. We're talking about the death penalty. We're getting new audiences by doing this so that's what matters here." She added: "A lot of people have hardline positions. They don't get anything done."

Many interviewees for this project, most engaged at the national level in work that would imply some coalition-building but also those involved in state- and local-level work expressed support—some using the same quote from Frederick Douglass—for working on reform with those with whom they might have vehement disagreements on other issues. Jeffrey Deskovic, who spent 16 years in prison for a murder he didn't commit, noted pointedly about his state-level coalitional work on wrongful conviction policy: "I work with who I can, when I can." Barbara Allan, who founded Prison Families Anonymous after her husband's incarceration in 1967, said, "I'll take help from a devil if it helps my prison families, if we can make progress. I won't go out of my way to meet the devil but if he comes to me...."[64] Referring to the FSA while giving his answer about working with those with whom he might profoundly disagree, the Fortune Society's Andre

Ward said emphatically "We [at Fortune] are in no way in agreement with the current—the *person*—who assumes the highest seat of office in this country. But we feel that there are some areas that may lean favorably to our people. We will acknowledge, we will continue to press our issues, but it's not a function of us accepting crumbs off the table and being satisfied. We will never satisfy ourselves with crumbs."

Of course, the notion of "doing right," per Frederick Douglass, is subjective and hinges on the ideologically relevant stories told by groups and individuals and then framed for others, as motivations for pursuing group action to change the criminal justice system. This affects the teleology of that activism as well as the group's beliefs about the steps needed. These stories do not have to align perfectly. They can be complementary, reaching a broader swath of people across value systems, or enhancing the story told by the other side. On the other hand, they can cause conflict when others' stories[65] and needs go unacknowledged. Examples of national advocacy group stories that derive from different tellings of the problem of mass/overincarceration (Figures 6.1 and 6.2) provide an illustration of these differences in underlying stories, which influence campaigns.

Figures 6.1 and 6.2, from the right-leaning organizations Prison Fellowship and the American Conservative Union (ACU), exemplify the Christian redemption story, invoking second chances, forgiveness, and human dignity. The ACU flyer, which was distributed during their Prison Reform CPAC conference in 2019, ties that story with other ideological correlates, like a concern with freedom, excessive government spending, and public safety. Figures 6.3 and 6.4, from the left-leaning ACLU and Critical Resistance, evince the exodus story, one of racial justice, where in the case of Critical Resistance, the criminal justice system's connection to slavery demands its entire abolition or, for the ACLU, a dramatic numerical reduction, with a focus on racial equity. They also demonstrate the connecting of the exodus story with the left's ideological critique of capitalism—the ACLU flyer showing a Black child holding a poster reading "World's Pri$on Capital" and the Critical Resistance flyer reading "Dismantle the Prison Industrial Complex." These illustrate the left advocacy groups' challenging of the relationship between government and industry in the carceral system and their especially strong critique of private prisons,

FIGURE 6.1. Prison Fellowship Toolkit image, 2021

despite evidence that these prisons, housing 8 percent of all incarcerated, are not the primary drivers of mass incarceration or materially worse than government-run prisons.[66]

Beyond the minor differences, such as the left's spirited insistence on less stigmatizing, more humanizing language in discussions and campaigns, some of the most salient points of fracture between left and right include, from a left perspective, were the lack of shared acknowledgment of and/or the *centrality* of the exodus story and thus of racial justice in demands for change by the right. From a right perspective, there is the lack of shared acknowledgment of and/or the centrality not of their story of redemption and second chances but of their overriding concern with "public safety" *first*.

FIGURE 6.2. American Conservative Union informational flyer, 2019

David Safavian observed, "The Soros folks' big initiatives are about something—'justice': racial justice, economic justice, environmental justice, immigration justice. And only *after* they get to that do they get to public safety."

Robert Rooks, looking back at the development of the racial justice focus among left-leaning national advocacy groups, pointed to the initial

FIGURE 6.3. ACLU Smart Justice campaign flyer, 2019

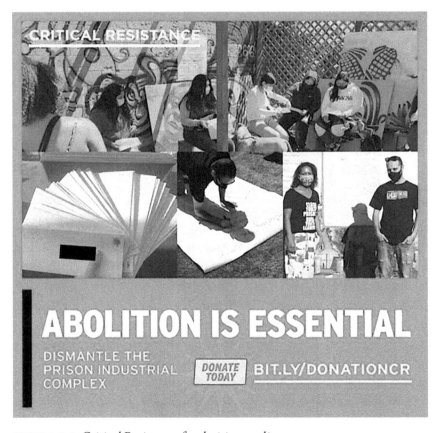

FIGURE 6.4. Critical Resistance fundraising media

steps taken by a few large organizations that "elevated the issue," such as the Drug Policy Alliance (DPA). DPA funded local groups like the Alliance for Safety and Justice, which decided to substantively incorporate racial justice into its criminal justice work in 2004. DPA itself, Rooks noted, started its racial justice focus, rather than a more universal concern with marijuana legalization and harm reduction, in 2006–2007, through the "trailblazing" leadership of Deborah Small, who would go on to found Break the Chains: Communities of Color and the War on Drugs. "We were all local leaders, local organizations; she was one of the first national leaders in drug policy and racial justice on this issue of people going to prison." We can hear the imperative of the racial justice/exodus narrative to left advocacy groups in the words of Jose Saldana, executive director of Releasing Aging People in Prison (RAPP) and a formerly incarcerated activist and prison abolitionist. While stating in our interview that he was on board with incremental reforms, trying to "take that wall down one brick at a time," he qualified, "[If I support a policy, it] will have to help me uproot the legacy of racism. Take the 'ban the chokehold.' That's a cosmetic reform. It doesn't address the legacy of racism in the criminal legal system. They'd just shoot us instead! If we don't take out the root of racism that justifies prisons, we'll always have them, because they were made for us."[67]

According to Bill Cobb, "The bipartisan shit is bullshit. . . . When the left says there's bipartisan cooperation, they have completely abandoned the fucking *nucleus* of our tension—it's minus the racism." He described a 2017 meeting of the bipartisan umbrella organization, Coalition for Public Safety, that took place at the TPPF during his tenure at the ACLU that exemplified the clash between right and left based on what he described as lacking a centering of a racial justice narrative in criminal justice and denying a racial root by some in the right's leadership: "One of the [leaders at Right on Crime] disagreed with racial disparities being a driver of incarceration. [He said] 'Racial disparities are a figment of your imagination, a left-leaning lie. Black people are in prison the most because they don't take care of their children.'" Cobb paused. "You know what every fiber of my being told me to do that day? Quit. The insult was horrible. Even worse was the sanctioning of it. . . . The ACLU continued to work with conservative organizations in an effort to be branded as bipartisan. But [right national organizations] co-opt our legislative efforts and bring in the White community bullshit, watering down the needs of the most impacted people. They're not my ally. They're my enemy."

David Safavian acknowledged disparate racial impacts in the criminal justice system, but expressed concern about centering and leading with a racial justice narrative when making outreach to right-leaning politicians and voters: "I don't think any thinking person who is reasonably well informed believes that racial bias doesn't exist," he stated "[But] there is a history of overusing the term racist. You don't like a tax increase, you're a racist. You don't like Obamacare, you're a racist. When you use race in the context of advocacy, immediately for conservatives a shield goes up. It's not fair, it's not right, but it is a natural reaction when you've been unfairly labeled a racist for so long." According to Safavian, it was therefore a tactical movement error, when trying to advance reforms that needed the support of the right, to lead with narratives of racial justice, as it could have sabotaged policy advances: "Let's say the ACU partners with a left-wing group. We make a joint pitch to a Republican who, as long as it is kind of bipartisan, might be able to get behind it. And then they read the racial stuff that doesn't advance the substantive policy case but it's in there to make people on the left *feel* good. The policy-maker goes—wait a minute, this isn't really bipartisan. It blows away any credibility that it's a left-right project. You lose [supporters]." It may be for this reason—fear of losing credibility when race and criminal justice have become litmus-test left issues—that during a day-long ACU Prison CPAC conference in Philadelphia in 2019, the only participants who talked about race were those who had been invited from left groups, and the term "mass incarceration" was not used even though individual reformers on the right privately acknowledged the racial dynamics of incarceration.

There were thus competing diagnoses of the etiology and continued problem of US incarceration. For the left, the origin point of the problem was slavery and the injustices that followed that historical legacy, compounded by capitalism. For the right, the problem was the disproportionately harsh, costly overreaction of the 1970s, a mistake that did not allow for human dignity and second chances and redemption, which capitalism might have helped to remedy by providing work to give meaning. And just as these diagnoses could either complement or clash with each other, the national movement showed that there could also be a clash of solutions.

"You're not going to get to long-term system change if people don't want to change systemic racism," said Laura Porter, a leader of several national organizations committed to abolishing the death penalty and promoting more wide-ranging progressive reforms, when she expressed what many left national advocates have posited. Because many on the left believe the criminal justice system is at its core racist and another form of slavery, their more aggressive decarceration goals stand in contrast to, and are unsupported by the right, and are articulated with a racial imperative. Udi Ofer of the ACLU pointed out that at least three major national advocacy organizations on the left during the 2010s had a literal "cut 50" decarceration goal: JustLeadershipUSA, #cut50, and the ACLU, which would go on to create a "50-state blueprint" data tool and campaign that provided a pathway toward that objective, going so far as to persuade most Democratic presidential candidates in 2020 to commit to that number, including Joe Biden. Ofer noted that he added a racial justice objective, ending racial disparities in the system, when he took over as director of the ACLU Justice Division, naming it coequal with the goal of a 50 percent cut in incarceration.

Among right and centrist advocates, there was a sense that the left advocacy groups were, as Kevin Ring of FAMM said, "getting over their skis," with their demands, fraying bipartisanship, especially with the 2020 demands after the George Floyd murder by police officer Derek Chauvin to "defund" the police by some but not all liberal advocacy groups (the NAACP declined to support "defund," and the ACLU promoted "divesting" from police and reinvesting in Black and Brown communities).[68] David Safavian saw the left as overreaching, and getting out of step with the position of politicians and average voters. "I'm not casting aspersions," he insisted, "but when you overreach, you're giving an opportunity to the 'bad' [antireform] guys to say, 'See, we told you.' Conservatives tend to be more measured, and that's why you saw criminal justice reform spread to 33 states, primarily driven by Southern 'red' governors."

Just as the right's decentering of race as a focus (and therefore its preference for the term "overincarceration" as noted in Chapter 1) entirely ignores the very raison d'être for much left advocacy, so right national advocates feel that left advocacy groups that become rigid and orthodox about what reform means, ignoring right-leaning advocate and voter rationales for and concerns about reform, risk losing all but their base. Safavian recalled a meeting he had with progressive Philadelphia district attorney Larry Krasner, who campaigned on a reform platform in 2017. Krasner was skeptical of the need to learn to communicate with conservatives outside of progressive frames on reform, as he could turn out his base for elections. "I shot back at him: that's well and good in Philadelphia. But if Democrats make this a litmus test issue a matter of dogma, it will become highly polarized. We'll have a stalemate, and nothing will get done to fix the *system*. You take that position, you're throwing all the people who live in Republican governor states under the bus. They will never get more reform."

For all the friction among national advocacy groups, some base areas of agreement are discernible, independent of ideological and practical justifications for them. In fact, areas of agreement among advocates may be much larger than exists in the political arena, as evidenced by, for example, bipartisan pushback against the antireformist contingent of the Republican Party during the FSA, or similar resistance to Attorney General Jeff Session's 2017 attempts to seek maximum penalties for federal drug offenses.[69] According to Dagan and Teles in their 2017 study of the conservative reform movement, "the notion that the US unnecessarily incarcerates far too many people is becoming standard conservative fare,"[70] which is obviously a key principle of liberal advocacy. Left advocacy groups are more likely to press for drug decriminalization or outright legalization, especially of marijuana (as the ACLU, the LCCHR, the NAACP, and others did in 2020), but right national groups such as those in Holly Harris's JAN have been part of a push to scale back drug laws, reducing harsh penalties and mandatory minimums.[71] The new libertarian Cannabis Freedom Alliance coalition backed by Charles Koch is also pushing for marijuana legalization.[72]

On even more "unlikely" topics like the benefits of restorative, noncarceral alternatives in response to violent crime, an issue one would assume to be the purview of the left, advocates saw limited convergence: "There are some tensions around decarceration particularly for violent offenders, but

I don't know if that's a complete fissure because I've seen more conservative groups starting to talk about the need to look at that," said Jolene Forman of the Chan Zuckerberg Initiative. Right on Crime's Marc Levin saw multiple areas of commonality. He invoked the liberal Common Justice as a model of success. This organization, based in Brooklyn, focuses on violent felonies in adult courts, providing alternatives to incarceration, and has a strong racial justice component. It is now being modeled in Texas. "Not every violent offense needs to result in incarceration," Levin said. He also offered that right advocacy groups by 2020 were agreeing that too many people were under correctional supervision, for too long, with excessive conditions and fees attached. Philanthropist Laura Arnold, whose foundation has funded JAN's "across the aisle" work, said that she saw many political "windows" for bipartisanship, which she was trying to pry open. "I'll be honest with you," she conferred, "there is sadly so much low-hanging fruit in criminal justice reform that needs focus."

WITHER BIPARTISANSHIP?

Sociologist Arlie Hoschchild in *Strangers in Their Own Land,* takes on the importance of deeply *felt* stories told by people on the right and the left to construct their understanding of history, current politics, and indeed their moral universe. These are stories that transcend objective conditions and are the emotional anchor of our political and social perspectives. The dominant story of the left now is one where many participants believe the system is working as intended, as an extension of slavery. Breaking the chains of people of color and especially Black people, then, is the ultimate objective and anything less is felt deeply as moral affront. The dominant story of the right is of second chances, redemption for the fallen, but fallen who have, after all, made a *mistake*, and the belief that the overreaction of the criminal justice system has been a costly error. Therefore, the remedy must restore dignity through engagement in work, faith, and family, but must also ensure a deeply felt concern for the safety of the community. Anything other than that is, for them, a moral affront.

This battle of stories and linked solutions was played out in the passage of the FSA and has also been played out nationally. At the same time,

Strange Bedfellows

because both sides have compelling arguments based on different traditions for reform of the system, there are complementary justifications for overhauling mass/overincarceration. According to billionaire reform philanthropist Michael Novogratz, "to get shit done, we need to win Republicans over. You can't be 'fuck you' to Republicans. You have to convince them in a way that's authentic that they're going to be safe, that people deserve a second chance, and this will be more economically efficient, and it's the right thing to do." The same need applies to Republicans toward the left. This doesn't imply the need for lockstep consensus, as social movement scholars have pointed out that heated debate can exist while moving toward a goal: "The civil rights movement was a lively band of rebels, united under the umbrella of a cause but with many differing ideas about how and why they should proceed. However, they had spent years working together and had a shared culture of mutual respect—even if it was quite tense at times," sociologist Zeynep Tufekci argues.[73]

The Sentencing Project's Marc Mauer hinted at how the damage of disagreement might be mitigated without either side "conceding" ground for engagement and objectives: "The pollsters tell us, 'Race is the *least* effective messaging [for reform]. Don't talk about race if you want to win them over.' The image [that] always comes to my mind is 1954: Dr. King and civil rights leaders are getting ready to launch major actions. But then the pollster comes back and says, 'Don't talk about race. White people in Alabama won't hear that.' Fortunately, they didn't have any polling. They did what needed to be done. Partly we *need* to talk about race. *And* we also need to talk about public safety. Current policies are very destructive in both those areas."[74]

In other words, in spite of much effort among technocratically focused reformers to present the public and politicians with rational, quantified evidence-based assessments and cost-centered arguments urging fiscal responsibility, incarceration and crime control are ultimately "gut," emotionally laden issues, and so without appeals based on emotions, tied to ideological stories, larger movement building is difficult. None of the national reform advocates on either side interviewed for this project said that they became involved because they felt swayed by rational or fiscal arguments, a finding Dagan and Teles also reported from their interviews with conservative leaders.[75] And so it is puzzling why some might think the general electorate is any different. Rationalizations based on evidence appear to be post hoc.[76] Criminologist Michael Tonry has also argued that instrumental arguments about cost savings and reductions in crime and recidivism will eventually fail because the harsh policies that have led to the explosion of imprisonment were premised on moral arguments.[77]

There are two key questions for the movement. First, even with an openness to bipartisanship and humanistic appreciation for deep stories, how should these understandings be expanded beyond the elite "grasstops" of the national movement to the general population? Second, can this do more than, as Andre Ward said, produce crumbs of reform? Consensus may be wide but not deep, as some have charged that "elite-led bipartisan deal cutting" has been grossly insufficient to the task of major change.[78]

In the final chapter, this book moves away from the "unlikely bedfellows" thus far analyzed—the unusual political alliances and stakeholder groups not traditionally associated with criminal justice reform nevertheless brought together through mainstreamization. It gives the stage to the group that should have been central to discussions of reforming criminal justice and yet, until the post-2000s, were primarily at the periphery: the formerly incarcerated. At the start of the 2020s, they were more consciously incorporated through their stories, lived experiences, and increasingly, leadership. Chapter 7 gives them the final say as we assess the significance of the changes in the post-2000 national criminal justice reform movement. We then step back from the First Step Act to look at what the reform movement's current configuration means and what it portends for the future of incarceration in the United States, for social movements, and for democracy.

SEVEN

FORMERLY INCARCERATED ACTIVISTS AND THE FUTURE OF CRIMINAL JUSTICE REFORM

THE DIRECTLY IMPACTED AND THE FIRST STEP ACT

At the signing of the Second Chance Act of 2007, President Bush was flanked by US Senators, the attorney general, and members of his cabinet. In his remarks, he pointed to a man in the audience, the formerly incarcerated Thomas Boyd, whom Bush had met while visiting a faith-based program supported by his administration's Prison Reentry Initiative. "He's working, back with his family, he's a good guy," Bush praised. Though he was not standing next to the president, another formerly incarcerated person's influence on the federal reform was even more significant: Pat Nolan, a Republican leader in the California State Assembly who had spent 29 months in federal custody after his conviction in 1993 for racketeering. Nolan had been a powerhouse as president of the faith-based advocacy group Prison Fellowship, using his political know-how and network, identity as a conservative, and personal story to contribute "substantially" to the success of the SCA and other federal legislation.[1] Before the SCA's passage, he advocated for it as a witness at the Joint Economic Committee's hearing in 2007, "Mass Incarceration in the United States: At What Cost?" "Others have discussed the financial cost of mass imprisonment," Nolan's statement read, "I will try to give you some perspective on the human toll it is taking."

Nolan continued in the 2010s to play a role in federal reform and in the First Step Act. As he stood alongside politicians and advocates near the president's desk in the Oval Office in 2018 for the FSA's signing, it was clear, though, that the optics—and reality—of formerly incarcerated people (FIPs), and those who had been directly impacted by mass/over-incarceration's influence in the mainstreamization/nationalization of the criminal justice reform movement, had changed in at least some respects. Nolan was invited by President Trump to give comments, but so were other FIP national advocacy leaders and individuals who had supported the coalition to advance the FSA. Among these were David Safavian, of the ACU's Nolan Center for Justice, John Koufos of Right on Crime, former NYPD commissioner Bernard Kerik, Georgetown professor Shon Hopwood—tapped by the White House to engage in reform policy after a 60-minute special on Hopwood's story aired in 2017—and Topeka Sam of #cut50. "I thank Jessica Jackson and Van Jones from #cut50 who have believed in formerly incarcerated leadership and have invested to make sure we were put in the front of this," Sam commented, before alluding to another constituency that had been key in pushing the FSA standing beside her: the directly impacted. "The reason why this happened was because of Jared [Kushner]." Addressing him directly, she said, "You experienced incarceration through your father, and you fought like you were in there just like we were. . . . We have been fighting and we will continue to fight. This is just a first step."

Outside of the Oval Office in December 2018, the influence of FIP advocates was further evident. Forty such advocates, including all of those at the FSA signing, and others like FAMM president Kevin Ring, founder of JLUSA Glenn Martin, How Our Lives Link Altogether! (H.O.L.L.A) founder Cory Greene, and #cut50 consultant and Decarceration Nations podcast host Joshua Hoe had added their names to a letter to Senate leaders urging action on the FSA before year's end, noting its imperfections but maintaining that it would provide relief to people in federal prison and their families. And, of course, the individual stories of then-incarcerated people like Alice Marie Johnson and Matthew Charles were first used by

Formerly Incarcerated Activists and the Future

advocates to gain support for the FSA. Later their personal stories became part of the public relations campaign praising its successes, with Johnson speaking at the Republican National Convention in 2020 and featured in a Super Bowl commercial praising Trump's criminal justice reforms. Matthew Charles would be a guest at the 2020 State of the Union address, where Trump pointed to his accomplishments in prison, saying, "Welcome home." Jared Kushner thanked Charles for being able to "utilize his story" to promote passage of the FSA. Charles would soon after pen an op-ed for *The Washington Post*, describing his vision for the next steps beyond the FSA. While the motives for centering the stories of Johnson and Charles were at least partially political, the fact that emphasizing second chances and letting people out of prison would be seen as a politically winning move and not harmful to reelection is in itself instructive.

As Chapter 6 showed, the FSA became a flashpoint for disagreement among advocacy groups about what criminal justice reform should look like and who should be its standard-bearers. Formerly incarcerated and directly impacted leaders were as much a part of the pushback to the act as some were part of the advocacy strategy. "We are so fractured as a community as a direct result," said Bill Cobb, himself incarcerated for seven years. "Formerly incarcerated people vehemently opposed—we are still vehemently opposed—to this day to the First Step Act." Andrea James, the formerly incarcerated leader of the National Council on Incarcerated and Formerly Incarcerated Women, wrote for the *Yale Law Journal*: "The answer in 2019 by Congress to the racist, harmful, and discriminatory criminal legal system, was to offer up . . . the First Step Act [which] keeps the system trained on the most vulnerable among us and sends the message that there is no need to fix the system itself."[2]

Incarcerated and formerly incarcerated people have been anything but passive bystanders in the hundreds of years since the establishment of prisons in the US. The long history of their involvement in prison reform movements makes this clear. There were the prison uprisings across the United States in the 1950s against deplorable conditions, which led to media and political attention and public demands for action, as well as growing political and legal activism and unity among the incarcerated in the 1960s. There were also sit-down strikes, insurrections, and calls for "convict power" in the 1970s, epitomized by the Attica uprising, the racial justice demands inspired by the Black Panthers in the Queens House of Detention, and the Folsom Prison strike in California, where the incarcerated forged an interracial unity, made demands about conditions, legal rights, racism, and violence, and formed a nascent labor movement.[3] This work would continue within and outside prisons in the 1980s and 1990s, "back when we were the lepers of society," DeAnna Hoskins of JustLeadershipUSA described derisively.

Many FIP leaders on the left who had been in the work since the 1990s felt that there was not enough deference and recognition in the "new" post-2000s movement configuration of the autonomous, grassroots organizing of the incarcerated and FIPs before criminal justice reform became a mainstreamed issue. "I remember the difficulties and challenges in even getting an article written in the paper in 2003 on criminal justice reform . . . we had lots of 'experts,' but not a lot of voices," Robert Rooks of the Alliance for Safety and Justice reflected. Bill Cobb pointed to the largest, most active umbrella coalition of FIPs and FIP-led organizations in the "reform" movement, the Formerly Incarcerated, Convicted People and Families Movement (FICPFM), as an example of a powerhouse organization that had its origins with activists within prisons. "It's taken minimally 20 years to get FICPFM to the degree where it has enough capacity to be recognized among philanthropic institutions, perceived to be leaders. The work that is driving across the country is deeply rooted in the Pennsylvania prison system, within the Angola prison system, people who came out of those institutions, like Malik Aziz and Norris Henderson. . . . We have all this momentum because we *made* criminal justice a shiny object."

AT THE TABLE? PHILANTHROPY AND "CENTERING" THE FORMERLY INCARCERATED

As Bill Cobb's statement implies, even if those who had been heroically pushing the cause of reform up the mountain, when all forces were against them, were still unsung, a major change in the post-2000 criminal justice reform movement was the move *within* organizations and institutions of power, money, and influence away from the highly limited inclusion, or outright exclusion, of the formerly incarcerated. It was a move away from dominance by "experts" from the academy, law, or professional nonprofit management to one where direct "lived" experience mattered. It meant that large philanthropy/philanthropists, as we saw in Chapter 3, were more willing to invest in that leadership (The Jordan Brand, for instance, donated $1 million in 2020 to FICPFM). The recent shift meant, according to Andre Ward of the Fortune Society, FIPs being at the "table where decisions are being made," a seeking of their voices and stories and cultivation of skills by philanthropy and within nonprofit advocacy organizations. Ward described this change as one that had developed in the mid- 2000s, when "our leadership was recognized, the analysis we were putting forth was honored and respected, where we were being consulted to inform the discussion, versus leaning on criminologists and the 'brain trust.'" Robert Rooks agreed: "There's been a lot of shifts in this field from 2010 to 2020, and one is the increasing of investments in people directly impacted." This has seen replication in international movements for reform, as Incarceration Nations Network founder Baz Dreisinger observed during our 2020 interview: "That is starting to have ripple effects around world. In the UK, which is most following in our footsteps in terms of popularization of the issue, there's a lot of directly impacted leaders in the movement that are being supported and brought to the fore of the movement." She pointed out that, in activist and academic panels on mass incarceration, she has been finding herself much more frequently the only person without incarceration experience, "which I'm thrilled about. It's been a tangible, radical shift."

The disconnect, being addressed only in the past 10 years, between those discussing and deciding criminal justice reform and those with justice involvement, has been described by advocates on the left and the right. "If you look at the amount of money being spent, we would convene meetings with all the biggest funders, and recipients of funding—$125 million a year—dealing with reform and I was the only person who has ever spent time in jail at the table," Bill Cobb noted with exasperation. Craig DeRoche of Justice Fellowship described hearings at the MacArthur foundation in 2011: "I was the only one with a criminal conviction, the only one who had been addicted and was in recovery. They love being in a university where they can meet all these smart people, I'm like, what the hell, have they never talked to somebody like me?"

"I've definitely seen a shift around lending the voices of people who are impacted. As people who have been impacted are trained, developed, and speaking up or utilizing their experience to empower the community, I feel like legislation will change," said Topeka Sam when I interviewed her in her Ladies of Hope Ministries (LOHM) office in Harlem in 2019. She had taken criticism for going to the Trump White House, but argued, "If I didn't go there, no one who looked like me was going to be there, who has been through what I've been through." Her personal example appeared to demonstrate the institutionalized inclusion of the formerly incarcerated by philanthropy and advocacy organizations. She had recently taken a position as senior adviser to New Yorkers United for Justice, a coalition of national and local reform organizations advocating for moderate reforms in the state, with funding from philanthropist Dan Loeb. As noted in Chapter 3, LOHM was in a corporate partnership with Loeb's Third Point.[4] In previous years, she had been a Soros fellow and was supported by celebrity John Legend and Bank of America's "Unlocked Futures" accelerator program, receiving advice and funding to "grow the impact and reach"[5] of her program. She was also on the board of directors of The Marshall Project.

Liberal-leaning philanthropies and mainstream advocacy organizations "searching for FIPs to elevate and have a voice"[6] have brought with them commitments to hire FIPs, which has a ripple effect. Bill Cobb, hired as deputy director of the ACLU's Smart Justice project, was positioned to then hire more FIPs and change institutional culture. This pivot has brought additional apparatuses to brand, market, and scale the work of "impactful" organizations created and led by FIPs. It has been infusing their organizations with funding and cultivating these individuals as leaders and social entrepreneurs under institutionally agreed upon theories of change. Funders assist with capacity building, for instance. This manifests differently according to organizational "need" but includes training in "storytelling," "narrative development," "infrastructure development," financial training and management, coaching in organizing, building up membership bases, network building, and "movement capacity building," such as moving different organizations toward shared goals.[7]

Jolene Forman, director of criminal justice policy at the Chan Zuckerberg Initiative (CZI), pointed to CZI's emphasis on the leadership of FIPs in such work through their movement and capacity-building team under the leadership of Gina Schwartz. Among the individuals and organizations Schwartz's team had recently worked with was the FICPFM. "They are an incredible network of impacted leaders who are fighting to extend their status," Schwartz imparted.[8] "They're asking for resources and ways of growing their infrastructure and power. We're able to work with trusted trainers and allies and people within their movement to help them gain the additional skills that they need to get to their goals. When they ask for the tools and resources to help them build narrative, we provided them with expert coaches and expert campaign strategists and people who can help them develop their own trajectories."[9]

The language used by some funders, including to describe their interventions in the space and among FIPs is frequently borrowed from that used to describe business startups, demonstrating the philanthrocapitalist ethos, with corporate culture and "quasi-entrepreneurial" structures dominating.[10] The term "accelerator," for instance, describes help given in the form of education, mentorship, and funding for startup companies with promising products. But it is now being used across large philanthropy to characterize "incubating" FIP-led, reform-oriented nonprofits,[11] also demonstrating the growing weight of tech-philanthropists in the space. In 2021, CZI launched its $350 million Justice Accelerator Fund, underscoring the shift to conscious "centering" of FIPs, especially racial minorities. The fund was established on the principle that "those closest to the problems have the best solutions" (a spinoff of the slogan of JustLeadershipUSA),[12] and appointed a formerly incarcerated leader, previously a manager in CZI's "Formerly Incarcerated People Program" as its strategic advisor.

A STORY, A HUMAN FACE . . . A TOKEN?

There were obvious advantages and ethical imperatives to movement participants and advocacy groups of such "humanization" work,[13] facilitated by FIPs telling their stories to educate the public or politicians. Often with a relatable, tragic narrative arc,[14] these stories were seen as empowering, since FIPs could assert ownership over them and define a contribution to the movement, allowing transformation of the wounds of incarceration into a means to help others.[15] It took incarcerated people out of the realm of the abstract, stigmatized Other to become the "human face" of an issue,[16] imbuing a sense of "there but by the grace of God go I" (or my daughter, son, brother, sister). They gave testimony to injustices, inhumanities, and the overall ineffectiveness of the system, with stories that were meant to change "hearts and minds," and the culture of punitiveness generally, but also to win specific reforms. FAMM had been founded in 1991 by Julie Stewart, whose brother had been sentenced under a mandatory minimum statute to five years for growing marijuana plants. Now led by formerly incarcerated Kevin Ring, it has long used Stewart's and Ring's stories of involvement, and those of other FAMM members, as arguments for change. "When the US Sentencing Commission is considering changes to the guidelines, we will write to our members and say, 'Who was sentenced under this guideline? Tell us your story.' When we do our amicus briefs at the Supreme Court or other levels, we use personal stories to put a human face on the arguments. One of the main provisions in the First Step Act was the 924(c) stacking charge. Julie Stewart was at Weldon Angeles's sentencing in 2003. Calling attention to the misuse of 924(c) was making Weldon a household name," Ring described.

Wrongfully convicted FIPs, who became prominent as advocates post-2000 when DNA technology allowed them to more readily prove their innocence, had morally unassailable, empathetic claims to the necessity of extensive reforms. Thus, they were highly valued and used by reform organizations on a spectrum of issues, for lobbying, public education, and fundraising,[17] in addition to forming their own exoneree-led organizations and coalitions. The Central Park Five and their fellow New Yorker exonerees Marty Tankleff and Jeffrey Deskovic, for instance, have been active in pushing for innocence-related state reforms and have worked as lobbyists and speakers for anti-death penalty organizations. Exoneree-advocates like them have had a discernible impact in shifting the debate around this topic and others. They have testified in all state hearings where death penalty abolition has recently passed.[18]

Formerly Incarcerated Activists and the Future

The impact of exonerees' and FIPs' stories on the movement was due partially to their bearing direct witness to what they were describing, as opposed to an academic or other professional outsiders' assessment. "If I was to try to be an advocate without that experience, some nameless person that's working at some nonprofit, how effective would I be at that?" Jeffrey Deskovic asked rhetorically. This helped with legislative lobbying, as well as in reaching the general public. David Safavian, who felt that his incarceration gave him more passion to pursue reforms, remarked: "Objectively, you have more credibility, when you are talking to policy makers, [if you] say, 'I've been there, I know what it's like' . . . it's not to say people who haven't been there can't make the same case, but it doesn't resonate as much as my experience." The credibility of formerly incarcerated leaders Safavian, Pat Nolan, and Kevin Ring among Republican policy-makers may be enhanced by life circumstances and ideological backgrounds that closely approximate those of the people to whom they are making appeals: each was prosecuted for white collar offenses, and each had come from a Republican background. In the case of Nolan and Ring, their preincarceration careers had been marked by advocating and writing legislation for harsh mandatory minimum sentencing. They were in a unique position to "identity vouch"[19] for the need for change before skeptical GOP policy-makers who believed that criminal justice reform wasn't needed for people "like" them. Marc Levin of Right on Crime had evidence for the credibility of formerly incarcerated advocates with the public. In 2018 his organization had polled the question of who were the most trusted messengers with right-leaning members of the public. He found that the police were most trusted. But second most trusted were formerly incarcerated people. On the other hand, he explained, "Republicans basically said that when they heard something from the ACLU or BLM, they would be *less* likely to support it."

With the established primacy of those with direct experience, with large funder-backed support for their narrative/story building, and with cultivation of select individuals and organizations in the leadership "pipeline,"[20] several concerns were expressed. Exoneree Jeffrey Deskovic found recounting his story "cathartic": "It's voluntary . . . and I feel like it is meaningful. It's a way of making suffering count." But others pointed to the toll of these recountings. "There are lots of needs within the movement around the trauma of storytelling," according to Michael Mendoza, national director of #cut50. Mendoza, who had been sentenced at 15 and spent 17 years in prison for his involvement in a gang-related homicide, was not alone in his concern. FIP activists being encouraged to "leverage" their stories, burdened with psychological anguish and often suffering from PTSD, sometimes felt they were being used as tools in the arsenal of the movement, and came away with emotional distress.[21] In some instances, there was a perceived exploitation of stories. "You really engage in that trauma porn every day. I'm on the panel, because I need to tell you about the time that I was raped, and you're gonna give me $100 for that, and I do that six times a week. That's no way to live," Dominique Morgan of Black and Pink said. This "trauma porn" was often poorly compensated or uncompensated, leading some FIP leaders like Topeka Sam or death row exonerees, through the organization Witness to Innocence, to form their own speakers' bureaus.

As Morgan implied in her statement about being "on the panel *because* I need to tell you I was raped," a related concern about the storytelling imperative for some FIP leaders, especially Black and non-White Latino leaders, is that within large advocacy groups or within government, all or most of what they are seen as bringing to the table *is* a story, in essence being used as a token.[22] DeAnna Hoskins of JLUSA was critical of the way in which some FIPs themselves, selected by those in positions of institutional power to be the "face" of an issue, were not doing enough with that status: "If you're the face of criminal justice, how are you using your platform to change policies and not just be tokenized to be out in front?" she asked. Among those who shared this perspective, many felt ancillary to policy-making or institutional leadership, excluded from control or input regarding the use of institutional resources. Michael Mendoza, while expressing gratitude for the opportunities he and FIPs had been given to "have a voice," in the movement, felt strongly that FIPs were lacking recognition and influence: "We need to provide access for FIPs to be at the table of policy and strategic meetings, associated with what's next in the criminal justice reform movement," he posited. "I believe there is more room for us to be included in every [nook] and cranny that defines the vision of what we do."

Formerly Incarcerated Activists and the Future

Just how much FIPs were to guide the direction of the movement, and who among the over 5 million of these individuals living in the US should be recognized as leaders and/or spokespeople remained a question. Abolitionist FIPs of color in this space and logically connected to the racial-justice linked exodus story felt that they should determine the direction of change. Said Bill Cobb with passion: "We should not have people who have not spent time in jail lead [these] efforts. Get the fuck out of the way of people that are the most impacted by this. Just because you went to school, just because you're part of this organization, doesn't give you insight, influence, or power. . . . Our fight is diluted when institutions carry *my* voice, my needs, the outcomes I must have. I don't have a choice whether or not to fight for my life. For everyone else it's just a job." Releasing Aging People in Prison's Jose Saldana largely concurred, believing that FIPs should be at the "forefront of the movement to end mass incarceration," but qualified pointedly, "you have to *earn* leadership," as he did; it isn't conferred or implicit by virtue of just having been incarcerated.[23]

Among those who disagreed with a focus on leadership predominantly by FIPs was David Safavian. As noted earlier, he acknowledged the credibility he had as a FIP leader, but said, "I am not of the mind that only directly impacted people should be doing this, that this is 'our' fight and we're leading the charge. That's bunk. Rich people should never help poor people, because only poor people should be fighting for poor people? Everyone has a stake in public safety, don't tell me the only people qualified to talk about it are those who have actually been locked up. If that's the case, we'll never get anything done."

Questions of who would lead among FIPs, whose stories would be heard, in what direction they would take the movement, what goals they should pursue—these bring us back to the central concerns of this book. Because of the nationalization and mainstreamization of the movement and its entry into pop culture, groups and individuals that are able to gain widespread attention are positioned to be celebritized within philanthropic circles. They may be ideal "poster children" or groups that have the infrastructure to absorb funding and scale in era of philanthrocapitalism, activating preexisting prominent connections or gaining new ones, acquiring networking, mentoring, and corporatizing skills. Indeed, sometimes they are celebritized by actual celebrities. As expected, these individuals will have an outsized influence. Concomitantly, because of the reform movement's changes in an era of post-democratic concentration of power in limited circles, with overlapping networks among pop culture, politics, philanthropy, business, and national advocacy, FIPs who are within those circles have more access to change-making. Furthermore, they are insulated from some of the collateral consequences of being formerly incarcerated, such as in securing housing or employment.

We can see these dynamics in the FSA's passage. They can also be observed in the way in which pardons were granted in 2018–2019. Six pardons handed down by President Trump were to FIPs who had been central to the Act's story and success and were now in philanthropic/advocacy/political positions of prominence. Charles Kushner, whose incarceration motivated Trump's son-in-law Jared to work on reform, was given a full pardon. Alice Marie Johnson, Pat Nolan, David Safavian, Bernard Kerik, and Topeka Sam were pardoned. So was music producer Weldon Angeles, a signatory to the FIP letter to Congress, whose harsh-sentencing had been used, as mentioned, by advocates for 924(c) sentencing reforms in the FSA, and who would use funding from Koch Industries and celebrities and other activists to form his marijuana justice reform nonprofit.[24] Watching the pardons come down in the wake of the FSA victory led JAN's Holly Harris to "an introspective moment": "I have a complicated—*more* complicated— view of this movement than I have in a long time . . . The work we focus on are policies that will have a broad impact. So when you see a handful of partisan clemencies and many of the executive actions focused on people who are well connected or who have money or who are celebrities . . . all of those cases underscore how broken our criminal justice system is; but some of these people didn't need this."

"COMPLICATED": BRINGING TOGETHER THE THREADS OF THE CRIMINAL JUSTICE REFORM MOVEMENT, AND LOOKING TOWARD THE FUTURE

Holly Harris's view of the national reform movement as complicated in response to the contradictions inherent in working on an issue affecting,

Formerly Incarcerated Activists and the Future

for the most part, millions of the most politically *dis*empowered—the incarcerated and formerly incarcerated; the poor; Blacks, non-White Latinos, and Native Americans; people without education; people without networks. But seeing a handful of those *with* education, connections, and wealth at the helm of national reform efforts become the recipients of clemency denied to the disempowered provides a fitting departure point for assessing the criminal justice reform movement of the 2000s to the early 2020s. There is no way, with academic hubris, to use this final chapter to suggest bullet point steps that if taken would result in "success."

The movement *is* complicated.

It is complicated by the daunting enormity of the carceral system and its decentralized nature, by the number of federal, state, and local laws, policies, practices, and institutional cultures that need to be revised in order to see a substantial dent made in the total number under correctional supervision. It is complicated by the way in which criminal justice reform as an issue cannot be siloed. Law creation and law breaking are often reflective of far deeper and devilishly difficult to eradicate social and public health problems, from unmet mental health needs, trauma, lack of social and familial bonds, substance abuse, and economic and racial disparities. And it is complicated by an imperative of not doing *further* harm to the communities it purports to help.

Despite nationalization, it is complicated by the lack of specific agreed-upon goals or outcomes. Former Vera Institute of Justice director Michael Jacobson saw this lack of a quantitative goal and a cohesive strategy among advocacy groups as the stymying of the national movement's progress, made worse by funders giving money in a way that didn't contribute to the objective of getting government to change. "Whatever your number . . . of reducing the incarcerated, it's a *big* goal," he emphasized. "You're not going to end mass incarceration at this rate. How can you ever achieve that if you don't talk about it? How can you achieve a goal if you don't set one? It can't be vague. It can't be 'Let's end mass incarceration.'"

What would it mean to end "overincarceration" or "mass incarceration"? Conservative advocates on panels and when interviewed for this project often echoed Doug Deason: "We need to lock up people we're scared of, not those who we are mad at."[25] While a logical introduction for those who may be skeptical of reform, this has little to offer in thinking about concrete inroads toward ending mass/overincarceration or what the goal of a reform movement should be. This is especially true for the most influential conservative reform group, Right on Crime, which steers away from serious discussion of numerical reductions. "We actually have reduced juvenile incarceration rates by half over the last 30 years," Marc Levin of Right on Crime noted. "[With] incarceration, I guess we would say we don't want to set an arbitrary target, we want to continue to advance sustainable policies by which we're continuing to reduce crime and not to increase crime." And so Right on Crime argues for the outright legalization of almost comical, rarely prosecuted business "crimes" like shipping lobster tails in plastic bags, but takes highly qualified positions on drug offenses, supporting alternatives to incarceration but not explicitly calling for, say, marijuana legalization or decriminalization of possession. Libertarian goals, also vaguely articulated, are generally and predictably more decarceratory, given their antistatism and the fact that they have "long opposed the War on Drugs."[26] Libertarian Hannah Cox of Conservatives Concerned About the Death Penalty, when asked what criminal justice would look like if she could reinvent it, said she would like a different system entirely, pointing to "revolutionary" European models as aspirational. "I would love to burn this thing down and start from scratch, to have a system that has mental health care and understanding of trauma at its base. There should be very few people in prison." Like other libertarians, she felt nonviolent property crimes and victimless crimes should not be dealt with via incarceration. Some liberal/progressive advocacy groups, as noted in Chapter 6 have chosen a quantitative goal, like the 50 percent decarceratory goal of #cut50, JLUSA, and the ACLU. Still, these differed in the timeline and means to achieve that goal, with the ACLU's 50 States Blueprint being the most clearly defined policy plan.[27] It's unclear why that number would be selected, however. The number of those in prison went from 197,245 in 1970 to 1.3 million in 2019, when the rate of violent crime committed was the same as in 1970: around 370 per 100,000 and there was a much lower rate of violent crime than in 1970: 2,110 versus 3,351 per 100,000. The homicide rate was in fact lower in 2019 than in 1970: 5 versus 7.1 per 100,000.

Cutting 50 percent would lead to 650,000 people in prison, more than three times the number in 1970.

Even the goals of prison abolitionist groups and advocates, already in tension with reformist advocates, are not uniform as one might expect, since "abolition means different things to different people."[28] While all embrace the aspirational goal of a prison-free and police-free US, they are divided in whether or not to reject "nonreformist reforms," in itself a subjective concept. Most interviewed for this project supported reforms that would "neutralize" the harm done by the criminal justice system,[29] so long as it did not contribute to *more* incarceration or more punitiveness for certain populations of incarcerated people, so long as it did not "throw them under the bus," such as those convicted of violent crimes or sex crimes versus drug crimes.[30] Dominique Morgan of Black and Pink, herself a convert to abolition after processing being sexually assaulted in prison, pointed out that abolitionists in positions of economic comfort and physical safety easily theorize about ending prisons, but "abolitionist values are not black and white. There's so much *yes* and *too*. People were saying initiatives like housing were not abolitionist. Listen—if I starve the system of things that keep perpetuating harm, it's the same as going and burning the building down, while people harmed by the system are centered; their needs are being met." According to fellow abolitionist Emily Galvin-Almanza, whose Partner for Justice trains volunteer-advocates to expand the wraparound services of public defender offices, "I believe in taking every improvement we can get, anything we do to make the system less and less horrific, culminating in hopefully its dismantling."[31] Some disagreed with the abolitionist focus on burning things down but not with what should be created afterwards,[32] leading to what Rebecca Weiker of Re:Store Justice said were "academic and disconnected" questions that were not of use in working toward articulable goals.[33]

The movement is perhaps most challenged, in spite of a post-democratic milieu, by a voter turnout that is much lower than in other established democracies, and a criminal justice system that is nevertheless highly responsive to public opinion and shifts in voters' attitudes[34] in response to perceived crime increases and decreases. In the two years between 2020 and 2022 alone, there was a whiplash of opposing sentiment about crime and some reforms. The summer of 2020 following George Floyd's murder was described by some movement participants as an "inflection point,"[35] a serious society-wide reckoning with the racial justice/exodus narrative of the left, where abolitionist demands to defund the police got a "respectful" mainstream hearing in the liberal media.[36] Crime had also been decreasing for several decades, leading to low issue salience, and a tight labor market was making the formerly incarcerated labor valuable, as noted in Chapter 5. Less than a year later, some retrenchment and even major backlash showed. "My sense was that the pendulum swung way out, in our favor, and we're starting to see it come back," David Safavian mused. Mid-2020 and 2021 headlines were marked by reportage of "surges" and "a crime wave" across the country, for which some criminal justice reforms, like the 2019–2020 bail reforms in New York, were blamed.[37] There was retreat from public support of "defund the police": in June 2020, majorities of Democrats, Black people, and people under 50 supported decreasing police spending in their area, but by 2021 majorities of all three groups supported increased funding.[38] Pledges to fight crime by Democrat and Republican politicians resurfaced even in the liberal bastion of New York City, where a former police captain, Eric Adams, was elected mayor. In October of 2020, Van Jones, emphasizing the importance of having acted during a moment of bipartisan convergence and unique political opportunities on the FSA in 2018, was concerned for the future of the movement: "Now we're in a world of rising crime, and high unemployment. And partisan divergence on the issue. It's 'defund the police' versus 'law and order': it's very bad."

Given the mercurial attitudes toward penality, the exuberance, akin to that of long bull markets, for the continued unfettered progress of the reform movement as it became mainstreamed and bipartisan in the 2000s was misplaced. It may have been tempting to think about main-streamization of reform as a linear effort, with earlier movement partici-pants pushing progress slowly for years, without major successes but with incremental progress—eventually leading to a tipping point after which a snowball effect ensued as the movement gained momentum and social contagiousness, increasing its speed and potential impact. Certainly we can identify some elements of this model in criminal justice reform—for example, in the work of movement actors during the "lock-'em-up" era of

Formerly Incarcerated Activists and the Future

the 1980s and early 1990s who were doggedly pushing against mass incarceration. A movement for penal reforms was certainly not absent in those days. However, unlike tipping points in science that lead to an irreversible change in state, there can be no such assumption about the progress of criminal justice, as the model of change in Chapter 2 illustrates. The tipping point model doesn't apply to the reform movement, and there is a danger in perceiving it as doing so.

It is easy to neglect the lessons of penal reform history and therefore keep reinventing the proverbial wheel or infer the newness of movement characteristics. Only the oldest in the movement have personal memories of a time before mass /overincarceration's start in the 1970s, so it may seem that incarceration on the scale we see it in the twenty-first century is the naturally exceptional punitive state of the US. This is the "normal," against which criminal justice reform is staking its claim to change, normatively and institutionally. But prison reform movement actors have been pressing for reforms since the founding of the republic. As we have seen, those considered "unique" stakeholders pressing for change today— philanthropists, celebrities, conservatives, and the formerly incarcerated— have been involved in earlier iterations of the movement. Also present in the history of penal reform was advocacy of (albeit with different language) "evidence-based practices" and classification systems, and rehabilitative or training-focused models that only seem new. Writing in 1990 during the tough-on-crime period, prison movement scholar Larry Sullivan made a pessimistic prediction: "If we have learned anything from the history of prison reform, it is that someday the rehabilitative model will return in some form, just as the 'just deserts model' is a throwback to retribution theories of the past. They will in all likelihood be a failure today, just as they were before."[39]

The prediction that the return of a rehabilitative ideal would occur was accurate following the 2000s. And there are signs that, in the post-2020 pandemic landscape, decarceratory, and ameliorative national reforms face predictable headwinds given that crime increased in salience during and after the pandemic. Writing in the mid-2010s, sociologist David Green observed that "much about US penality remains unchanged. Critics [contend] that concrete reforms have so far been superficial. . . . California,

CHAPTER SEVEN

New York, and Texas alone accounted for 90 percent of the reductions in state prison populations between 2010 and 2012. . . . If the brakes on government spending were to ease and/or if public concerns about crime and disorder were again to rise sufficiently, it is easy to imagine the return of an appetite for penal expansion and severity. So the prospects for continued reform remain decidedly precarious and contingent."[40]

Some interviewees from across the ideological spectrum and stakeholder groups acknowledged that precariousness, but were cautiously hopeful when asked if they saw "reform" as having taken root, or whether it was so fragile that it could easily return to where it had been in the 1980s. From philanthropy, Texas activist-investor Doug Deason said, "This will be hot for a long time; we've just scratched the surface. I see [reform] as more entrenched, more now than it's ever been. I see the federal government, just as we intended, leading the way for a lot of states." From advocacy, David Safavian agreed that going back was "always a concern," but he also saw anecdotal evidence that the work done by conservative advocates and their political allies may have begun to have lasting impact on the right. "Last summer there was someone released because of the First Step Act in Rhode Island, who is now wanted for a murder. Everybody on our side freaked out, worried what President Trump was going to do. Are we going to get a tweet from him? We convinced Senator Mike Lee to go talk to Trump. My understanding was that the president said, 'I get it. People do bad things.' That's a tremendously simple but positive sign." Marc Levin provided the practical insight, that the demographic trends he believed were partially responsible for the drop in crime would accelerate, leading to less salience of the crime issue in public discourse because of less actual crime in the long term. He also argued that state and local governments had seen with their own eyes the proof of concept—that they can save money with fewer people incarcerated and achieve good public safety outcomes. And from business, Heather Higginbottom of JPMorgan Chase, observed: "Everything's vulnerable to the political tides, [but] I think the more you get invested in issues or committed to things, the more invested you *are*." She noted a value shift among corporate leaders, so that CEOs like Jamie Dimon believed second chance hiring was the "right" thing to do and were seeing that these changes were good for the business landscape. "The political winds will

Formerly Incarcerated Activists and the Future

shift but that won't change the dynamic on this issue dramatically. Companies who are invested will continue to be."

Others from the left were more skeptical. Van Jones's remark in this chapter about the renewed partisanship of reform shows that he felt that the social forces of 2020–2021 were going to lead to national reforms but that changing the culture would be difficult. What is more, some felt that criminal justice reform as a mainstreamed, nationalized movement, attractive to major foundations, celebrities, and political figures, would lose its cachet. DeAnna Hoskins of JustLeadershipUSA asked, "What happens when the Koch money runs out, when this 'sexiness' [of criminal justice reform] changes?" Billionaire philanthropist/funder of Galaxy Gives Michael Novogratz agreed: "What always worries me is that people declare victory and go home."

VICTORY AND GO HOME? THE ADVANTAGES AND PERILS OF THE MAINSTREAMED REFORM MOVEMENT IN AN ERA OF PHILANTHROCAPITALISM AND POST-DEMOCRACY

The concerns and criticisms of Hoskins and Novogratz are well-founded. The pace and scale of decarceration, in all likelihood, will be far short of the mark in the next few decades in reducing the prison population by a million—the number needed just to get the US to where we were in 1970. Yet this book has demonstrated that the nationalized, mainstreamed justice reform movement provides qualified optimism that decarceratory, ameliorative trends can continue. There are some genuinely new, distinguishing features of this moment. The national movement configuration and the sociological realities facing the United States near the end of the first quarter of the twenty-first century give evidence that we're not headed toward another dark age of "three strikes and you're out" sentencing, capital punishment, and other excesses of American punitiveness.

The First Step Act story is ample illustration of the national movement dynamics that are in play: where mainstreamization was born of acknowledgment of the extreme excess of mass/overincarceration. The harms and inhumane degradation of incarceration were affecting a large swath of people and touching even the affluent or those with political connections.

The scale of incarceration recently peaked and is only slowly decreasing; it will continue to affect a significant percentage of US residents for the foreseeable future, keeping it a central concern. Acknowledgment of the problem of mass/overincarceration and the impetus for reform (or revolution) has meanwhile been enhanced by ideologically resonant stories of redemption and exodus that speak across political constituencies. According to Tinisch Hollins, executive director of Californians for Safety and Justice, "there are some universal issues. Black people are disproportionately impacted by some horrible stuff. But you have just as many folks of other ethnicities who have family members that are struggling with substance abuse, mental health, in need of housing. Those are universal issues that we've failed to address as a society. There becomes more of this collective reckoning and storytelling."

The change has been in large part a normative one. As David Green has remarked, a discursive shift has taken place across the ideological spectrum to oppose a punishment-only sensibility that isn't adequately reflected in the incarceration numbers.[41] But what sets this shift apart most from earlier periods of normative consensus around rehabilitation or reform are the structural characteristics of both the movement and the movement milieu.

What is new structurally, as demonstrated by the FSA, is the nationalization of the movement enabled by advocacy groups with the funding, support base, and infrastructure to support federal work and state campaigns. These groups have the political and social capital to wage lobbying campaigns, entrée to media outlets, and networks with other advocacy groups to form bigger coalitions.

What is new is the philanthrocapitalist moment that has made ameliorating or ending mass/overincarceration an object of large-scale funding and other forms of support, like CZI's capacity-building teams and the Arnolds' own research and policy work. Philanthropists and philanthropies, once solely grantors, giving to both national and state/local nonprofits, have grown in size and number since the 2000s and are now simultaneously doers.[42]

What is new is an increasingly post-democratic milieu, where celebrity and pop culture have an outsized reach and importance, where economic,

Formerly Incarcerated Activists and the Future

political, and cultural elites occupy many of the same spaces. "Reform" has crossed over to where it affects celebrities and has become an issue celebrities use their platform to address. The overlap between Hollywood and nonprofit spaces for the purposes of fundraising is demonstrated by gala events with red carpets featuring A- and B-listers.

What is new is that formerly incarcerated people and activists have been more centered in national advocacy work and in philanthropy. FIPs have been celebritized in the utilization of story and direct experience through new media platforms.

What is new is that large businesses and corporations, in the same political spaces as large philanthropy, but also affected by the sheer number of humans kept out of the labor pool by a criminal conviction, have joined the ranks of those pushing openly for decarceratory and ameliorative policies.

What is also new, but harder to empirically establish, is how "evolving standards of decency," to borrow a concept used by the Supreme Court to determine whether a particular punishment practice violates the Eighth Amendment, may be at play as well. Gradual cultural shifts that have moved the nation away from executing children, performing executions in a public square using a guillotine, banning interracial marriage, or other practices now seen as regressive by most may also be at play in buoying the reform movement.

The provocative contradiction of the post-2000 reform movement is that part of what is aiding its mainstreamization and nationalization is its embeddedness in its post-democratic and philanthrocapitalist milieu, and that it generally acquiesces to and works within that framework. Traditional social movement scholarship holds that the hallmark of mass movements is the pursuit of change through *noninstitutional* means.[43] There is the sense in this literature that a major element of movements, as opposed to interest groups, is a grassroots component where people *organically* organize, in nonprofessionalized/noncareerized fashion, with tactics that are to varying degrees disruptive. In this account, there may exist professional movement organizations, which "tend to prioritize resource mobilization over tactical efficiency, [and] focus on financial donations and media representation,"[44] but these are not dominant.

CHAPTER SEVEN

In the current reform movement, among the national, state, and local advocacy groups examined for this book, the vast majority, including those with the most radical objectives, had institutional ties to foundations or wealthy individuals that financed their work, as noted in Chapter 3. The traditional notion of "grassroots" as organizing and leadership as autonomous and separate from institutional sources has been eroded. But this is not to wantonly lob a Molotov cocktail and suggest that an entirely institutionally unfunded, elite-free movement might occur tomorrow and lead to the end of mass/overincarceration. It would deny the realities of a lack of sustained civic and political participation in this country and the influence of political, economic, and cultural elites on major institutions and government, which are ultimately responsible for implementing criminal justice reforms as changed institutional practices, policies, and day-to-day bureaucratic procedures.

Throughout this book we have seen glimpses of how philanthrocapitalist, post-democratic factors abet the reform movement. Big philanthropy can promote "discovery," providing a testing ground and risk capital for policy innovations with a long horizon, without the individual or party fears about losses and backlash that lead to extreme conservatism. "[Philanthropy] can promote, in a first-best sense, the aims of liberal democracy, and when it does, it is compatible with and plays an essential role in a flourishing liberal democratic state," Rob Reich argues.[45] "Influencers" and celebrities like Kim Kardashian, Meek Mill, John Legend, or Alyssa Milano who use their "brand" to advocate around an issue and call attention to flaws and injustices can reach millions and further popularize and mainstream it. Having those with outsized economic power from business lobby for reform in some guise is certainly better than having them lobby against it or remain on the sidelines, especially as they can revise their own institutional practices to benefit formerly incarcerated people. Philanthropic billionaires like Michael Novogratz, who toured the correctional system in Norway, where he was influenced by seeing more humane, less carceral regimes of accountability, and then funneled money toward the "army" amassing for reform can be part of the solution. JPMorgan, Kroger, Walmart, Butterball, and Verizon vocally committing to "second chances"

Formerly Incarcerated Activists and the Future

is part of institutionalizing a cultural attitude, much like consumer products that normalize reform.

But D. Winston, writing about consumer politics and commercialization in the gay rights' movement points out a tension in the reform movement: "From a rights perspective, the LGBT movement has been a success story. With each win, the gay community merges further into mainstream America, which is how Pride Month found fans from Taylor Swift to Target. But it came at a cost. Protestors at Stonewall . . . wanted a revolution; they got rainbow Nikes."[46]

There are perils in a movement structure that takes those from among the formerly incarcerated and the community who would be "grassroots" leaders and integrates them into the professional class of celebritized and funded leaders, one that adopts a corporate structure and ethos focused on building the capacity of nonprofits to accept grant money and scale an idea considered "actionable," one that is moved so much by the particular interests of a foundation at a moment in time. First, unlike the marriage equality movement, where demands relate to personal matters, the harms of crime are shared and carry a deeply felt primordial fear. Crime control responses similarly affect entire communities, which may experience disparate harm from that response, as has been seen in poor and Black and Latino communities. There is a problem not only with those having power, money, and prestige being removed from concerns about interpersonal or social control–based harm, but also with bubbles that can form around insulated groups advocating with like-minded colleagues. They can become out of touch with how those in nonactivist circles feel about an issue. And so the deeper the disconnect between the movement and the masses, and between the incarcerated, formerly incarcerated, and their families, and those who have no direct connection to someone who has been incarcerated, the less effective the movement becomes. It is crucial that the movement understand and respond to the wants, needs, fears of the larger community. This includes the need for safety—a term which some in the movement like Tinisch Hollins and Robert Rooks are enriching far beyond a narrow focus on more police and incarceration, but which is still notably deprioritized in left-leaning campaigns.

GETTING PAST THE "REMOVE" IN THE MOVEMENT FOR REFORM

Bill Cobb was drinking out of a plastic water bottle as our interview finished. A candidate for state representative whom he was helping organize a campaign for in Philadelphia was leaving for the evening. I asked him about his final thoughts on the reform movement. He paused, finished the bottle, took a Sharpie from the table, and wrote the words "criminal justice reform" on its cap. He then proceeded to crush the bottle slowly in his fist while maintaining eye contact. Directing his comments to the national movement, he declared: "Get the fuck out of your office and get the fuck out in the street. . . . Be a person that doesn't make a decision based on your paycheck or to get check marks for the next employment opportunity and not be responsible for having shit to do with these people that you're here with right now. Y'all believe you're doing something to transform a community. It's not possible. You've gotta be rooted in community in order to drive change. You're gonna pass a piece of legislation and one dollar for implementation? No one knows if the law changes our lives, how it works for us. I know people with arrests and convictions who are still unemployed, the doors they're knocking on won't open." He added sarcastically, "The experts call that shit 'service gaps.' Motherfucker, I *live* here! They are so far removed, not having to fight every day."

Advocacy leaders like Taina Angeli Vargas, co-founder of the California-focused Initiative Justice, even within an institutional milieu, have presented models for trying to rectify the distance from the incarcerated and formerly incarcerated Cobb alluded to *and* counteract some of the excesses of post-democratic civic and political disengagement. She had been working as a volunteer for reform work in the California legislature during the seven-year prison sentence of her partner, abolitionist Richie Reseda. She had been unexpectedly drawn into more systematically educating and organizing families of incarcerated people around legislation while visiting Reseda in prison. This organizing was transferred into the prison though Reseda, who handed out postcards describing reform legislation up for vote, provided information about how loved ones could vote, and distributed surveys asking the incarcerated about their policy priorities. Soon, those inside were providing Vargas with thousands of surveys, and in 2020, 28,000 incarcerated people were members of Initiate Justice, receiving newsletters that explained actions they could take and how political processes worked.

Formerly Incarcerated Activists and the Future

Vargas and Reseda worked to formalize a training program for those outside and inside prisons on how to do legislative work. For those inside, that program would grow to include 150 "boots on the ground" organizers inside all 35 California prisons, who developed facility campaigns and encouraged members' engagement. Vargas was adamant that those directly impacted on the outside, and even the formerly incarcerated, should not be "the voice" of the currently incarcerated. Instead, those inside would participate in a type of enfranchisement, expressing their views on legislative priorities and actions that could continue when they were released. She pointed to how funder-driven prioritizing of initiatives might not reflect the needs of those inside: "A few years ago funders decided that bail reform was what they really wanted to do. We [gave a survey to those inside members]. We listed 10 policy areas and had people rank them from the highest to lowest importance. By far the lowest importance was bail reform."[47] Initiate Justice therefore stayed out of bail reform. Vargas mirrored inside organizing with outside organizing for anyone who wished to participate. In response to feedback from members, six groups were formed according to member preferences, including political advocacy, organizing, outreach, fundraising, and healing and restorative work.

Tinisch Hollins, executive director of Californians for Safety and Justice, had lost both of her brothers to gun violence. Witnessing the inadequacy of the formal criminal justice system in providing justice and healing, she articulated the need for reform to be ultimately rooted in a rejection of post-democratic forms in favor of deep community engagement. "I align with bringing us back to practices and structure that allow us as human beings to come together and restore ourselves from harm and that requires a 360-degree approach," she conferred. "You got to include victims, you got to include the offender and the corrections conspirators. The *whole* community. You got to bring everybody in to achieve that." Her colleague Robert Rooks agreed: "The solution has to come from this expanded network of stakeholders that are elevating real safety solutions for how we respond to issues within the community."

While actively pursuing enfranchisement, organically rooted civic participation in humanistic responses to harm, an additional consideration for expanding the movement and countering post-democratic limitations was raised by Dominique Morgan. She expressed that what *constitutes* "being *in* the movement" must at the same time expand, and individuals must be encouraged to participate in "micro-level" practices, which in the aggregate produce culture change. "There are people doing the work, but they're not doing it on the level that is affirmed by philanthropy. I ain't doing 'mutual aid.' I'm helping a sister out. They'll say—'But the theory of change is'—I'm always gagging. It's like—I've been doing this shit forever. I know a whole bunch of Black trans women that have five kids in they home . . . stretching they check to feed and house these people, make sure they get in school. They're not a nonprofit, but they're doing the work. We need to start affirming and recognizing [that] *the work* looks different ways. The movement isn't always the panel. The movement is also—'listen, sis. I got two suits. You get one.' That's how I survived prison!"

The criminal justice reform movement—encompassing those engaged in the human-to-human, unsung practices of keeping kids from the carceral state by providing them with housing, as Morgan pointed out, as well as advocacy organizations working from both right and left ideological imperatives, billionaire philanthropists motivated to add their capital, the formerly and currently incarcerated, the business leaders advertising their second chance practices and offering wraparound services to employees—is not a monolith. As Michael Novogratz said in our interview, "the army has gotten really fucking big." Its contradictions and paradoxes, with nationalization and mainstreamization, have become writ large, with debates about the future of the movement playing out across the US. These contradictions and tensions do not have to result in a zero-sum game between visions. As long as post-democracy and the strong link between financial resources, government, and political victories exist,[48] with low civic engagement and the outsized influence of cultural elites—rejecting the involvement of those who can provide connections, or rejecting the "story" of one's ideological opponent, does not help to address the massive, immediate human suffering at hand. It requires the mainstreamization provided by this current movement and the pop cultural work it has done, and the access to power that it has given to people with direct experiences of incarceration that can influence gatekeepers. But the movement should also reflect on how it might become a *mass* movement, as well as one with

Formerly Incarcerated Activists and the Future

strong institutional actors, not in the limited sense of institutional action officially acknowledged, professional, compensated, and formally trained. So far, there haven't been mass demonstrations against overincarceration or over any aspect of the criminal justice system other than police brutality. What's more, these often don't make immediate, explicit connections to ending mass/overincarceration and connecting to other issues articulated at the very beginning of this book: those issues at the periphery of the "reform" umbrella.

But because of the fickleness of elite interest, the fear that "they will declare victory and go home," having a movement that is as independent, self-sustaining, and appealing to a broad public cannot be deprioritized. Tinisch Hollins reflected, "There will be a time that comes around, again, where the conversation is not sexy as it is now. When that happens, how many people will be actually looking at how we define safety and how do we do it *not* at the expense of others? That's the conversation that should be happening right now." And as Baz Dreisinger of the Incarceration Nations Network cautioned, "a movement doesn't necessarily lead to anything. One of my biggest critiques of the movement in the US is that it's very focused on what we're abolishing, and not focused on what we're building. We need more attention [on] that future vision."

The scale of the now mainstreamed, nationalized opposition to the carceral state and its ravages in the United States; the moral imperative of its ideological stories; its economic and political resources; the expansion of stakeholders and voices in the "chorus"—these factors position criminal justice reform in the 2020s at least as strongly as it has been since the start of the incarceration binge beginning in the 1970s, to begin the slow work to remove the US from its distinction as the world's only advanced democracy that is simultaneously a brutal jailer. The "army" now amassed should be thinking about the war on all fronts and levels, with all the urgency demanded by a war with so many millions of lives hanging in the balance.

ACKNOWLEDGMENTS

A book about a living, messy, evolving movement such as that to reimagine what justice looks like in the United States necessarily could not be a solitary project.

Without my participants from across a range of experiential and ideological perspectives and ways of engaging in the reform movement, this work would not have been possible. And so my deepest thanks go to them, for their trust in me to document and present in good faith their insights and stories: Barbara Allan, Sue Ellen Allen, Laura Arnold, Juan Cartagena, Bill Cobb, Hannah Cox, Zuri Davis, Doug Deason, Craig DeRoche, Jeffrey Deskovic, Baz Dreisinger, Taina Angeli Vargas, Jolene Forman, Joshua Hoe, DeAnna Hoskins, Emily Galvin-Almanza, Bob Gangi, Holly Harris, Heather Higginbottom, Tinisch Hollins, Rayshun Holt, Jessica Jackson, Michael Jacobson, Elissa Johnson, Van Jones, Jesse Kelley, Adnan Khan, Jenny Kim, Marc Levin, Serena Liguori, Dan Loeb, Cliff Maloney, Marc Mauer, Jeff Cook-McCormack, Michael Mendoza, Alyssa Milano, Dominique Morgan, Michael Novogratz, Udi Ofer, Laura Porter, Jason Pye, Kevin Ring, Robert Rooks, David Rothenberg, David Safavian, Jose Saldana, Topeka Sam, Katie Schad, Gina Schwartz, Jeremy Travis, Andre Ward, Billy Watterson, and Rebecca Weiker.

My first formal foray into reform came while working for New Yorkers Against the Death Penalty under executive director David Kaczynski, now a lifelong friend. His humanism and empathy in seeking common ground solutions to violence were deeply influential. I'm grateful for his providing me with that experiential starting point and his warm cultivation of me, and that he was able to contribute to this book by reviewing several chapters. I also appreciate former colleagues from the anti-death-penalty space: Laura Porter, Marie Verzulli, and "the" Barbara Smith for their shared advocacy, camaraderie, and wisdom; Barbara Allan for her motherly embracing of my work and decades-long, tireless advocacy for humanity in prisons; Jared Feuer for his encouragement of the prism the book brings to the movement; and the formerly incarcerated advocates whose friendships from the early days of the journey impacted me indelibly, especially Serena Liguori, Lawrence Ghana Hayes, and Jeff Deskovic.

I am grateful for the support I've received from my editors at Stanford University Press: Michelle Lipinski, for her enthusiasm for the proposal and belief in me, and Marcela Cristina Maxfield, who ushered the book to the finish line. My thanks to the executive director of Stanford's Criminal Law Center, Debbie Mukamal, for her valuable suggestions for the manuscript, as well as the two anonymous reviewers who also lent their expertise to strengthening this project. Ellen Adler at the New Press also was of great assistance in providing publication data about *The New Jim Crow.*

Thanks to colleagues, friends, and former students who have given moral support and encouragement, even as the higher education landscape has made research and writing difficult for all but the few.

Death and illness reveal the small circle of people most deserving of appreciation in life, for whom what we do is always secondary to who we are. Thanks to Şaban Eren and Vincent Duggan for their warm encouraging of their niece to follow their path into academics. My deepest gratitude always to my mother, Patricia Duggan-Eren, and to my sister Meg Eren, also my generous and hawk-eyed proofreaders. And to my husband, Elias Hernandez, always my unwavering supporter, dearest friend, and love.

APPENDIX:
INTERVIEWEES, TITLES, AND AFFILIATIONS

Barbara Allan	Founder/director, Prison Families Anonymous
Sue Ellen Allen	Founder, Reinventing ReEntry
Laura Arnold	Philanthropist/cofounder, Arnold Ventures LLC
Juan Cartagena	President/ general counsel, LatinoJustice PRLDEF
William Cobb	Former deputy director, ACLU Campaign for Smart Justice
Hannah Cox	National manager, Conservatives Concerned About the Death Penalty
Zuri Davis	Communications strategist, CJ Reform, ACLU of Florida
Doug Deason	Philanthropist/president, Deason Capital Services, LLC
Craig DeRoche	President, Justice Fellowship
Jeffrey Deskovic	Exoneree/founder, Jeffrey Deskovic Foundation for Justice

Appendix

Baz Dreisinger	Founder, Incarceration Nations Network
Taina Angeli Vargas	Cofounder, Initiate Justice
Jolene Forman	Manager of Criminal Justice Policy, Chan Zuckerberg Initiative
Joshua Hoe	Policy analyst, Safe and Just Michigan
Emily Galvin-Almanza	Cofounder and executive director, Partners for Justice
Bob Gangi	Founder, Police Reform Organizing Project
Holly Harris	Executive director, Justice Action Network
Heather Higginbottom	Managing director, JPMorgan Chase Policy Center
Tinisch Hollins	Executive director, Californians for Safety and Justice
Rayshun Holt	Program director, Beacon of Hope Business Alliance
DeAnna Hoskins	President and CEO, JustLeadershipUSA
Jessica Jackson	Cofounder, #cut50
Michael Jacobson	Executive director, CUNY Institute for State & Local Governance
Elissa Johnson	Director of campaigns & advocacy, CJ Reform, FWD.us
Van Jones	Cofounder, #cut50/CEO, REFORM Alliance
Jesse Kelley	Manager, Criminal Justice & Civil Liberties, R Street
Adnan Khan	Founder and executive director, Re:Store Justice
Jenny Kim	Vice president of public policy, Koch Companies Public Sector, LLC
Marc Levin	Founder, Right on Crime
Serena Liguori	Founder, New Hour for Women and Children
Dan Loeb	Philanthropist/founder and CEO, Third Point LLC
Cliff Maloney	President, Young Americans for Liberty
Marc Mauer	Executive director, The Sentencing Project
Jeffrey Cook-McCormack	Head of public affairs, Third Point LLC

Appendix

Michael Mendoza	National Director, #cut50
Alyssa Milano	Actress/activist/producer
Dominique Morgan	Executive director, Black and Pink
Michael Novogratz	Philanthropist/CEO, Galaxy Investment Partners
Udi Ofer	Director, Justice Division, ACLU
Laura Porter	Policy director, 8th Amendment Project
Jason Pye	Vice president of legislative affairs, FreedomWorks
Kevin Ring	President, Families Against Mandatory Minimums
Robert Rooks	Cofounder, Alliance for Safety and Justice
David Rothenberg	Founder, The Fortune Society
David Safavian	Director, ACU Foundation's Nolan Center for Justice
Jose Saldana	Director, Releasing Aging People in Prison
Topeka Sam	Founder/executive director, Ladies of Hope Ministries
Katie Schad	Manager, Beacon of Hope Business Alliance
Gina Schwartz	Director, Movement & Capacity Building, Chan Zuckerberg Initiative
Jeremy Travis	Executive vice president of criminal justice, Arnold Ventures LLC
Andre Ward	Associate vice president, David Rothenberg Center, The Fortune Society
Billy Watterson	Executive director, Galaxy Gives
Rebecca Weiker	Program director, Re:Store Justice

NOTES

Preface

1. A. Philip, "George Floyd Protests Have Made Police Reform the Consensus Position," *CNN*, June 9, 2020; L. Buchanan, Q. Bui, and J. K. Patel, "Black Lives Matter May Be the Largest Movement In U.S. History," *The New York Times*, July 3, 2020.

2. J. A. Kingson, "$1 Billion-Plus Riot Damage Is Most Expensive in Insurance History," *Axios*, September 16, 2020.

3. P. G. Cassell, "Explaining Recent Homicide Spikes in U.S. Cities: The 'Minneapolis Effect' And The Decline In Proactive Policing," *Federal Sentencing Reporter* 33 (2020): 83–127.

4. A. Grawert and N. Kim, "Myths and Realities: Understanding Recent Trends in Violent Crime," Brennan Center, July 12, 2022, http://www.brennancenter.org/our-work/analysis-opinion/how-first-step-act-became-law-and-what-happens-next.

5. A. Chabria, "No, The Criminal Justice Reform Movement Isn't Dead. But It May Need to Grow Up," *Los Angeles Times*, June 9, 2022.

6. J. J. Donohue, "Comey, Trump, and the Puzzling Pattern of Crime In 2015 and Beyond," *Journal of Labor Economics* 117, no. 5 (2017): 1297–345.

7. E. Kilgore, "Sessions as AG Means Criminal Justice Reform Is Dead," *Intelligencer*, November 2016.

8. J. M. Seibler, "No, Jeff Sessions as Attorney General Won't Mean Criminal Justice Reform Is Dead," *Daily Signal*, December 12, 2016.

Notes to Preface and Chapter One

9. A. Lenore, "Criminal Justice Reform Is Dead? Not So Fast," *Governing*, November 23, 2016, https://www.governing.com/gov-institute/voices/col-criminal-justice-reform-state-ballot-measures-legislation.html.

10. D. Safavian and C. Culver, "Is Criminal Justice Reform Dead?" *Washington Times*, July 6, 2022.

11. Gallup, "Crime," poll, 2022, https://news.gallup.com/poll/1603/crime.aspx.

Chapter One

1. "FIRST STEP" originally was an acronym, standing for "The Formerly Incarcerated Reenter Society Transformed Safely Transitioning Every Person."

2. Video and transcripts of the First Step Act signing ceremony are available through C-SPAN's video library: https://www.c-span.org/video/?456225-1/president-trump-signs-step-juvenile-justice-reform-acts.

3. As of January 2021, #cut50 became Dream.Org, which also focuses on climate change and poverty.

4. In addition to the First Step Act, the Juvenile Justice Reform Act was signed the same day.

5. *New York Times* Editorial Board, "A Real Chance at Criminal Justice Reform," November 14, 2018; *Wall Street Journal* Editorial Board, "A Prison Reform Opening," November 16, 2018.

6. R. Bort, "Kim Kardashian, Alyssa Milano, Van Jones among 50+ Celebrities Lobbying for Prison Reform Legislation, *Rolling Stone*, November 14, 2018.

7. M. Haberman and A. Karni, "Trump Celebrates Criminal Justice Reform amid Doubts It Will Be Fully Funded," *The New York Times*, April 1, 2019.

8. D. M. Cohen, "Justice, Not Jailbreak: The Context And Consequence Of The First Step Act," *Victims & Offenders*, 14, no. 8 (2019): 1084–98; J. Jefferson-Bullock, "Perspectives on the FIRST STEP Act: Consensus, Compassion, and Compromise?" *Federal Sentencing Register* 80 (December 2018):70-75.

9. J. Pfaff, *Locked In: The True Causes of Mass Incarceration And How To Achieve Real Reform* (New York: Basic Books, 2017).

10. D. Dagan and S. Teles, *Prison Break: Why Conservatives Turned against Mass Incarceration* (New York: Oxford University Press, 2017), 173.

11. While signing the FSA, Trump cited Kentucky's, Texas's, and Georgia's criminal justice reform efforts as among the successful models that he had looked to when considering endorsing reform-based legislation.

12. M. Jacobson, interview, September 17, 2020. All further quotations from Jacobson are taken from this interview.

13. P. K. Enns, *Incarceration Nation: How the United States Became the Most Punitive Democracy in the World* (New York: Cambridge University Press, 2016).

14. M. D. Ramirez, "Punitive Sentiment," *Criminology*, 51, no. 2 (2013): 329–64; Enns, *Incarceration Nation*.

Notes to Chapter One   199

15. In his 2016 inaugural speech, Trump painted a bleak image: "Crime and the gangs and the drugs [have] stolen too many lives and robbed our country of so much unrealized potential. This American carnage stops right here and stops right now." His campaign had positioned him as the "law and order president" against the specter of what he presented incorrectly in 2015 as a spiraling number of homicides. John Donohue (2017) raised the question whether this renewed apprehension about crime among Americans may have been enough to give Trump his narrow electoral victory.

16. Cohen, "Justice, Not Jailbreak," 1084.

17. Jefferson-Bullock, "Perspectives on the First Step Act," 70.

18. Hopwood, "Effort to Reform," 791.

19. H. Harris, personal interview, February 5, 2020. All further quotations from Harris are taken from this interview.

20. H. Cox, personal interview, October 14, 2019. All further quotations from Cox are taken from this interview.

21. V. Jones, personal interview, August 31, 2020. All further quotations from Jones, unless otherwise indicated, are taken from this interview.

22. C. Crouch, *Post-Democracy* (Cambridge, UK: Polity, 2020); C. Crouch, *Post-Democracy after the Crisis* (Cambridge, UK: Polity, 2020).

23. M. Bishop and M. Green, *Philanthrocapitalism: How Giving Can Save the World* (Bloomsbury Press, 2008); Bishop and Green, "Philanthrocapitalism Rising," *Society* 52, no. 6 (2008): 541–48.

24. M. D'Oliveira-Martins, "Interview with Arlie Hoschschild," *Sociologia, Problemas e Praticas* 83, no. 1 (2017): 181-91.

25. Pew Research Center. "America's Incarceration Rate Falls to Lowest Level Since 1995," 2021, https://www.pewresearch.org/fact-tank/2021/08/16/americas-incarceration-rate-lowest-since-1995/.

26. M. Tonry, cited in M. Gottschalk, *Caught: The Prison State and the Lockdown of American Politics* (Princeton University Press, 2015), 132.

27. J. McCurdy, "The First Step Act Is Actually the 'Next Step' after 15 Years of Successful Reforms to the Federal Criminal Justice System," *Cardozo Law Review* 41 (2019): 189–241.

28. C. Doyle, "Federal Mandatory Minimum Sentences: Safety Valve and Substantial Assistance Exceptions, Congressional Research Service, July 5, 2022, https://fas.org/sgp/crus/misc/R41326.pdf.

29. McCurdy, "The First Step Act Is Actually the 'Next Step.'"

30. Cohen, "Justice, Not Jailbreak."

31. American Bar Association (ABA), "Federal Sentencing Reform," August 2010, https://americanbar.org/advocacy/governmental_legislative_work/publications/washingtonletter/august_2010_WL/first_step_act_article/.

32. J. Gehrke, "Dems in the Driver's Seat on Criminal Justice Reform Bill, *Washington Examiner*, April 22, 2016.

33. K. Gotsche, "One Year after the First Step Act: Mixed Outcomes," The Sentencing Project, 2019, https://www.sentencingproject.org/publicatoins/one-year-after-the-first-step-act/.

34. This section, in addition to drawing on the text of the First Step Act itself, relies on N. James's excellent summary of the First Step Act: "The First Step Act of 2018: An Overview," Congressional Research Service, March 4, 2019, https://crsreports.congress.gov/product/pdf/R/R45558.

35. The Hudson Institute, a conservative think tank, was selected by the DOJ and NIJ to host the independent review committee required by the First Step Act. Concerns were raised by House Judiciary Committee chair Jerry Nadler (D-New York) and Congresswoman Karen Bass (D-California), chair of the House Judiciary Subcommittee on Crime, Terrorism and Homeland Security, after it was revealed that the DOJ and NIJ had selected the Hudson Institute, without evidence that the organization had any experience in the development of risk assessment tools, or why it was chosen given its opposition to sentencing reform from its leadership. See their statement here: https://judiciary.house.gov/news/documentsingle.aspx?DocumentID=350. Former senior fellow at the Hudson Institute J. H. Anderson wrote "Why Trump Should Oppose Criminal Justice Reform," Hudson Institute, May 18, 2016, (https://www.hudson.org/research/12506-why-trump-should-oppose-criminal-justice-reform), which raised the specter of increases in "drug crime."

36. The Prisoner Assessment Tool Targeting Estimated Risk and Needs (PATTERN) includes 6 static and 11 dynamic factors. A description of those factors, their weighting, and how they affect individuals can be found through Families Against Mandatory Minimums' "PATTERN Tool FAQ," n.d., https://famm.org/wp-content/uploads/PATTERN-Tool-FAQ.pdf.

37. Age of first arrest was initially included, but removed after a "wave" of criticism, according to J. Paperny in "Big Developments under the First Step Act," January 18, 2022, https://www.youtube.com/watch?v=dlZRMFdYEt8&t=292s.

38. Families Against Mandatory Minimums (FAMM), "PATTERN Tool FAQ," n.d., https://famm.org/wp-content/uploads/PATTERN-Tool-FAQ.pdf.

39. Indeed, throughout the FSA we can infer of attempts to wrestle power away from the BOP's "reading" of the law in the least advantageous way possible to those incarcerated. As Jefferson-Bullock notes, the intentions of legislators are often hamstrung by the BOP, mockingly referred to as a "bureau of jailers," that implements the most restrictive interpretation of the Act in its guidelines (2018). See Jefferson-Bullock, "Perspectives on the First Step Act."

40. J. Pye, "Unjust, Cruel, and Even Irrational: Stacking Charges under 924c,"-FreedomWorks, October 22, 2015, https://www.freedomworks.org/unjust-cruel-and-even-irrational-stacking-charges-under-924c/.

41. Public defenders are not provided for these petitions, and so any counsel that is retained to assist in the process is privately funded.

Notes to Chapters One and Two

42. President Franklin Roosevelt established Federal Prison Industries in 1934 through executive order. It is a corporation, entirely owned by the US government, whose mission is "to protect society and reduce crime by preparing inmates with job training and practical work skills for reentry success."

43. Bureau of Prisons (BOP), "Work Programs,", 2021, https://www.bop.gov/inmates/custody_and_care/work_programs.jsp.

44. Section 604 of the FSA, "Identification for Returning Citizens" amended Section 231 (b) of the Second Chance Act of 2007. It requires the BOP to help those leaving prison or a halfway house obtain Social Security cards, driver licenses, and birth certificates.

45. N. James, "The First Step Act of 2018: An Overview," Congressional Research Service, 2019, https://crsreports.congress.gov/product/pdf?R/R45558

46. James, "The First Step Act," 15.

47. #cut50, "#Homefortheholidays: A Celebration of Freedom Made Possible by the First Step Act," 2019.

48. Gotsche, "One Year after the First Step Act: Mixed Outcomes"; Department of Justice (DOJ), "Press Release: Department of Justice Announces Release of 3,100 Inmates under First Step Act, Publishes Risk and Needs Assessment System," press release, July 19, 2019.

49. DOJ, "Press Release."

50. Cohen, "Justice, not Jailbreak."

51. Jefferson-Bullock, "Perspectives on the FIRST STEP Act."

52. M. Cohen, E. Danya-Perry, and J. Perry, "This Is an Unmistakable Win for Incarcerated People," CNN, January 19, 2022.

53. ABA, "Federal Sentencing Reform."

54. Excellent books on aspects of the criminal justice reform movement, even though they are not characterized as such, include H. Haines, *Against Capital Punishment: The Anti-Death Penalty Movement in America, 1972–1994* (Oxford, UK: Oxford University Press, 1996), and L. E. Sullivan, *The Prison Reform Movement: Forlorn Hope* (Woodbridge, CT: Twayne Publishers, 1990).

Chapter Two

1. S. G. Stolberg and A. W. Herndon, "'Lock the S.O.B.'s Up': Joe Biden and the Era of Mass Incarceration," *The New York Times*, June 25, 2019.

2. K. Miller, "Joe Biden Told a Voter He'll 'Go Further' Than Cutting Incarceration by 50 Percent," *Buzzfeed News*, July 19, 2019, https://www.buzzfeednews.com/article/katherinemiller/joe-biden-incarceration-prison-population-cut-aclu.

3. J. Haltiwanger, "Biden Played Key Role in Pushing US to Take Hardline Stances on Crime in 1990s, and Now He's Apologizing as 2020 Looms," *Business Insider*, January 22, 2019, https://www.businessinsider.com/biden-apologizes-for-pushing-hardline-laws-on-crime-immigration-in-1990s-2019-1?op=1.

Notes to Chapter Two

4. N. Portner, "Top Trends in State Criminal Justice Reform, January 2019," The Sentencing Project, https://www.sentencingproject.org/wp-content/uploads/2020/01/Top-Trends-in-State-Criminal-Justice-Reform-2019.pdf.

5. B. Sutherland and B. Chappatta, "Why Jamie Dimon, McDonald's and Walmart Want to Hire Ex-Convicts," *Chicago Business*, April 26, 2021.

6. Chan Zuckerberg Initiative (CZI), "Chan Zuckerberg Initiative Announces $450 Million to Accelerate Criminal Justice & Immigration Reform," January 27, 2021, https://chanzuckerberg.com/newsroom/chan-zuckerberg-initiative-announces-450-million-to-accelerate-criminal-justice-immigration-reform/

7. D. Loeb, "Effective Giving Requires Rolling Up Your Sleeves," *The Wall Street Journal*, October 16, 2020.

8. Pew Research Center, "Budget Deficit Slips as a Public Priority," January 1, 2016, https://www.pewrsearch.org/politics/2016/01/22/budget-deficit-slips-as-public-priority/.

9. "New Poll Shows that 94 Percent of Americans Back Criminal Justice Reform," *MarketWatch*, June 23, 2020, https://www.marketwatch.com/story/new-poll-shows-94-of-americans-back-criminal-justice-reform-2020-06-23.

10. E. Mintz, "New Polling Finds Extraordinary Bipartisan Support for Policing Reforms," *News and Stories*, Arnold Ventures, August 25, 2020, https://arnoldventures.org/stories/new-polling-finds-extraordinary-bipartisan-support-for-policing-measures.

11. P. B. McGuigan and R. R. Rader, eds., *Criminal Justice Reform: A Blueprint* (Chicago: Regnery/Gateway Books, 1983).

12. W. J. Nicholls, J. Ultermark, and S. van Haperen, "Going National: How the Fight for Immigrant Rights Became a National Social Movement," *Journal of Ethnic and Migration Studies* 46, no. 2 (2019): 1–23.

13. P. K. Enns, *Incarceration Nation: How the United States Became the Most Punitive Democracy in the World* (New York: Cambridge University Press, 2016).

14. M. Jacobson, personal interview, September 21, 2020.

15. A. Ward, personal interview, December 19, 2019. All further quotes from Ward are taken from this interview.

16. W. Cobb, personal interview, February 28, 2020. All further quotes from Cobb are taken from this interview.

17. C. Maloney, personal interview, October 28, 2019. All further quotes from Maloney are taken from this interview.

18. D. Hoskins, personal interview, February 12, 2020. All further quotes from Hoskins are taken from this interview.

19. S. E. Allen, personal interview, May 29, 2020. All further quotes from Allen are taken from this interview.

20. I avoid the term "broken" or "dysfunctional" here because part of the resonant ideological story that is told by some participants in the movement is that

Notes to Chapter Two   203

the criminal justice system is functioning as intended and is not "broken" from the vantage point of those whom it disproportionately affects.

21. Enns, *Incarceration Nation*.

22. Mackinac Center for Public Policy, "A Brief Explanation of the Overton Window," 2021, https://www.mackinac.org/OvertonWindow.

23. B. Dreisinger, personal interview, September 14, 2020. All quotes from Dreisinger are drawn from this interview.

24. J. Q. Whitman, *Harsh Justice: Criminal Punishment and the Widening Divide between American and Europe* (Oxford, UK: Oxford University Press, 2005).

25. Enns, *Incarceration Nation*, 162.

26. L. E. Sullivan, *The Prison Reform Movement: Forlorn Hope* (Woodbridge, CT: Twayne Publishers).

27. Enns, *Incarceration Nation*, 3. It should be noted that this comparison was made excluding jail populations.

28. Enns, 5.

29. D. Dagan and S. Teles, *Prison Break: Why Conservatives Turned against Mass Incarceration* (Oxford, UK: Oxford University Press), 160.

30. LatinoJustice PRLDEF, formerly the Puerto Rican Legal Defense & Education Fund, was founded in 1972 to protect the civil rights of Puerto Ricans. Its name was changed in 2008.

31. J. Cartagena, personal interview, August 23, 2020. All further quotes from Cartagena are taken from this interview.

32. T. Sam, personal interview, January 17, 2020. All further quotes from Sam are taken from this interview.

33. M. Gottschalk, *Caught: The Prison State and the Lockdown of American Politics* (Princeton, NJ: Princeton University Press), 241.

34. S. Raphael and M. A. Stoll, *Why Are So Many Americans in Prison?* (New York: Russell Sage Foundation, 2013).

35. R. Brame, S. D. Bushway, R. Paternoster, and M. G. Turner, "Demographic Patterns of Cumulative Arrest Prevalence by Ages 18 and 23," *Crime & Delinquency* 60, no. 3 (2014): 471–86.

36. N. McCarthy, "Over Half a Million Americans Have Had a Family Member Incarcerated," *Forbes*, December 7, 2018.

37. A. Cohen, "When Heroin Hits the White Suburbs," The Marshall Project, August 12, 2015, https://www.themarshallproject.org/2015/08/12/when-heroin-hits -the-white-suburbs.

38. J. Netherland and H. Hansen, "The War on Drugs Wasn't Wasted: Whiteness, 'Dirty Doctors,' And Race in Media Coverage of Prescription Opioid Misuse," *Culture, Medicine, and Psychiatry* 40 (2016): 656–86.

39. S. Liguori, personal interview, October 21, 2019. All further quotes from Liguori are taken from this interview.

40. C. Maloney, personal interview, October 29, 2019. All further quotes from Maloney are taken from this interview.

41. Marc Levin, personal interview, November 18, 2019. All further quotes from Levin are taken from this interview.

42. Holly Harris, personal interview, February 19, 2020. All further quotes from Harris are taken from this interview.

43. J. Travis, A. Crayton, and D. A. Mukamal, "A New Era in Inmate Reentry," *Corrections Today* 71 (2009): 6.

44. Ideology: "The concept of ideology focuses attention on the content of whole systems of beliefs, on the multiple dimensions of these belief systems, and on the ways the ideas are related to each other." Also, "When people are thinking ideologically, they are explicitly concerned with a theory of society, values, and norms, and with creating a comprehensive and consistent understanding of the world." Both quotes are from P. Oliver and H. Johnston, "What a Good Idea! Ideologies and Frames in Social Movement Research," *Mobilization: An International Quarterly* 5 (2000): 37–54.

45. C. DeRoche, personal interview, August 12, 2020. All further quotes from DeRoche are taken from this interview.

46. U. Ofer, personal interview, February 3, 2020. All further quotes from Ofer are taken from this interview.

47. B. Cobb, personal interview, February 28, 2020. All further quotes from Cobb are taken from this interview.

48. F. Polletta, "Contending Stories: Narratives in Social Movements," *Qualitative Sociology* 21, no. 4 (1998): 419–46.

49. F. W. Mayer, *Narrative Politics: Stories and Collective Action* (Oxford, UK: Oxford University Press, 2014).

50. M. Alexander, *The New Jim Crow: Mass Incarceration in the Age of Colorblindness* (New York: The New Press, 2010).

51. The New Press, "The New Jim Crow: Mass Incarceration in the Age of Colorblindness. A Case Study on the Role of Books in Leveraging Social Change," November 2014, https://mediaimpactfunders.org/wp-content/uploads/2014/12/The-New-Press-NJC-Case-Study-Nov20141.pdf, 2.

52. A. Romero, "Reimagining the Role of Police," *ACLU: News & Commentary*, June 5, 2020, https://aclu.org/news/criminal-law-reform/reimagining-the-role-of-police.

53. A. Milano, personal interview, September 10, 2020. All further quotes from Milano are taken from this interview.

54. "It would be hard to overstate what a remarkable achievement this is for any book at any time, but even more so for a book about mass incarceration and its impact on people of color," Ellen Adler, publisher at The New Press described. The initial print run of the book was slightly over 3,000 copies.

Notes to Chapter Two

55. New Press, "New Jim Crow," 7.

56. Also information provided by Ellen Adler on January 4, 2023. See note 55.

57. The New Press, "New Jim Crow."

58. D. Garland, "Introduction: The Meaning of Mass Imprisonment," in *Mass Imprisonment: Social Causes and Consequences*, ed. D. Garland (London: Sage, 2001).

59. Enns, *Incarceration Nation*.

60. The New Press, "New Jim Crow," 5.

61. M. Cadden, "Books about Race Flying off Shelves, Climbing Best-Seller Lists after the Death of George Floyd," *USA Today*, June 4, 2020.

62. N. Gross and M. Mann, "Is There a "Ferguson Effect?" Google Searches, Concern about Police Violence, and Crime in U.S. Cities, 2014–2016," *Socius,* 2017. https://doi.org/10.1177/2378023117703122.

63. C. Madar, "A Republican against Prisons," *The American Conservative*, 2015, https://www.theamericanconservative.com/articles/a-republican-against-prisons/.

64. Pew Research Center, "About the Religious Landscape Study," n.d., https://www.perform.org/religious-landscape-study/party-affiliation.

65. J. Pye, personal interview, November 15, 2019. All further quotes from Pye are taken from this interview.

66. S. E. Allen, personal interview, May 29, 2020. All further quotes from Allen are taken from this interview.

67. D. Mukamal, from her written comments as a peer reviewer, July 2022.

68. Gottschalk, *Caught*.

69. M. Ball, "Do the Koch Brothers Really Care about Criminal Justice?" *The Atlantic*, March 3, 2015.

70. Tides, "Californians for Safety and Justice," 2021, https://www.tides.org/story/californians-safety-justice/.

71. JustLeadershipUSA (JLUSA), "JLUSA's 2021–2024 Roadmap," 2021, https://jlusa.org/roadmap.

72. In 2021, Diann Rust-Tierney, executive director of National Coalition to Abolish the Death Penalty listed "criminal justice reformer" in her Twitter profile, as did Rebecca Brown of the Innocence Project on her Twitter page, Molly Gill, vice president of policy at Families Against Mandatory Minimums, Candice Jones, CEO of the Public Welfare Foundation, and others.

73. Jeremy Travis, one of the pioneers in the reentry space, described reentry as a social movement in 2007, calling attention to its bipartisan appeal and support.

74. C. P. Eren, "The Right Anti-Death Penalty Movement?" *New Politics* 15, no. 2 (2015): 58. https://newpol.org/issue_post/right-anti-death-penalty-movement/.

75. M. Brenan, "Support for Marijuana Legalization Inches Up to a New High," Gallup, November 9, 2020, https://news.gallup.com/poll/323582/support-legal-marijuana-inches-new-high-aspx.

Notes to Chapters Two and Three

76. D. Morgan, personal interview, September 25, 2020.

77. D. Morgan, personal interview, September 25, 2020.

78. Gottschalk, *Caught*, 193.

79. BBC News, "Trump Urges Death Penalty for Drug Dealers," March 19, 2018.

80. L. Porter, personal interview, October 24, 2019. All further quotes from Porter are taken from this interview.

81. M. Mendoza, personal interview, February 20, 2020. All further quotes from Mendoza are taken from this interview.

82. Deferred Action for Childhood Arrivals (DACA) protects undocumented people who arrived in the US as children from deportation and allows them to get legal work permits.

83. T. Hollins, personal interview, July 24, 2020. All further quotes from Hollins are taken from this interview.

84. P. Wright, "'Victims' Rights' as a Stalking Horse for State Repression," *Journal of Prisoners on Prisons* 9, no. 2 (1998): 17–22.

85. C. A. Rentschler, *Second Wounds* (Durham, NC: Duke University Press, 2011).

86. T. Hollins, personal interview, July 10, 2020. All further quotes from Hollins are taken from this interview.

87. R. Weiker, personal interview, June 25, 2020. All further quotes from Weiker are taken from this interview.

88. J. Levenson, Y. N. Brannon, T. Fortney, and J. Baker, "Public Perceptions about Sex Offenders and Community Protection Policies," *Analyses of Social Issues and Public Policy* 7, no. 1 (2007): 1–25.

89. D. P. Connor and R. Tewksbury, "Public and Professional Views of Sex Offender Registration and Notification," *Criminology, Criminal Justice, Law & Society* 18, no. 1 (2017): 1–27.

Chapter Three

1. Bryan Stevenson in 2017 defined proximity in his talk "The Power of Proximity" for the CEO Initiative: "We have to find more ways to get proximate to the poor and the vulnerable . . . we have to find ways to get closer to the disfavored, the marginalized and the excluded, the poor, the disabled." https://www.youtube.com/watch?v=1RyAwZIH04Y.

2. D. Deason, personal interview, December 6, 2019. Unless otherwise noted, all quotes from Deason are taken from this interview.

3. Ray Washburne, an investor from Texas, was appointed by Trump as president and CEO of OPIC (Overseas Private Investment Corporation), having joined the agency in 2017.

4. J. Colvin and C. Long, "Trump Pardoned his Son-In-Law's Dad," *Chicago Tribune*, December 24, 2020.

Notes to Chapter Three

5. J. Jackson, personal interview, May 21, 2020. Unless otherwise noted, all quotes from Jackson are taken from this interview.

6. R. Bernstein, "Democrats Split over Trump's Prison Pitch, *The Atlantic*, May 23, 2018.

7. D. Loeb, personal interview, March 5, 2020. Unless otherwise noted, all quotes from Loeb are taken from this interview.

8. J. Nash, "The Prison Has Failed: The New York State Prison, in the City of New York, 1979–1828," *New York History* 98 (2016): 71–89.

9. L. E. Sullivan, *The Prison Reform Movement: Forlorn Hope* (Woodbridge, CT: Twayne Publishers).

10. M. Novogratz, personal interview, July 28, 2020. Unless otherwise noted, all quotes from Novogratz are taken from this interview.

11. R. Rooks, personal interview, June 20, 2020. Unless otherwise noted, all quotations from Rooks are taken from this interview.

12. A. Smith, "The NGO-ization of the Palestinian Liberation Movement: Interviews with Hatem Bazian, Noura Erekat, Atef Said, and Zeina Zaatari," in *The Revolution Will Not be Funded*, ed. INCITE! Women of Color Against Violence (New York: South End Press, 2007), 165–84.

13. M. Ming Francis, "The Price of Civil Rights: Black Lives, White Funding, and Movement Capture," *Law & Society Review* 35 (March 2019): 275.

14. R. Costello and C. P. Eren, *The Impact of Supreme Court Decisions on U.S. Institutions* (London: Routledge, 2021).

15. Noble was sentenced to 13 years of hard labor under Louisiana's habitual offender law for carrying a few joints worth of marijuana after prior arrests for possession of small amounts of drugs.

16. M. J. de la Merced, "Daniel Loeb's Third Point Bets on Criminal Justice," *The New York Times*, February 27, 2021.

17. K. Grow, "Meek Mill's Legal Troubles," *Rolling Stone*, March 14, 2018.

18. "Michael Rubin Talks Business Come-Up, Friendship with Meek Mill & REFORM Alliance," *Power 105.1 FM Breakfast Club*, January 30, 2019, https://www.youtube.com/watch?v=Hm4wPgv94_w.

19. K. Walsh, J. Hussemann, A. Flynn, J. Yahner, and L. Golian, "Estimating the Prevalence of Wrongful Conviction," research report, National Institute of Justice, 2017, https://nij.ojp.gov/library/publications/estimating-prevalence-wrongful-convictions.

20. Private foundations are nongovernmental nonprofit corporate entities endowed with private funds whose main role is to financially support, in the form of grants, other charitable and civil society organizations. They took form with the Carnegie and Rockefeller Foundations at the beginning of the twentieth century, according to Rob Reich in *Just Giving: Why Philanthropy Is Failing Democracy and How It Can Do Better* (Princeton, NJ: Princeton University Press, 2018).

208   *Notes to Chapter Three*

21. N. Nambiampurath, "Bitcoin Bull Michael Novogratz Donates 36 Million to Criminal Justice Reform," *Beincrypto.com*, November 19, 2019, https://beincrypto.com/bitcoin-bull-michael-novogratz-donates-36-million-to-criminal-justice-reform-and-philanthropy/.

22. L. Setaro, "How Jay-Z and Meek Mill's Reform Organization Plans to Improve the Criminal Justice System," *Complex*, February 15, 2019.

23. J. Jackson, personal interview, May 21, 2020.

24. J. Travis, personal interview, January 16, 2020.

25. M. Ball, "Do the Koch Brothers Really Care about Criminal Justice Reform?" *The Atlantic*, March 3, 2015.

26. M. Clarke, "Madoff Fraud Bankrupts JEHT Foundation," *Prison Legal News*, June 15, 2009.

27. L. Arnold, personal interview, April 16, 2020. Unless otherwise noted, all quotes from Arnold are taken from this interview.

28. B. Watterson, personal interview, February 12, 2020. Unless otherwise noted, all quotes from Watterson are taken from this interview.

29. D. Donovan, "Billionaire Donors Laura And John Arnold Support Far More in Maryland Than Police Surveillance," *Baltimore Sun*, August 26, 2016; E. Opilo, "Texas Philanthropists Say They're Backing Out of Financing Surveillance Plane Technology That Flew Over Baltimore," *Baltimore Sun*, January 26, 2021; Arnold Ventures, "Grants: Persistent Surveillance Systems, LLC," July 12, 2021, https://arnoldventures.org/grants/persistent-surveillance-systems-llc.

30. The most prominent abolitionist organization in the US, Critical Resistance, while taking in a sizable percentage of its funding from small grassroots donations, receives 25 percent from a limited number of funders, such as the Hull Family Foundation (https://localwiki.org/oakland/Critical_Resistance). M. Blair Hull, with a net worth of $400 million, founded Hull Trading Company, a market-making business that used advanced quantitative models, which he sold to Goldman Sachs for over $500 million.

31. K. Whitlock, and N. A. Heitzig, "Billionaire-Funded Criminal Justice Reform Actually Expands The Carceral System," *TruthOut*, November 21, 2019, https://truthout.org/articles/billionaire-funded-criminal-justice-reform-actually-expands-carceral-system/.

32. Bridgespan Group, "Risk Tolerance: Laura and John Arnold Are Open to Failure in Their Philanthropy," November 11, 2013, https://www.bridgespan.org/insights/library/remarkable-givers/profiles/john-and-laura-arnold/risk-tolerance-laura-and-john-arnold-are-open-to.

33. P. Rojc, "Quantitative Advocacy: How an Effective Altruist Funder Backs Criminal Justice Reform," *Inside Philanthropy*, April 30, 2020.

34. Bridgespan Group, "Where to work: When Choosing Causes, Laura and John Arnold Search for Viable Paths," November 27, 2013, https://www.bridgespan.org/insights/john-and-laura-arnold/where-to-work-when-choosing-causes-laura-and-joh.

Notes to Chapter Three

35. De la Merced, "Daniel Loeb's Third Point."

36. Reich, *Just Giving*, 19.

37. A. Khan, personal interview, June 17, 2020. Unless otherwise noted, all quotes from Khan are taken from this interview.

38. D. Hoskins, personal interview, February 13, 2020. Unless otherwise noted, all quotes from Hoskins are taken from this interview.

39. Sullivan, *Prison Reform Movement*, 25–26.

40. Sullivan, 33.

41. M. Mendoza, personal interview, February 21, 2020. Unless otherwise noted, all quotes from Mendoza are taken from this interview.

42. L. M. Salamon and C. L Newhouse, "2020 Nonprofit Employment Report," *Nonprofit Economic Data Bulletin*, no. 48 (June 2019).

43. INCITE! Women of Color Against Violence (eds.), *The Revolution Will Not Be Funded* (Durham, NC: Duke University Press, 2017).

44. P. X. Rojas, "Are the Cops in Our Heads and Hearts?" in *The Revolution Will Not Be Funded*, ed. INCITE! Women of Color Against Violence (Duke University Press, 2017), 206.

45. Z. Tufekci, "'Not This One': Social Movements, the Attention Economy, and Microcelebrity Networked Activism," *American Behavioral Scientist* 57 (2013): 848–70. By networked microcelebrity, Tufekci is referring to "politically motivated actors who successfully use affordances of social media to engage in a presentation of [their] political and personal [selves] to garner attention to a cause."

46. R. Putnam, "Civic Disengagement in Contemporary America," in *Crime, Inequality, and the State* (London: Routledge, 2020), 92–98.

47. F. F. Piven and R. Cloward, *Poor Peoples' Movements: Why They Succeed, How They Fail* (New York: Vintage Books, 1979).

48. R Wilson-Gilmore, "In the Shadow of the Shadow State," in *The Revolution Will Not Be Funded*, ed. INCITE! Women of Color Against Violence (Durham, NC: Duke University Press, 2017), 49–51.

49. A. H. Perez and Sisters in Action for Power, "Between Radical Theory and Community Praxis: Reflections on Organizing and the Nonprofit Industrial Complex," in *The Revolution Will Not Be Funded*, ed. INCITE! Women of Color Against Violence (Durham, NC: Duke University Press, 2017), 91–100.

50. David Callahan argues that there are way too many nonprofits, across all sectors, leading to massive amounts of waste, duplication, fighting internally for resources, and ultimately not having a big enough impact. This is because there is pressure against consolidation from those working in them. Grants are spread thinly without much thought about strategy. See Callahan, "There Are Way Too Many Nonprofits. What Are Funders Going to Do about That?" *Inside Philanthropy*, January 14, 2015.

51. H. H. Haines, "Black Radicalization and the Funding of Civil Rights: 1957–1970," *Social Problems* 32 (1984): 31–43.

52. I. Parmar and I. Choudhury, "Black Lives Matter Must Avoid Being Co-Opted by American Corporate Philanthropy," *The Conversation*, July 15, 2020, https://theconversation.com/black-lives-matter-must-avoid-being-co-opted-by-american-corporate-philanthropy-141927.

53. Reich, *Just Giving*, 7.

54. K. Ring, personal interview, July 7, 2020. Unless otherwise noted, all quotes from Ring are taken from this interview.

55. H. H. Haines, "Black Radicalization."

56. M. Levin, personal interview, November 18, 2019. Unless otherwise noted, all quotes are taken from this interview.

57. A. Ward, personal interview, February 7, 2020. All further quotes from Ward are taken from this interview.

58. T. Angeli Vargas, personal interview, July 24, 2020. Unless otherwise noted, all quotes from Vargas are taken from this interview.

59. N. Burrowes, M. Cousins, and I. R. Rojas, "On Our Own Terms: Ten Years of Radical Community Building," in *The Revolution Will Not Be Funded*, ed. INCITE! Women of Color Against Violence (Durham, NC: Duke University Press, 2017), 227–34.

60. D. Safavian, personal interview, February 20, 2020. Unless otherwise noted, all quotes from Safavian are taken from this interview.

61. T. Carlson, "Normal People Don't Want Criminal Justice Reform, They Want Criminal Justice Enforcement," Fox News, January 3, 2020.

62. P. K. Enns, *Incarceration Nation: How the United States Became the Most Punitive Democracy in the World* (New York: Cambridge University Press, 2016).

63. M. Bishop and M. Green, *Philanthrocapitalism: How Giving Can Save the World*. New York: Bloomsbury Press, 2008), 9.

Chapter Four

1. J. Bennett, "Alyssa Milano, Celebrity Activist for the Celebrity Presidential Age," *The New York Times*, May 23, 2018.

2. Artists & Athletes Alliance, "Celebrities Come Together to Continue the Fight for Criminal Justice Reform," July 25, 2019, https://www.globenewswire.com/en/news-release/2019/07/25/1888429/0/en/Celebrities-come-together-to-continue-the-fight-for-criminal-justice-reform.html.

3. A. Apatoff, "Met Gala 2014: Ivanka Trump's Ridiculously Glamorous Photo Diary," *People*, May 8, 2014.

4. B. Bennet, "The Inside Story of How Unlikely Allies Got Prison Reform Done," *Time*, December 21, 2018.

5. L. Carroll and A. A. Edwards, "This Lawyer Is Helping Kim Kardashian with Her Legal Career," *Refinery29*, April 29, 2019, https://www.refinery29.com/en-us/2019/04/230602/jessica-jackson-kim-kardashian-cut-50-incarcerated-women.

Notes to Chapter Four

6. J. Jackson, personal interview; *The View*, interview with K. Kardashian, March 31, 2020, https://youtube.com/watch?v=6xpTIBQIrc; *Mic*, Interview with K. Kardashian, May 30, 2018, https://t.co/We2Lom6bFV?amp=1.

7. M. Wheeler, *Celebrity Politics* (Cambridge, UK: Polity, 2013).

8. M. D. Atkinson and D. DeWitt, "Does Celebrity Issue Advocacy Mobilize Issue Publics?" *Political Studies* 67 (2019): 83–99, https://doi.org/10.1177/0032321717751294.

9. J. Street, "Celebrity Politicians: Popular Culture and Political Representation," *British Journal of Politics & International Relations* 6, no. 4 (2004): 435–52.

10. Joan Baez took part in a protest at San Quentin in 1992 to stop the execution of the first person to be killed after the reinstatement of the death penalty.

11. Wheeler, *Celebrity Politics*, 31, 45.

12. L. L. Gould, "JFK: Celebrity in the White House," BBC News, November 21, 2013, https://www.bbc.co.uk/history/worldwars/coldwar/kennedy_celebrity_01.shtml.

13. M. Boardman, "Before Bruce Springsteen and Stacey Dash: A Brief History of Politically Minded Celebrities," *Huffington Post*, November 1, 2012.

14. A. Cooper, "Celebrity Diplomacy and the G8: Bono and Bob as Legitimate International Actors," working paper no. 29, Center for International Governance and Innovation, University of Waterloo, Waterloo, ON, September 2007.

15. M. D. Atkinson and D. DeWitt, "Celebrity Issue Advocacy."

16. Wheeler, *Celebrity Politics*, 34.

17. A. Goudsouziam, *Sidney Poitier: Man, Actor, Icon* (Durham, NC: University of North Carolina Press, 2011).

18. Wheeler, *Celebrity Politics*, 54.

19. Ali joined the Nation of Islam in 1964, even establishing a boxing promotion company that was a source of funding for the organization. He faced prison and fines and was stripped of his titles and suspended from boxing for years for very publicly refusing to be drafted during the Vietnam era on political/moral grounds. See A. Dobuzinskis, "FBI Kept Tabs on Muhammad Ali in 1966 during Nation of Islam Probe," Reuters, December 16, 2016, https://www.reuters.com/article/us-usa-muhammadali-idUSKBN145I22.

20. Wheeler, *Celebrity Politics*. Wheeler provides a thorough overview of the controversies around celebrities and celebritized politicians.

21. D. Siegfried, "Anti-apartheid and the Politicization of Pop Music: Controversies around The Mandela Concert in 1988," in *Apartheid and Anti-Apartheid in Western Europe*, ed. K. Andresen, S. Justke, and D. Siegfried, (London: Palgrave Macmillan, 2021), 139–62.

22. In an interview, Van Jones described himself as a former "rowdy Black nationalist" who had spent 10 years "trying to be a revolutionary," having belonged to a socialist collective, Standing Together to Organize a Revolutionary Movement, in

Notes to Chapter Four

the mid-1990s. With a law degree from Yale, he founded the Ella Baker Center in 1996 in Oakland, California. Among the programs established by the center was Bay Area Police Watch, which assisted victims of police violence, and Books Not Bars to transform youth prisons in California into rehabilitation centers. See E. Strickland, "The New Face of Environmentalism," *Easy Bay Express*, November 2, 2005, https://eastbayexpress.com/the-new-face-of-environmentalism-1/. Jones noted in our 2020 interview that "the Ella Baker Center for Human Rights wound up helping to close five abusive youth prisons. Stopped them from building the super jail for youth in Oakland. Helped to reform the San Francisco Police Department."

23. R. van Krieken, *Celebrity Society* (London: Routledge, 2012), 54–55.

24. Q. Bui, J. Katz, M. Ruby, "Can You Identify These Politicians, Activists, and Celebrities?" *The New York Times*, December 23, 2019.

25. O. Driessens, "Celebrity Capital: Redefining Celebrity Using Field Theory," *Theory and Society*, 42 (2013): 543–60.

26. A. Alleyne, "Met Gala Red Carpet: A history of One of New York's Most Glamorous Affairs," CNN, May 2, 2019, https://www.cnn.com/style/article/met-gala-red-carpet-history/index.html.

27. Y. Lee, "The Doe Fund's 2016 Gala," *Socially Superlative*, October 31, 2016, https://www.sociallysuperlative.com/2016/10/31/the-doe-funds-2016-gala/.

28. Red Carpet Report, "14th Annual A New Way of Life Fundraising Gala," 2012.

29. Driessens, "Celebrity Capital."

30. Atkinson and DeWitt, "Celebrity Issue Advocacy."

31. T. Waldrop, "'Free Rodney Reed:' Celebrities Use Star Power to Try to Stop Execution of Man on Death Row in Texas." *CNN*, November 4, 2019, https://www.cnn.com/2019/11/04/entertainment/free-rodney-reed-petition-stars-trnd/index.html.

32. D. Brockington, "The Politics of Celebrity Advocacy," *E-International Relations*, March 21, 2014, https://www.e-ir.info/2014/03/21/the-politics-of-celebrity-advocacy/.

33. Strickland, "New Face of Environmentalism."

34. Proposition 21 dealt with the treatment of juveniles who broke the law in California. One of its provisions allowed children over 14 to have charges filed directly in adult court for certain serious violent offenses; among others were increased prison sentences for gang-related offenses committed by juveniles, prohibition of informal probation for juveniles who committed felonies, and reduced confidentiality of records for those over 14 for certain "serious" offenses.

35. D. Siegfried, "Anti-Apartheid," 139.

36. K. G. Tomaselli and B. Boster, "Mandela, MTV, Television, and Apartheid," *Popular Music and Society*, 17 (1993): 1–19.

37. David and Christina Arquette, Seth Green, Tina Knowles-Lawson (Beyoncé's mother), Al Sharpton, Martin Luther King III, Kim Kardashian, Alyssa Milano, Van Jones, and Demi Lovato.

Notes to Chapters Four and Five

38. Dream Corps, "#DayofEmpathy2020—Alyssa Milano," May 15, 2020, https://www.youtube.com/watch?v=o17rk3VqbQ&t=39s.

39. J. Ben-Menachem, "How Legislation Meant to Overhaul Probation and Parole in Pennsylvania Strayed from Its Roots," *The Appeal*, September 16, 2020, https://theappeal.org/probation-pennsylvania/.

40. G. Pender, "JAY-Z, Meek Mill Group Wants Mississippi Lawmakers to Override Reeves Prison Reform Veto," *Mississippi Today*, July 17, 2020; S. Grant, "Yo Gotti Teams Up with Meek Mill's Reform Alliance for Mississippi Reform Campaign," *The Source*, August 27, 2020, https://thesource.com/2020/08/27/yo-gotti-teams-with-meek-mills-reform-alliance-for-mississippi-reform-campaign/.

41. B. Dreisinger, personal interview, September 13, 2020. All further quotes are taken from this interview.

42. Z. Tufekci, "Not This One," 857.

43. *The View*, interview with K. Kardashian.

44. DreamCorps Zoom event, March 25, 2020, streamed online.

45. A. Khan, personal interview, June 17, 2020. All further quotes are taken from this Interview.

46. D. Trejo, "Vote Yes on Prop 25," October 22, 2020, https://facebook.com/watch/?v=826226388144076.

47. A. Armstrong, "A Letter to Jay-Z: Don't Keep This Promise," *The Appeal*, April 10, 2018, https://theappeal.org/a-letter-to-jay-z-dont-keep-this-promise-93bee11e20bd/.

48. T. Dinki, "NY Republicans Demand Repeal of Bail Reform, Offer Anecdotes, Not Evidence—It's Behind Increased Crime," *WBFO-FM 88.7*, December 18, 2021, https://www.wbfo.org/crime/2021-12-18/ny-republicans-demand-repeal-of-bail-reform-offer-anecdotes-not-evidence-its-behind-increased-crime.

49. *Rolling Stone*, "Jay-Z's Roc Nation Support App to Improve Criminal Justice System," March 19, 2018.

50. A. Armstrong, "Letter to Jay-Z."

51. B. Sullivan, "CBS Backtracks on 'The Activist' after a Backlash, Including from One of Its Hosts," *WABE*, September 17, 2021, https://www.wabe.org/cbs-backtracks-on-the-activist-after-a-backlash-including-from-one-of-its-hosts/.

52. K. G. Tomaselli and B. Boster, "Mandela, MTV," 3.

Chapter Five

1. L. Kaye, "How This Lawyer Became a Force of Nature for Second Chance Hiring," *Triple Pundit*, October 19, 2019, https://www.triplepundit.com/story/2019/how-lawyer-became-force-nature-second-chance-hiring/85221.

2. J. Kim, personal interview, April 24, 2020. All further quotes from Kim are from this interview.

214   *Notes to Chapter Five*

3. P. Menon, "A Discussion on Criminal Justice Reform with Mark Holden," *Just Thoughts* (blog), American University Justice Programs Office, October 4, 2018, https://jpo.blogs.american.edu/2018/10/04/a-discussion-on-criminal-justice-reform-with-mark-holden/.

4. K. Walker, "A 'First Step' towards Criminal Justice Reform" (blog), *The Keyword*, December 20, 2018, https://www.blog.google/outreach-initiatives/public-policy/first-step-towards-criminal-justice-reform/.

5. D. Hininger, "Statement from CoreCivic President and CEO Damon Hininger on the First Step Act," 2021, https://www.corecivic.com/statement-first-step-act.

6. L. Segura, "The First Step Act Could Be a Big Gift to CoreCivic and the Private Prison Industry," December 22, 2018, *The Intercept*.

7. Segura.

8. A. Katz, *The Influence Machine: the U.S. Chamber of Commerce and the Corporate Capture of American Life* (New York: Spiegal & Grau, 2015).

9. US Chamber of Commerce (USCOC), "Letter Supporting the Bipartisan First Step Act of 2018," November 20, 2018, https://www.uschamber.com/letters-congress/letter-supporting-the-bipartisan-first-step-act-of-2018.

10. Business Round Table (BRT), "BRT Letter in Support of the First Step Act," December 17, 2018, https://www.businessroundtable.org/brt-letter-in-support-of-first-step-act-and-meaningful-criminal-justice-reform.

11. D. Mukamal, from her comments as a reviewer of the manuscript in July 2022.

12. M. Eilert and A. Nappier Cherup, "The Activist Company: Examining a Company's Pursuit of Societal Change through Corporate Activism Using an Institutional Theoretical Lens," *Journal of Public Policy & Marketing* 39 (2020): 461–76.

13. According to law professor Tom C. W. Lin, businesses "played a crucial role with Presidents Kennedy and Johnson in the run-up, passage, and enforcement of civil rights legislation that became the landmark Civil Rights Acts of 1964 and 1968." See Lin, "Incorporating Social Activism," *Boston University Law Review* 98 (2018): 1535–605: "Major corporations like Avon, McDonald's, and Xerox led the way in integrating African Americans into their hiring practices, marketing plans, and investment initiatives" (p. 1543).

14. D. Siegfried, "Anti-Apartheid and the Politicisation of Pop Music: Controversies around the Mandela Concert in 1988," In *Apartheid and Anti-Apartheid in Western Europe*, ed. Knud Andresen, 139–62 (London: Palgrave Macmillan).

15. In 1986, for example, General Motors pulled out of South Africa, with the GM chairman citing the slow progress of ending apartheid and sanctions by the US government. At the time, GM was the world's largest industrial company and the largest American employer in South Africa. Yet in 2012 it paid $1.5 million to victims of South Africa's apartheid-era government for helping keep the White

Notes to Chapter Five

minority state afloat, demonstrating the complexity of corporations' relationships with movements.

16. K. Komiya, "A Majority of Customers Expect Brands to Take a Stand on Issues before Purchasing, Survey Finds," *Barron's*, July 7, 2020.

17. T. Jan, J. McGregor, and M. Hoyer, "Corporate America's $50 Billion Promise," *The Washington Post*, August 23, 2021.

18. J. Korzenik, *Untapped Talent: How Second Chance Hiring Works for Your Business and the Community* (New York : HarperCollins Leadership, 2021).

19. D. C. Dwyer and R. B. McNally, "Public Policy, Prison Industries, and Business: An Equitable Balance for the 1990s," *Federal Probation*, 57 (1993): 30.

20. S. Mihm, "America's Rocky Relationship with For-Profit Prisons," *Bloomberg View*, January 9, 2019, https://www.bloomberg.com/opinion/articles/2016-08-26/america-s-rocky-relationship-with-for-profit-prisons#xj4y7vzkg.

21. Korzenik, in *Untapped Talent*, says that JBM Envelope had been calling its initiatives "second chance" programs but decided to change to "fair chance" as they "felt it was too easy to conflate second chance with second rate" (p. 151). He uses the two terms interchangeably. Based on the use of the two terms to refer to similarly purposed programs and policies, I will stick with "second chance" as it has a slightly longer history in criminal justice reform and therefore may be more readily recognizable to readers.

22. J. Travis, "Reflections on the Reentry Movement," *Federal Sentencing Reporter*, 20 (2007): 2.

23. Congressional Research Service (CRS), "The Work Opportunity Tax Credit," 2018, https://sgp.fas.org/crs/misc/R43729.pdf.

24. D. Mukamal, from her comments as a reviewer of this manuscript in July 2022.

25. S. Marshall, "Permanent Prison: New Attitudes, Bad Economy Mean Released Prisoners Can't Find Jobs," *Crain's New York Business*, October 21, 2002.

26. G. W. Bush, State of the Union Address, January 20, 2004, https://2001-2009.state.gov/r/pa/ei/wh/rem/28276.htm.

27. Korzenik, *Untapped Talent*.

28. D. Deason, "Ruining Peoples' Lives with Criminal 'Justice,'" *The New York Times*, July 30, 2015.

29. A. Looney and N. Turner, "Work and Opportunity before and after Incarceration," Brookings, March 14, 2013, https://www.brookings.edu/wp- content/uploads/2018/03/es_20180314_looneyincarceration_final.pdf.

30. R. Simon, "The Company of Second Chances," *The Wall Street Journal*, January 25, 2020.

31. R. Holt, personal interview, April 17, 2020. All further quotes from Holt are taken from this interview.

32. S. Fister Gale, "A Second Chance: How Nehemiah's Unconventional Hiring Program is Slashing Turnover and Changing Lives," *Talent Management*, June 17,

2021, https://www.talentmgt.com/articles/2021/06/17/a-second-chance-how-nehemiahs-unconventional-hiring-program-is-slashing-turnover-and-changing-lives/.

33. Simon, "Company of Second Chances."

34. Fister Gale, "A Second Chance."

35. R. Holt, personal interview, April 17, 2020.

36. Simon, "Company of Second Chances."

37. Society for Human Resource Management (SHRM), "Second Chance Hiring from the Consumer Perspective," 2021, https://www.shrm.org/hr-today/trends-and-forecasting/research-and-surveys/pages/getting-talent-back-towork---consumer-persepective.aspx.

38. J. Pfaff, *Locked In: The True Causes of Mass Incarceration and How to Achieve Real Reform* (New York: Basic Books, 2017).

39. K. Schad, personal interview, March 30, 2020. All further quotes from Schad are taken from this interview.

40. SHRM, "Workers with Criminal Records," 2018, https://www.shrm.org/hr-today/trends-and-forecasting/research-and-surveys/Pages/Second-Chances.aspx.

41. H. Higginbottom, personal interview, December 5, 2019. All further quotes from Higginbottom are taken from this interview.

42. Federal Deposit Insurance Corp (FDIC), "Overview of the Final Rule," July 24, 2020, https://www.fdic.gov/news/section19-7-24-20.pdf.

43. K Broughton, "JPMorgan Has 'a Responsibility' to Recruit Ex-Cons, Dimon Says," *American Banker*, April 5, 2018.

44. J. Dimon and A. Duncan, "Hiring Returning Citizens Is Good for Business," *Chicago Tribune*, June 13, 2018.

45. T. Angeli Vargas, personal interview, July 24 2020. All further quotes from Vargas are taken from this interview.

46. M. Heimer, "Why JPMorgan Chase Wants to Give More Former Criminals a Second Chance," *Fortune*, October 2019.

47. L. Couloute, "Getting Back on Course: Educational Exclusion and Attainment among Formerly Incarcerated People," *Prison Policy Initiative*, 2018, https://www.prisonpolicy.org/reports/education.html.

48. Business Roundtable (BRT), "Business Roundtable and Partners Launch Second Chance Business Coalition," 2021, https://www.businessroundtable.org/business-roundtable-and-partners-launch-second-change-business-coalition-to-improve-access-to-employment-advancement-for-people-with-criminal-records.

49. L. Moynihan, "Jamie Dimon Launching Coalition That Aims to Boost Hiring of Ex-Cons," *New York Post*, April 27, 2021.

50. SHRM, "Second Chance Hiring."

51. SHRM, "Second Chance Hiring"; "Workers with Criminal Records."

Notes to Chapter Five

52. J. Dimon, "If You Paid Your Debt to Society, You Should Be Allowed to Work," *The New York Times*, August 4, 2021.

53. Under President Bill Clinton's 1994 Violent Crime Control and Law Enforcement Act (also known as the 1994 Crime Bill), the federal government was prohibited from providing Pell Grants to the incarcerated. In December of 2020, after 26 years, the ban was lifted.

54. JPMorgan Chase Policy Center, "Giving People with Criminal Backgrounds a Second Chance," 2021, https://www.jpmorganchase.com/content/damn/jpmc/jpmorgan-chase-and-co/documents/jpmc-policycenter-overview-V1-ada.pdf.

55. #Next20, "Criminal Justice Reform," July 8, 2020, https://www.yahoo.com/entertainment/next20-criminal-justice-reform-215855888.html.

56. USCOC, "U.S. Chamber Launches National Initiative To Address Inequality Of Opportunity," press release, June 5, 2020.

57. USCOC, "U.S. Chamber Calls on Congress to Pass Bills To Address Race-Based Opportunity Gaps," press release, August 4, 2020.

58. BRT, "Letter in Support."

59. "Randall Stephenson addresses the Racial Tension in American Society," YouTube, September 24, 2016, https://www.youtube.com/watch?v=ThO74-oFt_Q&t=48s.

60. Jan, McGregor, and Hoyer, "Corporate America's $50 billion promise."

61. AT&T, "Our Advocacy on Policing Reform," July 1, 2020, https://about.att.com/story/2020/business_roundtable.html.

62. In 2019 Verizon expanded its pro bono program to include criminal justice issues, focusing on helping the formerly incarcerated seal or expunge their record and eliminating extreme sentences for juveniles. While sealing or expunging of records might be linked to employment, it is difficult to see how eliminating extreme sentences for juveniles bears on Verizon directly and hence is indicative of corporations expanding beyond direct interest. See C. Sillman, "Working for More Justice in the Criminal Justice System," News Center: Verizon, June 12, 2019.

63. Walmart, "Criminal Justice Grants," 2020, https://walmart.org/center-for-racial-equity-center-for-racial-equity-grants.

64. It was symbolic because private prisons do not drive incarceration and are not necessarily qualitatively worse than public prisons.

65. D. Henry and I. Moise, "JP Morgan Backs away from Private Prison Finance," Reuters, March 5, 2019.

66. W. Yakowicz, "Billionaire Charles Koch on Why Cannabis Should Be Legal," *Forbes*, July 27, 2021.

67. Ben & Jerry's, "Defund the Police and Invest in Our Communities," *What's New*, June 19, 2020, https://www.benjerry.com/whats-new/2020/06/defund-the-police.

68. #REFORM Alliance, "PUMA X Meek Mill," 2021, https://us.puma.com/us/en/puma-x-meek-mill.

69. A. Agan and S. Star, "Ban the Box, Criminal Records, and Racial Discrimination: A Field Experiment," *Quarterly Journal for Economics*, 133(2018): 191–235.

70. Jan, McGregor, and Hoyer, "Corporate America's $50 billion Promise."

71. E. Strickland, "The New Face of Environmentalism," *East Bay Express*, November 2, 2005, https://eastbayexpress.com/the-new-face-of-environmentalism-1/.

72. Eilert and Nappier Cherup, "Activist Company," 465.

Chapter Six

1. E. Strickland, "The New Face of Environmentalism," *East Bay Express*, November 2, 2005, https://eastbayexpress.com/the-new-face-of-environmentalism-1/; V. Jones, personal interview.

2. F. Barbarsh and H. Siegel, "Van Jones Resigns amid Controversy," *Politico*, September 6, 2009.

3. In fact, in 2021, Amazon founder Jeff Bezos gave him a $100M "Courage and Civility" award for "trying to be a unifier in a divisive world" (Darcy, 2021).

4. Among many other examples, the Comprehensive Crime Control Act of 1984 and the Anti-Drug Abuse Act of 1986 passed both houses of Congress with bipartisan majorities. Republican Strom Thurmond, who had supported racial segregation and voted against the Civil Rights and Voting Rights Acts, sponsored the Comprehensive Crime Control Act, but it was cosponsored by Democrats Edward Kennedy and Joe Biden.

5. Altman, 2015.

6. The bill drew on, and improved, the SRCA's prison reform portions, which were approximately half of SRCA.

7. J. Jackson, personal interview; Families Against Mandatory Minimums (FAMM), "H.R. 4261: SAFE JUSTICE ACT OF 2017 (115th Congress)," fact sheet, 2017, https://famm.org/wp-content/uploads/SAFE-Justice-Act-Factsheet-2017-1.pdf.

8. D. Green, "Penal Optimism and Second Chances: The Legacies of American Protestantism and the Prospects for Penal Reform," *Punishment & Society* 15 (2013), 125.

9. D. Dagan and S. Teles, *Prison Break: Why Conservatives Turned Against Mass Incarceration* (Oxford, UK: Oxford University Press, 2016), 162.

10. C. Page, "Conservatives, NAACP Agree: Too Much Spent on Prisons," *Dayton Daily News,* April 15, 2011, https://www.daytondailynews.com/lifestyles/philosophy/clarence-page-conservatives-naacp-agree-too-much-spent-prisons/W5VekIBEomlisbyIP4E5CN/?outputType=amp.

11. Targeted News Service, "NAACP Report Ties State Spending on Prisons to Low Educational Achievement," March 29, 2011.

Notes to Chapter Six

12. Dagan and Teles, *Prison Break*.

13. Prominent counterexamples exist, though, that were religiously rooted. A national organization on the right can be found in the work of former Nixon special counsel Chuck Colson. Incarcerated on an obstruction of justice charge and impelled by religious fervor after becoming a born-again Christian, his faith-based Prison Fellowship and its subsidiary, Justice Fellowship, founded in 1976 and 1983, respectively, lobbied for prison reform, with a national headquarters, regional directors, and an international presence. Wheaton BCG Archives. "Records of Prison Fellowship Ministries—Collection 274," n.d., https://www2 .wheaton.edu/bgc/archives/GUIDES/274.htm#4. The American Friends Service Committee of the Quakers is another counterexample, with its a century-long history of reform involvement nationally, establishing local committees to focus on prison issues in the 1940s, underscoring racial and class differences in punishment as early as the 1960s, and calling for sweeping changes like decriminalizing drug offenses in the 1970s. The executive director of The Sentencing Project, Marc Mauer, in fact, first got involved in criminal justice issues as a student in the 1970s through a local AFSC office in Ann Arbor, Michigan, which was already organizing a "fledgling movement around bail reform": The AFSC's book, *Struggle for Justice* [New York: Hill & Wang, 1971], raised some fundamental questions about the purpose of incarceration and discretionary decision making and all those kinds of things and was quite influential." The book also heavily criticized the criminal justice system's role in "perpetuating the second-class status of people of color" (Bolante, 2015).

14. N. Alford, "Van Jones on Being Called a 'Sellout': 'I'm More Worried about Outcomes Than Outrage,'" *The Grio*, November 27, 2019; D. Hoskins, personal interview.

15. M. Novogratz, personal interview; A. Milano, personal interview.

16. Z. Linly, "Van Jones Goes on The View and Gets Roasted Like a Two-Faced Potato Because Ain't No Such Thing as Halfway Activist," *The Root*, February 5, 2021; D. Young, "Van Jones Is Aaron Burr," *The Root*, August 28, 2020.

17. This perspective was by no means uniform. Prominent civil rights leader Jesse Jackson and formerly incarcerated activist Shaka Sengor remained supporters, appearing as guests at #cut50's days of empathy, and some liberal organization leaders praised his national work for producing mainstreamization.

18. C-SPAN, "Presidential Campaign Announcement Full Speech," June 16, 2015.

19. D. Durbin, "Press Release: President Obama Signs Durbin's Fair Sentencing Act into Law," August 3, 2010, https://www.durbin.sesnate.gov/newsroom/press-releases/president-obama-signs-durbins-fair-sentencing-act-into-law.

20. Jones, personal interview.

21. C-SPAN, "Conservative Political Action Conference Straw Poll Results," February 25, 2017, https://www.c-span.org/video/_424471-10/conservative-politi cal-action-conference-2017-strawpoll.

22. M. Gottschalk, *Caught: The Prison State and the Lockdown of American Politics* (Princeton, NJ: Princeton University Press, 2015), 162.

23. L. Owens, "How the National Urban League Missed the Mark with Its State of Black America Report," *Political Machine*, March 19, 2012.

24. Vera Institute of Justice, "Marc Levin," 2021, https://www.vera.org/justice -in-focus-crime-bill-20/the-bigger-picture/marc-levin.

25. J. Pye, personal interview.

26. Politicians who were important to the passage of the First Step Act included Senators Cory Booker (D-New Jersey), Mike Lee (R-Utah), Rand Paul (R-Kentucky), Sheldon Whitehouse (D-Rhode Island), and Dick Durbin (D-Illinois). Because this book is focused on the movement outside of political institutions of power, they are not included in the general discussion.

27. From here on, I leave out the quotation marks in describing the right, but the umbrella is large and, especially in the case of libertarians, by no means a settled designation. As Hannah Cox from Conservatives Concerned About the Death Penalty said, "The Republican party is quite fractured. You have your social conservatives which overlaps with Christian conservatives. You have your libertarians, who are budget hawks. Tea Party Types. You have your more moderate, big-business, neo-con Republicans. Different things work with each of them; it really depends on who you're talking to."

28. Dagan and Teles, *Prison Break*, 8.

29. Dagan and Teles, 161.

30. Dagan and Teles, 8.

31. Stacking Provisions under 924c of the US Code triggered lengthy mandatory minimums for the "separate" crime/charge of having a gun during a drug offense or violent offense. Even the presence of a legally purchased gun in the home of the defendant could result in an enhanced sentence under the old system. The charges were therefore "stacked," and sentences were to be served concurrently.

32. Norquist, an antitax activist who had championed tough-on-crime legislation in the 1990s, became involved with a small cadre of prominent conservatives like Richard Viguerie and Pat Nolan who met regularly to discuss criminal justice reform. According to Dagan and Teles, "As a result of listening to the conservatives he trusted, Norquist came around to the idea that the same principles he had about the rest of government should apply with equal force to criminal justice" (p. 60). His agreeing with Jason Pye about the need for sentencing reform is unsurprising as he, like conservative reform leader Pat Nolan, had previously endorsed reducing crack-cocaine disparities.

Notes to Chapter Six

33. A. Grawert and T. Lau, "How the First Step Act Became Law—And What Happens Next" (blog), Brennan Center, January 4, 2019, https://www.brennan center.org/our-work/analysis-opinion-/how-first-step-act-became-law-and-what -happens-next.

34. Levin, personal interview.

35. Safavian, personal interview.

36. Jones, personal interview; Jackson, personal interview.

37. As the president of FAMM, Kevin Ring described his group in this way in our interview: "The right thinks we're left, and the left thinks we're right. Because my background is in Republican politics, people assume we're conservative, but we spend all of our time trying to get Black and Brown people out of long prison sentences. Our staff is all over the map politically, so I don't blame them for not being able to place us."

38. Jackson, personal interview.

39. The bill drew on, and improved, the SRCA's prison reform portions, which were approximately half of the act.

40. Grawert and Lau, "How the First Step Act Became Law,"

41. *CNBC*, "Trump Addresses Criminal Justice at Prison Reform Summit," May 18, 2018, https://wwwcnbc.com/2018/05/18/watch-trump-addresses-crimi-nal-justice-at-prison-reform-summit.html.

42. Dear colleague letters are official correspondence sent from one member of Congress to all other members, in both chambers. They are used to persuade other members to endorse or oppose a bill.

43. Besides the LCCHR, two groups had letters attached to the Dear Colleague letter, whose role in reforms historically and contemporaneously should be the subject of scholarly inquiry but is outside the scope of this book. The groups were Law Enforcement Leaders to Reduce Crime and Incarceration and the American Federation of Government Employees, AFL-CIO, Council of Prison Locals.

44. Though its name did not appear in the oppositional letter, the Brennan Center leadership under Inimai Chettiar, director of its Justice program, was also opposed, according to Jackson.

45. Leadership Conference on Civil and Human Rights (LCCHR), "The Leadership Conference on Civil and Human Rights Voting Record, 115th Congress," 2018, https://civilrights.org/resources/civil-and-human-rights-coalition-scores-the -115th-Congress/.

46. LCCHR.

47. H. Jeffries, "Dear Colleague," *Politico*, May 18, 2018, https://www.politico .com/f/_id=0000163=73c9=d627-a5e3-7fcfc3110001.

48. This is an ironic flipping of what have been seen as progressive reforms, as discretion was initially eliminated to prevent bias.

49. LCCHR, "Leadership Conference Voting Record."

50. I. Chettiar and A. Grawert, "Letter to Chairman Goodlatte and Ranking Member Nadler," May 18, 2018, https://www.scribd.com/document/378632847/letter-to-congress-on-the-first-step-act&from_embed.

51. R. Berman, "Democrats Split over Trump's Prison Pitch," May 23, 2018, *The Atlantic.*

52. LCCHR, "Leadership Conference Voting Record."

53. J. Hoe, personal interview, December, 21, 2021. All further quotes are taken from this interview.

54. Cox, personal interview; Safavian, personal interview; Pye, personal interview; Jackson, personal interview.

55. This vote was taken under a House suspension of the rules, which is used to expeditiously pass noncontroversial bills expected to have supermajority support, limiting debates to 40 minutes. It does not allow amendments to be introduced on the floor and requires a two-thirds majority to pass.

56. M. Gill, "Threading the Needle: the FIRST STEP Act, Sentencing Reform, and Criminal Justice Reform Advocacy," *Federal Sentencing Reporter*, 31 (2018): 107.

57. J. Jackson, personal interview; H. Harris, personal interview.

58. H. Harris, personal interview.

59. R. Allen, "Full Criminal Justice Package, to Reduce State's Prison Population, Clears House and Senate," *The Advocate*, July 5, 2017.

60. T. Roelofs, "Hell Freezes over: GOP and ACLU Push Prison Reform," *Bridge Michigan*, August 20, 2015, https://www.bridgemi.com/michigan-government/hell-freezes-over-gop-and-aclu-push-prison-reform.

61. J. Horowitz, "Michigan Enacts Landmark Jail Reform," issue brief, Pew Research Center, https://www.pewtrust.org/en/research-and-analysis-issue-briefs/2021/09/michigan-enacts-landmark-jail-reforms.

62. J. Lester Feder, "In a Rare Show of Solidarity, Republicans and Democrats Are Working Together to Pass Sweeping Criminal Justice Reform in Michigan as the State's Jail Population Grows," *Business Insider*, December 17, 2020, https://www.businessinsider.com/michigan-to-keep-thousands-out-of-jail-with-sweeping-reform-2020-12?op=1.

63. Feder.

64. B. Allan, personal interview, October 27, 2019. All further quotes are taken from this interview.

65. A story is not necessarily a fictional account. However, every sequence of events has to be constructed by a human storyteller, linking together events, often in familiar narrative arcs with archetypes, villains, morals, and so forth.

66. J. Pfaff, *Locked In: The True Causes of Mass Incarceration and How to Achieve Real Reform* (New York: Basic Books, 2017).

Notes to Chapters Six and Seven

67. J. Saldana, personal interview, August 20, 2020. All further quotes are taken from this interview.

68. ACLU, "Petition," 2021, https://www.action.aclu.org/petition/divest-police-invest-Black-and-brown-communities; S. Peoples, A. Fram, and J. Lemire, "Key Democrats Spurn Push to Defund the Police amid Trump Attacks," *AP News*, June 9, 2020, https://apnews.com/article/american-protests-donald-trump-ap-top-news-elections-joe-biden-3e6226c495f63ea8551f0d997af9412b.

69. Justice Action Network (JAN), "NBC News: Republican States Make the Case against Trump's Drug Policy," May 19, 2017, https://www.justiceactionnetwork.org/news/nbc-news-republican-states-make-the-case-against-trumps-drug-policy.

70. Dagan and Teles, *Prison Break*, 111.

71. J. Schuppe, "Republican States Make the Case against Trump's Drug Policy," NBC News, May 19, 2017, https://www.nbcnews.com/news/us-news/republican-states-make-case-against-trump-s-drug-policy-n761651.

72. M. Zhang, "Koch-Backed Group Joins Marijuana Push after Zoom With Dogg," *Politico*, April 6, 2021.

73. Z. Tufekci, *Twitter and Tear Gas: The Power and Fragility of Networked Protest* (New Haven, CT: Yale University Press, 2017), 67.

74. M. Mauer, personal interview, July 15, 2020. All further quotes are taken from this interview.

75. Dagan and Teles, *Prison Break*, 61.

76. J. Haidt, *The Righteous Mind: Why Good People Are Divided By Politics and Religion* (New York: Pantheon Books, 2012).

77. M. Tonry, cited in Green, "Penal Optimism," 168.

78. Gottschalk, *Caught*, 162.

Chapter Seven

1. D. Dagan and S. Teles, *Prison Break: Why Conservatives Turned Against Mass Incarceration* (Oxford, UK: Oxford University Press), 143.

2. A. James, "Ending the Mass Incarceration of Women and Girls," *Yale Law Journal* 129 (2019).

3. L. E. Sullivan, *The Prison Reform Movement: Forlorn Hope* (Woodbridge, CT: Twayne Publishers).

4. M. J. de la Merced, "Daniel Loeb's Third Point Bets on Criminal Justice," *The New York Times*, February 27, 2021.

5. New Profit, 2017.

6. B. Cobb, personal interview.

7. G. Schwartz, personal interview, October 19, 2020.

8. Schwartz, personal interview.

9. Schwartz, personal interview.

10. D. Rodriguez, "The Political Logic of the Non-Profit Industrial Complex," in *The Revolution Will Not Be Funded*, ed. INCITE! Women of Color Against Violence (Durham, NC: Duke University Press, 2017), 27; Perez, 2017, 98.

11. In addition to the CZI Justice Accelerator Fund, see, for example, Justice Capital (https://justice.capital/accelerator-and-advisory/) and Amazon Black Business Accelerator (https://sell.amazon.com/programs/Black-business-accelerator).

12. See *The Appeal*, https://theappeal.org/those-closest-to-the-problem-are-clos est-to-the-solution-555e04317b79/.

13. Jackson, personal interview.

14. For the conservative perspective, see https://conservativejusticereform.org/lindsay-holloway-redemption/.

15. J. Schwartz and J. Chaney, *Gifts from the Dark: Learning from the Incarceration Experience* (Lanham, MD: Lexington Books, 2021).

16. Z. D. Convisser and W. Werry, "Exoneree Engagement in Policy Reform Work: An Exploratory Study of the Innocence Movement Policy Reform Process," *Journal of Contemporary Criminal Justice* 33, no. 1 (2016), https://doi.org/10.1177/1043986216673010.

17. Convisser and Werry.

18. P. Jonsson, "Debra Milke: Why Freedom Feels So Elusive for Death Row Exonerees," *The Christian Science Monitor*, March 26, 2014.

19. Dagan and Teles, *Prison Break*.

20. Schwartz, 2020.

21. In my time as an organizer for New Yorkers Against the Death Penalty, FIPs who had been released from death row due either to a commutation or to innocence were frequently invited to speak during days of lobbying, panels, and educational events.

22. Cobb, personal interview.

23. J. Saldana, personal interview.

24. J. Bryant, "Trump Pardons Cannabis Entrepreneur, Clemency Activist and Hip-Hop Producer Weldon Angeles," *Forbes*, December 24, 2020.

25. Deason, personal interview; Kim, personal interview.

26. I. Somin, "Conservatives Rethinking Mass Imprisonment and the War on Drugs," *The Volokh Conspiracy*, January 28, 2014.

27. ACLU, "About the 50 State Blueprint, 2022," https://50stateblueprint.aclu .org/about/.

28. Dreisinger, personal interview.

29. Saldana, personal interview.

30. Vargas-Edmond, personal interview.

31. Galvin-Amanza, personal interview.

32. Dreisinger, personal interview.

33. Weiker, personal interview.

Notes to Chapter Seven

34. Enns, *Incarceration Nation: How the United States Became the Most Punitive Democracy in the World* (New York: Cambridge University Press, 2016).

35. Galvin, personal interview.

36. M. Mauer, personal interview. Also see an example of this respectful hearing from M. Kaba, "Yes We Mean Literally Abolish the Police," *The New York Times*, June 12, 2020.

37. B. Latzer, "Will the Crime Wave Soon Crest? There's Already Backlash against Anti-Police Policies and Demographic Trends Are Encouraging," *The Wall Street Journal*, January 2, 2022; T. Dinki, "NY Republicans Demand Repeal of Bail Reform, Offer Anecdotes—Not Evidence—It's Behind Increased Crime." *WBFO NPR*, December 18, 2021, https://www.wbfo.org/crime/2021-12-18/ny-republicans-demand-repeal-of-bail-reform-offer-anecdotes-not-evidence-its-behind-increased-crime.

38. J. Lahut, "Defund the Police," *Business Insider*, October 26, 2021.

39. Sullivan, *Prison Reform Movement*, 137.

40. D. Green, "Penal Optimism and Second Chances: The Legacies of American Protestantism and the Prospects for Penal Reform," *Punishment & Society* 15, no. 2 (2013): 123–46

41. Green, 285.

42. Levin, personal interview.

43. D. McAdam and D. Snow, *Social Movements: Readings of their Emergence, Mobilization, and Dynamics* (Los Angeles: Roxbury Publishing, 1997), xxiv.

44. D. Wolfe, "Funders Are Backing a Push to Clear Criminal Records. For Many Involved, It's Personal," *Inside Philanthropy*, March 25, 2021.

45. R. Reich, *Just Giving: Why Philanthropy Is Failing Democracy and How It Can Do Better* (Princeton, NJ: Princeton University Press), 18.

46. D. Winston, "How Gay Rights Went Mainstream—And What It Cost," *The Washington Post*, June 30, 2019.

47. Vargas, personal interview.

48. R. Costello and C. Eren, *The Impact of Supreme Court Decisions on U.S. Institutions: A Sociology of Law Primer* (London: Routledge).

BIBLIOGRAPHY

Abramson, A. "Kanye West Calls President Trump 'My Brother' Then Tweets a Selfie in a MAGA Hat." *Time.* April 25, 2018.

Adams, C. "Ben & Jerry's Unveils New Flavor to Support Rep. Cori Bush's Public Safety Bill." *Today.* September 21, 2021.

Adeniji, A. "With Prisoners Facing New Risks, a Nonprofit Rallies Donors— Including a Tech Billionaire." *Inside Philanthropy.* June 25, 2020. https://www .insidephilanthropy.com/home/2020/6/24/with-prisoners-facing-covid-risks -a-nonprofit-rallies-donorsincluding-a-tech-billionaire.

Agan, A., and, S. Starr. "Ban the Box, Criminal Records, and Racial Discrimination: A Field Experiment." *The Quarterly Journal of Economics* 133, no. 1 (2018): 191–235.

Aguiar, L. M. and C. J. Schneider, eds. *Researching among the Elites: Challenges and Opportunities in Studying Up.* London: Ashgate, 2012.

Alexander, M. 2010. *The New Jim Crow: Incarceration in an Age of Colorblindness.* New York: The New Press.

Alford, N. "Van Jones on Being Called a 'Sellout': 'I'm More Worried about Outcomes Than Outrage.'" *The Grio.* November 27, 2019.

Allen, K. L. "Manager's Tool Kit: Truly Inside Workers. Across the Board." February 2000. https://advance-lexis-com.ezproxy.wpunj.edu/api/document?collec tion=news&id=urn:contentItem: -TFT0-00RH-F0K0-00000-00&context =1516831.

Bibliography

Allen, R.. "Full Criminal Justice Package, to Reduce State's Prison Population, Clears House and Senate." *The Advocate*. July 5, 2017.

Alliance for Safety and Justice (ASJ). 2022. "Nation's Largest Criminal Justice Reform Organization Makes History." Press release. March 1, 2022. https://allianceforsafetyandjustice.org/press-release/nations-largest-criminal-justice-reform-organization-makes-history/.

Allison, C. "Major Dallas Trump Donor Talks the Election." *DMagazine*, November 13, 2020.

American Bar Association (ABA). "Federal Sentencing Reform." 2022. https://www.americanbar.org/advocacy/governmental_legislative_work/priorities_policy/criminal_justice_system_improvements/federalsentencingreform/.

———. "First Step Act Already Shows Success." August 15, 2019. https://www.americanbar.org/advocacy/governmental_legislative_work/publications/washingtonletter/august_2010_WL/first_step_act_article/.

American Civil Liberties Union (ACLU). "ACLU Launches State-by-State Blueprints with Roadmaps for Cutting Incarceration by 50 Percent." Press release. September 5, 2018. https://www.aclu.org/press-releases/aclu-launches-state-state-blueprints-roadmaps-cutting-incarceration-50-percent.

———. "ACLU Awarded $50 Million by Open Society Foundations to End Mass Incarceration." Press release. November 7, 2014.

———. 2021. "Divest from the Police. Invest in Black and Brown Communities." Petition. https://action.aclu.org/petition/divest-police-invest-Black-and-brown-communities.

American Conservative Union (ACU). "Pat Nolan." 2021. http://acufoundation.conservative.org/center-for-criminal-justice-reform/pat-nolan/.

Anderson, L. "Criminal-Justice reform Is dead? Not So fast." *Governing.com*. November 23, 2016. https://www.governing.com/gov-institute/voices/col-criminal-justice-reform-state-ballot-measures-legislation.html.

Apatoff, A. "Met Gala 2014: Ivanka Trump's Ridiculously Glamorous Photo Diary." *People*. May 8, 2014.

Armstrong, A. "A Letter to Jay-Z: Don't Keep This Promise." *The Appeal*. April 10, 2018. https://theappeal.org/a-letter-to-jay-z-dont-keep-this-promise-93bee11e20bd/.

Arnold Foundation. "Arnold Foundation Statement on the First Step Act." December 19, 2018. https://www.arnoldventures.org/newsroom/arnold-foundation-statement-on-first-step-act/.

Artists & Athletes Alliance. "Celebrities Come Together to Continue the Fight for Criminal Justice Reform." July 25, 2019. https://www.globenewswire.com/en/news-release/2019/07/25/1888429/0/en/Celebrities-Come-Together-to-Continue-the-Fight-for-Criminal-Justice-Reform.html.

Bibliography

Associated Press. "New Poll Shows that 94 percent of Americans Back Criminal Justice Reform." June 23, 2020. https://www.marketwatch.com/story/new-poll-shows-94-of-americans-back-criminal-justice-reform-2020-06-23.

Atkinson, M. D., and D. DeWitt. "Does Celebrity Issue Advocacy Mobilize Issue Publics?" *Political Studies* 67, no. 1 (2019): 83–99.

AT&T. "Our Advocacy on Policing Reform." July 1, 2020. https://about.att.com/story/2020/business_roundtable.html.

Ball, M. "Do the Koch Brothers Really Care about Criminal Justice Reform?" *The Atlantic*, March 3, 2015.

Barbash, F., & H. Siegel. "Van Jones Resigns amid Controversy." *Politico*. September 9, 2009. https://www.politico.com/story/2009/09/van-jones-resigns-amid-controversy-026797.

Barry, E. "Women Prisoners on the Cutting Edge: Development of the Activist Women's Prisoners' Rights Movement." *Social Justice* 27, no. 3 (2000): 168–75.

BBC News. "Trump Urges the Death Penalty for Drug Dealers." March 19, 2018. https://www.bbc.com/news/world-us-canada-43465229.

Ben & Jerry's. "What's New: Defund the Police and Invest in Our Communities." June 19, 2020. https://www.benjerry.com/whats-new/2020/06/defund-the-police.

Ben-Menachem, J. "How Legislation Meant to Overhaul Probation and Parole in Pennsylvania Strayed from Its Roots." *The Appeal*. September 16, 2020. https://theappeal.org/probation-pennsylvania/.

Bennet, B. "The Inside Story of How Unlikely Allies Got Prison Reform Done—With an Assist from Kim Kardashian West." *Time*, December 21, 2018.

Bennett, J. "Alyssa Milano, Celebrity Activist for the Celebrity Presidential Age." *The New York Times*. November 4, 2019.

Berman, R. "Democrats Split over Trump's Prison Pitch." *The Atlantic*. May 23, 2018.

Bernstein, J. "Is Agnes Gund the Last Good Rich Person?" *The New York Times*. November 3, 2018.

Bishop, M., and M. Green. *Philanthrocapitalism: How Giving Can Save the World*. New York: Bloomsbury Press, 2008.

———. "Philanthrocapitalism Rising." *Society* 52, no. 6 (2015): 541–48. http://dx.doi.org.ezproxy.wpunj.edu/10.1007/s12115-015-9945-8.

Bridgespan Group. "Where to Work: When Choosing Causes, Laura and John Arnold search for Viable Paths." November 27, 2013. https://www.bridgespan.org/insights/john-and-laura-arnold/where-to-work-when-choosing-causes-laura-and-joh.

Boardman, M. "Before Bruce Springsteen and Stacey Dash: A Brief History of Politically Minded Celebrities." *Huffington Post*. November 1, 2012.

Bort, R. "Kim Kardashian, Alyssa Milano, Van Jones, among 50+ Celebrities Lobbying for Prison Reform Legislation." *Rolling Stone*. November 14, 2018. https://www.rollingstone.com/politics/politics-news/kardashian-prison--755934/.

Bradley, N. L., US Chamber of Commerce. "Letter Supporting the First Step Act to the United States Senate." November 20, 2018.

Brame, R., S. D. Bushway, R. Paternoster, and M. G. Turner. "Demographic Patterns of Cumulative Arrest Prevalence by Ages 18 and 23." *Crime & Delinquency* 60, no. 3 (2014): 471–86.

Brenan, M. "Support for Marijuana Legalization Inches up to a New High." Gallup. November 9, 2020. https://news.gallup.com/poll/323582/support-legal-marijuana-inches-new-high.aspx.

Brockington, D. *Celebrity and the Environment: Fame, Wealth, and Power in the Conversation*. New York: Zed Books, 2009.

———. "The Politics of Celebrity Advocacy." *E-International Relations*. March 21, 2014. https://www.e-ir.info/2014/03/21/the-politics-of-celebrity-advocacy/.

Broughton, K. "JPMorgan Has 'a Responsibility' to Recruit Ex-Cons, Dimon Says." *American Banker*. April 5, 2018.

Brown, C. "Is Criminal Justice Reform *Really* Dead?" *Cato Daily Podcast*. November 1, 2016. https://www.cato.org/multimedia/cato-daily-podcast/criminal-justice-reform-really-dead.

Bryant, J. "Trump Pardons Cannabis Entrepreneur, Clemency Activist, and Hip-Hop Producer Weldon Angelos." *Forbes*. December 24, 2020.

Buchanan, L., Q. Bui, and J. K Patel. "Black Lives Matter May Be the Largest Movement in U.S. History." *The New York Times*. July 3, 2020.

Bui, Q., J. Katz, and M. Ruby. "Can You Identify These Politicians, Athletes and Celebrities? Most Americans Can't." *The New York Times*. December 23, 2019.

Bureau of Prisons (BOP). "Work Programs." 2021. https://www.bop.gov/inmates/custody_and_care/work_programs.jsp#:~:text=percent20earn percent2012 percentC2 percentA2 percent20to,hour percent20for percent20these percent20work percent20assignments.

Burrowes, N., M. Cousins, P. X. Rojas, and I. Ude. 2017. "On Our Own Terms: Ten Years of Radical Community Building with Sista II Sista." *The Revolution Will Not Be Funded: Behind the Nonprofit Industrial Complex*. Edited by INCITE! Women of Color against Violence: 227–35. Durham, NC: Duke University Press.

Bush, G. W. "State of the Union." Video clip. January 20, 2004. https://www.c-span.org/video/?c4547106/user-clip-bush-speech-2.

Business Leaders against the Death Penalty. 2021. Signatories. https://www.businessagainstdeathpenalty.org/signatories.

Business Roundtable (BRT). "BRT Letter in Support of the First Step Act and Meaningful Criminal Justice Reform." December 17, 2018. https://www.busi

nessroundtable.org/brt-letter-in-support-of-first-step-act-and-meaningful-cri
minal-justice-reform.

———. "Business Roundtable and Partners Launch Second Chance Business
Coalition." 2021. https://www.businessroundtable.org/business-roundtable-and
-partners-launch-second-chance-business-coalition-to-improve-access-to-em
ployment-advancement-for-people-with-criminal-records.

———. "Justice System." 2021. https://www.businessroundtable.org/equity/justice.

Businesswire. "Dave's Killer Bread to Be Acquired by Flower Foods." August 12, 2015.
https://www.businesswire.com/news/home/20150812006425/en/Daveper
centE2 percent80percent99s-Killer-Bread-to-Be-Acquired-by-Flowers-Foods.

Bussert, T. "What the First Step Act Means for Federal Prisoners." *The Champion.* May 2019. https://www.nacdl.org/Article/May2019WhattheFirstStepAct
MeansforFederalPrisoner.

Cadden, M. "Books about Race Flying off Shelves, Climbing Best-Seller Lists after
the Death of George Floyd." *USA Today.* June 6 2020.

Callahan, D. "There Are Way Too Many Nonprofits. What Are Funders Going to
Do about That?" *Inside Philanthropy.* January 14, 2015.

Carras, C. "A Reality Show about Activism Starring Rich and Famous Celebs? 'No
One Asked for This.'" *Los Angeles Times.* September 10, 2021.

Carroll, L., and A. A. Edwards "This Lawyer Is Helping Kim Kardashian with
Her Legal Career." *Refinery29.* April 29, 2019. https://www.refinery29.com/en-
us/2019/04/230603/jessica-jackson-kim-kardashian-cut-50-incarcerated-women.

Carson, T. "Normal People Don't Want Criminal Justice Reform, They Want
Criminal Justice Enforcement." Fox News. January 3, 2020.

Cassell, P. G. "Explaining the Recent Homicide Spikes in U.S. Cities: The 'Minneapolis Effect' and the Decline in Proactive Policing." *Federal Sentencing Reporter* 33, no. 1 (2020): 83–127.

Chabria, A. "No, the Criminal Justice Reform Movement Isn't Dead. But It May
Need to Grow Up." *Los Angeles Times.* June 9, 2022.

Chan Zuckerberg Initiative (CZI). "Movement and Capacity Building." 2021.
https://chanzuckerberg.com/movement-capacity-building/.

———. "Chan Zuckerberg Initiative Announces $450 Million to Accelerate Crim-
inal Justice & Immigration Reform." January 27, 2021. https://chanzuckerberg
.com/newsroom/chan-zuckerberg-initiative-announces-450-million-to-accel
erate-criminal-justice-immigration-reform/.

Cheddar News. "Kim Kardashian West Mentor Says First Step Act Not the
Last for Prison Reform." February 12, 2020. https://cheddar.com/media/
kim-kardashian-mentor-says-first-step-act-not-the-last-for-prison-reform.

Chettiar, I., and A. Grawert. "Letter to Congress on the FIRST STEP Act." https://
www.scribd.com/document/378632847/Letter-to-Congress-on-the-FIRST
-STEP-Act#download&from_embed.

Ciesemier, K., and J. Horowitz. "Meet Alice Johnson, the Woman Kim Kardashian Wants Trump to Pardon." *Mic.* May 30, 2018. https://t.co/We2Lom6bFV?amp=1.

Clarke, M. "Private Prison Companies Face Stock Crash, Credit Crunch." *Forbes.* February 1, 2021.

———. "Madoff Fraud Bankrupts JEHT Foundation." *Prison Legal News.* June 15, 2009.

Cohen, D. M. "Justice, Not Jailbreak: The Context and Consequence of the First Step Act." *Victims & Offenders* 14, no. 8 (2019): 1084–98.

Cohen, M., D. E. Perry, and J. Perry. "This Is An Unmistakable Win for Incarcerated People." CNN. January 19, 2022.

Colvin, J., and C. Long. "Trump Pardoned His Son-In-Law's Dad. Here's What Charles Kushner Did." *Chicago Tribune.* December 24, 2020.

Congressional Research Service. "The Work Opportunity Tax Credit." September 25, 2018. https://sgp.fas.org/crs/misc/R43729.pdf.

Connor, D. P., and R. Tewksbury. "Public and Professional Views of Sex Offender Registration and Notification." *Criminology, Criminal Justice, Law and Society* 18, no. 1 (2017): 1–27.

Conservatives Concerned About the Death Penalty (CCADP). "The Right Way. More Republican lawmakers." 2021. https://conservativesconcerned.org/therightway/.

CoreCivic. "Statement from CoreCivic President and CEO Damon Hininger on the First Step Act." December 19, 2018. https://www.corecivic.com/news-releases/statement-from-corecivic-on-the-first-step-act.

Cooper, A. F. 2007: Celebrity Diplomacy and the G8: Bono and Bob as Legitimate International Actors. Working paper no. 29, Waterloo, Canada: The Centre for International Governance Innovation (CIGI).

Cordero, R. "Usher, Priyanka Chopra & Julianne Hough Set for 'The Activist.'" *Deadline.* September 10, 2021. https://deadline.com/2021/09/usher-priyanka-chopra-julianne-hough-the-activist-cbs-1234829647/#respond.

Costello, R., and C. Eren. *The Impact of Supreme Court Decisions on U.S. Institutions: A Sociology of Law Primer.* London: Routledge.

Couloute, L. "Getting back on Course: Educational Exclusion and Attainment among Formerly Incarcerated People." Press release. *Prison Policy Initiative.* October 2018. https://www.prisonpolicy.org/reports/education.html.

Crouch, C. 2004. *Post-Democracy.* Cambridge, UK: Polity.

———. 2020. *Post-Democracy after the Crises.* Cambridge, UK: Polity.

C-SPAN. "Conservative Political Action Conference Straw Poll." February 25, 2017. https://www.c-span.org/video/?424471-10/conservative-political-action-conference-2017-straw-poll.

———. "Donald Trump Presidential Campaign Announcement Full Speech." June 16, 2015. https://video.search.yahoo.com/search/video?fr=mcafee&ei=UTF

-8&p=%E2%80%9CPresidential+Campaign+Announcement+Full+Speech. %E2%80%9D&type=E210US1144G91709#id=1&vid=41cf9b73f4347baf fb8c02f59c9cb959&action=click.

———. "First Step Act of 2018 Signing." December 21, 2018. https://www.c-span .org/video/?456225-1/president-trump-signs-step-juvenile-justice-reform-acts.

———. "Presidential Campaign Announcement Full Speech." June 16, 2015.

———. "Second Chance Act of 2007 Signing." April 9, 2008. https://www.c-span .org/video/?204806-1/chance-act-2007-signing.

———. "Watch: Trump Addresses Criminal Justice at Prison Reform Summit." May 18, 2018. https://www.cnbc.com/2018/05/18/watch-trump-addresses-cri minal-justice-at-prison-reform-summit.html.

#Cut50. #HomeForTheHolidays: A Celebration of Freedom Made Possible by the First Step Act. December 2019.

Dagan, D., and S. Teles. "How Conservatives Turned against Mass Incarceration." *New America*. September 15, 2015. https://www.newamerica.org/political-reform/ policy-papers/how-conservatives-turned-against-mass-incarceration/.

———. *Prison Break: Why Conservatives Turned against Mass Incarceration*. Oxford, UK: Oxford University Press.

Darcy, O. "Bezos Donates $100 Million Each to CNN Contributor Van Jones and Chef Jose Andres." CNN. July 21, 2021. https://www.cnn.com/2021/07/20/ media/van-jones-bezos-100-million/index.html.

Deason, D. "Ruining Lives with Criminal 'Justice.'" *The New York Times*. July 30, 2015.

Decarceration Nation. "95 Jeffrey Korzenik." Podcast. February 15, 2012. https:// decarcerationnation.com/95-jeffrey-korzenik/.

De la Merced, M. J. "Daniel Loeb's Third Point Bets on Criminal Justice." *The New York Times*. February 27, 2021.

Department of Justice (DOJ). "Department of Justice Announces the Release of 3,100 Inmates under First Step Act, Publishes Risk and Needs Assessment System." Press release. July 19, 2019.

———. "Justice Department Announces New Rule Implementing Federal Time Credits Program Established by the First Step Act." Press release. January 13, 2020. https://www.justice.gov/opa/pr/justice-department-announces-new-rule-im plementing-federal-time-credits-program-established.

Department of Justice Archive. "The President's Prisoner Re-entry Initiative." n.d. https://www.justice.gov/archive/fbci/progmenu_programs.html#1.

Diamond, J., and A. Rogers. "How Jared Kushner, Kim Kardashian West, and Con-gress Drove the Criminal Justice Overhaul." CNN. December 18, 2018. https:// www.cnn.com/2018/12/18/politics/criminal-justice-overhaul/index.html.

Dimon, J. "If You Paid Your Debt to Society, You Should Be Allowed to Work." *The New York Times*. August 4, 2021.

Dimon, J., and A. Duncan. "Hiring Returning Citizens Is Good for Business." *Chicago Tribune.* June 13, 2018.

Dinki, T. "NY Republicans Demand Repeal of Bail Reform, Offer Anecdotes—Not Evidence—It's Behind Increased Crime." NPR. December 18, 2021. https://www.wbfo.org/crime/2021-12-18/ny-republicans-demand-repeal-of-bail-reform-offer-anecdotes-not-evidence-its-behind-increased-crime.

Dobuzinskis, A. "FBI Kept Tabs on Muhammad Ali in 1966 during Nation of Islam Probe." Reuters. December 16, 2016. https://www.reuters.com/article/us-usa-muhammadali-idUSKBN145122.

Doleac, J. L., and B. Hansen. "The Unintended Consequences of "Ban the Box": Statistical Discrimination and Employment Outcomes When Criminal Histories Are Hidden." *Journal of Labor Economics* 38, no. 2 (2020): 321–74.

d'Oliveira-Martins, M. "Interview with Arlie Russell Hochschild." *Sociologia Problemas e Práticas* 83, no. 1 (2017): 181–91.

Donohue, J. J. "Comey, Trump, and the Puzzling Pattern of Crime in 2015 and Beyond." *Columbia Law Review* 117, no. 5 (2017): 1297–354.

Donovan, D. "Billionaire Donors Laura and John Arnold Support Far More in Maryland Than Police Surveillance." *Baltimore Sun.* August 26, 2016.

Dorman, S. "Verizon Promotes Defunding the Police and Idea America Is Fundamentally Racist: Report." Fox Business. August 26, 2021.

Doyle, C. 2019. "Federal Mandatory Minimum Sentences: Safety Valve and Substantial Assistance Exceptions." Congressional Research Service. 2019. https://fas.org/sgp/crs/misc/R41326.pdf.

Dream.Org. "#DayofEmpathy Online Town Hall with Van Jones and Special Guests." April 17, 2020. https://www.youtube.com/watch?v=tD5LSN9IrxI&t=1871s.

———. "#DayofEmpathy 2020—Alyssa Milano." May 25, 2020. https://www.youtube.com/watch?v=oxI7rk3VqbQ&t=39s.

Driessens, O. "Celebrity Capital: Redefining Celebrity Using Field Theory." *Theory and Society* 42, no. 5 (2018): 543–60.

Durbin, D. "President Obama Signs Durbin's Fair Sentencing Act into Law." Press release. August 3, 2010. https://www.durbin.senate.gov/newsroom/press-releases/president-obama-signs-durbins-fair-sentencing-act-into-law.

Dwyer, D. C., and R. B. McNally. "Public Policy, Prison Industries, and Business: An Equitable Balance for the 1990s." *Federal Probation* 57, no. 2 (1993): 30

Eilert, M., and A. Nappier Cherup. "The Activist Company: Examining a Company's Pursuit of Societal Change through Corporate Activism Using an Institutional Theoretical Lens." *Journal of Public Policy & Marketing* 39, no. 4 (2020): 461–76.

Enns, P. K. *Incarceration Nation: How the United States Became the Most Punitive Democracy in the World.* New York: Cambridge University Press, 2016.

Bibliography

Evers-Hillstrom, K. "For-Profit Prisons Strongly Approve of Bipartisan Criminal Justice Reform Bill." *OpenSecrets.* December 20, 2018.

Families Against Mandatory Minimums (FAMM). "First Step Formerly Incarcerated Leaders' Letter." June 6, 2018. https://famm.org/wp-content/uploads/First-Step-Formerly-Incarcerated-Letter.pdf.

———. "First Step Act Risk and Needs Assessment FAQ." 2019.

———. "Matthew Charles: Saved by the First Step Act." 2021. https://famm.org/stories/matthew-charles-saved-by-the-first-step-act/.

Federal Deposit Insurance Corp. (FDIC). "Fact Sheet." July 2020. https://www.fdic.gov/news/section19-7-24-20.pdf.

Fister Gale, S. "A Second Chance: How Nehemiah's Unconventional Hiring Program Is Slashing Turnover and Changing Lives." June 17, 2021. https://www.chieflearningofficer.com/2021/06/17/a-second-chance-how-nehemiahs-unconventional-hiring-program-is-slashing-turnover-and-changing-lives/.

Ford, J. "Exonerated Five, Others Endorse Legislation to Stop Wrongful Convictions; Another Case Could Be Overturned." *Pix11.* December 15, 2021. https://pix11.com/news/local-news/exonerated-five-others-endorse-legislation-to-stop-wrongful-convictions-another-case-could-be-overturned.

Fox Piven, F., and R. A. Cloward. *Poor Peoples' Movements: Why They Succeed, How They Fail.* New York: First Vintage Books, 1977.

FreedomWorks. "'Unjust, Cruel, and Even Irrational': Stacking Charges under 924c." October 22, 2015.

Gallup. "Crime." Poll. https://news.gallup.com/poll/1603/crime.aspx.

Galston, W. A. "Civic Knowledge, Civic Education, and Civic Engagement: A Summary of Recent Research." *International Journal of Public Administration* 30, nos. 6–7 (2007): 623–42.

Garcia, V. "Celebrities, Activists Urge Criminal Justice Reform at 'Day of Empathy.'" Fox News. March 5, 2019.

Garland, D. "Introduction: The Meaning of Mass Imprisonment. *Punishment & Society* 3, no. 1 (2001): 5–7.

Gehrke, J. "Dems in the Driver's Seat on Criminal Justice Reform Bill." *Washington Examiner.* April 22, 2016.

Geo Funders. "What We Care about: Capacity Building." 2021. https://www.geofunders.org/what-we-care-about/capacity-building.

Gill, M. "Threading the Needle: The FIRST STEP Act, Sentencing Reform, and the Future of Criminal Justice Reform Advocacy." *Federal Sentencing Reporter* 31 (December 2018): 107.

Giridharadas, A. *Winners Take All: The Elite Charade of Changing the World.* New York: Alfred A. Knopf, 2018.

Goodman P., J. Page, and M. Phelps. "The Long Struggle: An Agonistic Perspective On Penal Development." *Theoretical Criminology* 19, no. 3 (2015): 315–35.

Gotsche, K. "One Year after the First Step Act: Mixed Outcomes." The Sentencing Project. 2019. https://www.sentencingproject.org/publications/one-year-after -the-first-step-act/.

Gottlieb, A. "The Effect of Message Frames on Public Attitudes toward Criminal Justice Reform for Nonviolent Offenses." *Crime and Delinquency* 63, no. 5 (2017): 636–56.

Gottschalk, M. *Caught: The Prison State and the Lockdown of American Politics.* Princeton, NJ: Princeton University Press, 2015.

Goudsouziam, A. *Sidney Poitier: Man, Actor, Icon.* Chapel Hill, NC: University of North Carolina Press, 2011.

Gould, L. L. "JFK: Celebrity in the White House." BBC News. November 21, 2013. http://www.bbc.co.uk/history/worldwars/coldwar/kennedy_celebrity_0 1.shtml.

Grant, S. "Yo Gotti Teams up with Meek Mill's Reform Alliance for Mississippi Reform Campaign." *The Source.* August 27, 2020. https://thesourcecom/2020/ 08/27/yo-gotti-teams-with-meek-mills-reform-alliance-for-mississippi-reform -campaign/.

Grawert, A., and N. Kim. "Myths and Realities: Understanding Recent Trends in Violent Crime." Brennan Center for Justice. July 12, 2022. https://www.bren nancenter.org/our-work/research-reports/myths-and-realities-understand ing-recent-trends-violent-crime.

Grawert, A., and T. Lau. "How the FIRST STEP Act Became Law—And What Happens Next." Brennan Center for Justice. January 4, 2019. https://www .brennancenter.org/our-work/analysis-opinion/how-first-step-act-became-law -and-what-happens-next.

Green, D. "Penal Optimism and Second Chances: The Legacies of American Protestantism and the Prospects for Penal Reform." *Punishment & Society* 15, no. 2 (2013): 123–46.

———. "US Penal-Reform Catalysts, Drivers, and Prospects." *Punishment & Society* 17, no. 3 (2015): 271–98.

Gross, N., and M. Mann. "Is There a 'Ferguson Effect'? Google Searches, Concern about Police Violence, and Crime in U.S. Cities, 2014–2016." *Socius* 2017. https://doi.org/10.1177/2378023117703122;

Grow, K. "Meek Mill's Legal Troubles." *Rolling Stone.* March 14, 2018.

Haberman, M., and A. Karni. "Trump Celebrates Criminal Justice Overhaul amid Doubts It Will Be Fully Funded." *The New York Times.* April 1, 2019.

Haidt, J. *The Righteous Mind: Why Good People Are Divided by Politics and Religion.* New York: Pantheon Books, 2012.

Haines, H. "Black Radicalization and the Funding of Civil Rights: 1957–1970." *Social Problems* 32 (1984): 31–43.

———. *Against Capital Punishment: The Anti-Death Penalty Movement in America, 1972–1994*. New York: Oxford University Press, 1996.

Harris, E. "Inside Kim Kardashian's Prison-Reform Machine." *The New York Times*. April 2, 2020.

Heimer, M. "Why JPMorgan Chase Wants to Give More Former Criminals a Second Chance." *Fortune*. October 21, 2019. https://fortune.com/2019/10/21/jpmorgan-chase-ban-the-box-hiring/.

Henry, D., and I. Moise. "JPMorgan Backs away from Private Prison Finance." Reuters. March 5, 2019.

Hess, N. "Exodus and Incarceration: A Jewish View of Racial Justice." *New York Jewish Week*. October 22, 2020.

Hopwood, S. "The Effort to Reform the Federal Criminal Justice System." *Yale Law Journal Forum*. February 25, 2019.

Horowitz, J. "Michigan Enacts Landmark Jail Reforms." Pew Research Center. September 23, 2021. https://www.pewtrusts.org/en/research-and-analysis/issue-briefs/2021/09/michigan-enacts-landmark-jail-reforms.

Hunter, L., and E. Chung. "Trump Says One Thing and Does Another on Criminal Justice." *Center for American Progress*. February 3, 2020.

Inside Philanthropy. "Margaret and Daniel Loeb Foundation." n.d. https://www.insidephilanthropy.com/l-grants/margaret-and-daniel-loeb-foundation.

Inthorn, S., and J. Street. "'Simon Cowell for prime minister?' Young Citizens' Attitudes towards Celebrity Politics." *Media, Culture & Society* 33, no. 3 (2011): 479–89.

Jackson, J. "How the FIRST STEP Act Would Restore Dignity to Incarcerated Women." *Federal Sentencing Reporter* 31 no. 2 (2018): 116–18. https://doi.org/10.1525/fsr.2018.31.2.116.

James, A. "Ending the Incarceration of Women and Girls." *The Yale Law Journal* 128, February 25, 2019. https://www.yalelawjournal.org/forum/ending-the-incarceration-of-women-and-girls#_ftnref72.

——— "The First Step Act of 2018: An Overview." *Congressional Research Service Reports*. March 4, 2019. https://crsreports.congress.gov/product/pdf/R/R45558.

Jan, T., J. McGregor, and M. Hoyer. "Corporate America's $50 billion Promise." *The Washington Post*. August 23, 2021.

Jefferson-Bullock, J. "Consensus, Compassion, and Compromise? The First Step Act and Aging out of Crime." *Federal Sentencing Reporter* 32, no. 2 (December 2019): 70–75.

Jeffries, H. "Dear Colleague." May 18, 2018. https://www.politico.com/f/?id=00000163-73c9-d627-a5e3-7fcfc3110001.

Joint Economic Committee of the U.S. Congress. "Testimony of: Pat Nolan, Vice President of Prison Fellowship. 'Mass Incarceration in the United States: At What Cost?'" October 4, 2007.

Jones, J. M. "Trump Third Year Sets New Standard for Party Polarization." Gallup. January 21, 2020. https://news.gallup.com/poll/283910/trump-third-year-sets-new-standard-party-polarization.aspx

Jonsson, P. "Debra Milke: Why Freedom Feels So Elusive for Death Row Exonerees." *The Christian Science Monitor.* March 26, 2015.

JPMorgan Chase & Co. Policy Center. "Giving People with Criminal Backgrounds a Second Chance." 2021. https://www.jpmorganchase.com/content/dam/jpmc/jpmorgan-chase-and-co/documents/jpmc-policycenter-overview-v1-ada.pdf.

Justice Action Network. (JAN). "NBC News: Republican States Make the Case against Trump's Drug Policy." May 19, 2017. https://www.justiceactionnetwork.org/news/nbc-news-republican-states-make-the-case-against-trumps-drug-policy.

JustLeadershipUSA (JLUSA). "JustLeadershipUSA's 2021–2024 Roadmap." 2022. https://jlusa.org/roadmap/.

Kaba, M. "Yes, We Mean Literally Abolish the Police. *The New York Times.* June 12, 2020.

———. *We Do This 'Til We Free Us: Abolitionist Organizing and Transforming Justice.* New York: Haymarket Books, 2021.

Katz, A. *The Influence Machine: The U.S. Chamber of Commerce and the Corporate Capture of American Life.* New York: Spiegel & Grau, 2015.

Kaye, L. "How This Lawyer Became a Force of Nature for Second Chance Hiring." *Triple Pundit.* October 19, 2019. https://www.triplepundit.com/story/2019/how-lawyer-became-force-nature-second-chance-hiring/85221.

Kilgore, E. "Sessions as AG Means Criminal Justice Reform Is Dead." *Intelligencer.* November 2016. https://nymag.com/intelligencer/2016/11/sessions-as-ag-means-criminal-justice-reform-is-dead.html.

Kim, J. Panel Discussion for Alston & Bird. YouTube. June 20, 2017. https://www.youtube.com/watch?v=_Hrlo3wLt1s.

——— "Why I fight for Second Chances." YouTube. 2019. https://www.youtube.com/watch?v=fqh78flH6To.

Kingson, J. A. "$1 billion-Plus Riot Damage Is Most Expensive in Insurance History. *Axios.* September 16, 2020.

Komiya, K. "A Majority of Consumers Expect Brands to Take a Stand on Issues before Purchasing, Survey Finds." *Barron's.* July 7, 2020.

Korzenik, J. *Untapped Talent: How Second Chance Hiring Works for Your Business and the Community.* New York: HarperCollins Leadership, 2021.

Kushner, J. *Breaking History: A White House Memoir.* New York: Broadside Books.

Lahut, J. "Support for Defunding the Police Collapsed in 2021, with Steep Drops among Black Adults and Democrats, New Poll Shows." *Business Insider.* October 26, 2021. https://www.businessinsider.com/defund-the-police-polling-public-support-drop-democrats-pew-research-2021-10.

Bibliography

Laming, R. N. "Verizon Debuts #Next20 Series to Listen, Learn and Accelerate Systemic Change." 2020. https://www.verizon.com/about/news/verizon-debuts -next20-series.

Latzer, B. "Will the Crime Wave Soon Crest? There's Already a Backlash against Antipolice Policies, and Demographic Trends Are Encouraging." *The Wall Street Journal.* January 2, 2022.

Leadership Conference on Civil and Human Rights (LCCHR). "Civil and Human Rights Scores the 115th Congress." October 24, 2018. https://civilrights.org/ resource/civil-and-human-rights-coalition-scores-the-115th-congress/.

Lee, Y. "The Doe Fund's 2016 Gala." *Socially Superlative.* October 31, 2016. https:// www.sociallysuperlative.com/2016/10/31/the-doe-funds-2016-gala/.

Lethabo King, T., and E. Osayande. "The Filth on Philanthropy: Progressive Philanthropy's Agenda to Misdirect Social Justice Movements." In *The Revolution Will Not Be Funded: Beyond the Non-Profit Industrial Complex.* Edited by INCITE! Women of Color against Violence. 79–90. Durham, NC: Duke University Press, 2017.

Levenson, J., Y. N. Brannon, T. Fortney, and J. Baker. "Public Perceptions about Sex Offenders and Community Protection Policies." *Analyses of Social Issues and Public Policy* 7, no. 1 (2007): 1–25.

Lewis, N., and M. Chammah. "7 Years behind Bars for 2 Joints—and Now He's Free." *Nola.com.* April 12, 2018. https://www.nola.com/news/crime_police/article_efbbe0c5-09e8-5d90-827d-21c1a555d65c.html.

Lin, T. C. W. "Incorporating Social Activism." *Boston University Law Review* 98, no. 6 (2018): 1535–605.

Linly, Z. "Van Jones Goes on The View and Gets Roasted Like a Two- Faced Potato Because Ain't No Such Thing as Halfway Activists." *The Root.* February 5, 2021.

Loeb, D. "Effective Giving Requires Rolling Up Your Sleeves." *The Wall Street Journal.* October 16, 2020.

Looney, A., and N. Turner. "Work and Opportunity before and after Incarceration." Brookings. March 14, 2013. https://www.brookings.edu/research/work -and-opportunity-before-and-after-incarceration/content/uploads/2018/03/es _20180314_looneyincarceration_final.pdf.

Macedo, S. *Democracy at Risk: How Political Choices Undermine Citizen Participation, and What We Can Do about It.* Washington DC: Brookings Institution Press, 2006.

Mackinac Center for Public Policy. "A Brief Explanation of the Overton Window." 2021. https://www.mackinac.org/OvertonWindow.

Madar, C. "A Republican against Prisons." *The American Conservative.* February 3, 2013. https://www.theamericanconservative.com/articles/a-republican-against -prisons/.

Marshall, S. "Permanent Prison: New Attitudes, Bad Economy Mean Released Prisoners Can't Find Jobs." *Crain's New York Business.* October 21, 2002.

Mayer, F. W. *Narrative Politics: Stories and Collective Action.* Oxford, UK: Oxford University Press, 2014.

McAdam, D., and D. Snow. *Social Movements: Readings on Their Emergence, Mobilization, and Dynamics.* Los Angeles, CA: Roxbury Publishing, 1997.

McCarthy, N. "Over Half of Americans Have Had a Family Member Incarcerated." *Forbes.* December 7, 2018.

McCarthy, R. "Doug Collins Sponsored Radical Criminal Justice Reform Bill Alongside Rep. Hakeem Jeffries." *Townhall.* January 31, 2020.

McCurdy, J. "The First Step Act Is Actually the 'Next Step' after Fifteen Years of Successful Reforms to the Federal Criminal Justice System." *Cardozo Law Review* 41 (2019): 189–241.

Menon, P. "A Discussion on Criminal Justice Reform with Mark Holden." *Just Thoughts* (blog). October 4, 2018. https://jpo.blogs.american.edu/2018/10/04/a-discussion-on-criminal-justice-reform-with-mark-holden/.

Mihm, S. "America's Rocky Relationship with For-Profit Prisons." *Bloomberg View.* January 9, 2019.

Miller, K. "Joe Biden Told a Voter He'll 'Go Further' Than Cutting Incarceration by 50 Percent." *BuzzFeed News.* July 9, 2019. https://www.buzzfeednews.com/article/katherinemiller/joe-biden-incarceration-prison-population-cut-aclu.

Ming Francis, M. "The Price of Civil Rights: Black Lives, White Funding, and Movement Capture." *Law & Society Review* 35 (March 2019): 275.

Mintz, E. "New Polling Finds Extraordinary Bipartisan Support for Policing Reforms." Arnold Ventures. August 25, 2020. https://www.arnoldventures.org/stories/new-polling-finds-extraordinary-bipartisan-support-for-policing-reforms/.

Mosendez, P., and J. Robinson. "While Crime Fell, the Cost of Cops Soared." *Bloomberg Businessweek.* June 4, 2020.

Moskos, P. *In Defense of Flogging.* New York: Basic Books, 2011.

Moynihan, L. "Jamie Dimon Launching Coalition That Aims to Boost Hiring of Ex-Cons." *New York Post.* April 27, 2021.

Nambiampurath, N. "Bitcoin Bull Michael Novogratz Donates 36 Million to Criminal Justice Reform." *Beincrypto.com.* November 19, 2019. https://beincrypto.com/bitcoin-bull-michael-novogratz-donates-36-million-to-criminal-justice-reform-and-philanthropy/.

Nash, J. "'The Prison Has Failed': The New York State Prison, in the City of New York, 1797–1828." *New York History* 98 (2017): 71–89.

Netherland, J., and H. Hansen. "The War on Drugs That Wasn't: Wasted Whiteness, 'Dirty Doctors,' and Race in Media Coverage of Prescription Opioid Misuse." *Culture, Medicine, and Psychiatry* 40 (2016): 656–86.

New York Times Editorial Board. "A Real Chance at Criminal Justice Reform." November 14, 2018.

Nicholls, W. J., J. Ultermark, and S. van Haperen. "Going National: How the Fight for Immigrant Rights Became a National Social Movement." *Journal of Ethnic and Migration Studies* 46, no. 4 (2020) 705–27.

Office of National Drug Control Policy. "Arrestee Drug Abuse Monitoring Program II." 2014 Annual report. The White House. https://www.whitehouse.gov/ondcp/.

Office of the Press Secretary. "Remarks by the President at the NAACP Conference." July 14, 2015. https://obamaWhitehouse.archives.gov/the-press-office/2015/07/14/remarks-president-naacp-conference.

Oliver, P., and Johnston, H. "What a Good Idea! Ideologies and Frames in Social Movement Research." *Mobilization: An International Quarterly* 5, no. 1 (2000): 37–54.

Opilo, E. "Texas Philanthropists Says They're Backing Out of Financing Surveillance Plane Technology That Flew over Baltimore." *Baltimore Sun.* January 26, 2021.

Owens, L. "How the National Urban League Missed the Mark with Its State of Black America Report." *HuffPost*, March 9, 2012.

Page, C. "NAACP, Right-Wing Foes Get Friendly." *Chicago Tribune.* April 13, 2011.

——— "Conservatives, NAACP agree: Too Much Spent on Prisons," *Dayton Daily News.* April 15, 2011. https://www.daytondailynews.com/lifestyles/philosophy/clarence-page-conservatives-naacp-agree-too-much-spent-prisons/W5VekIBEomlisbyIP4E5CN/?outputType=amp.

Paperny, J. "Big Developments under the First Step Act." YouTube. January 18, 2022. https://www.youtube.com/watch?v=dlZRMFdYEt8&t=292s.

Parmar, I., and Choudhury, I. "Black Lives Matter Must Avoid Being Co-Opted by American Corporate Philanthropy." *The Conversation.* July 15, 2020.

Pender, G. "JAY-Z, Meek Mill Group Wants Mississippi Lawmakers to Override Reeves Prison Reform Veto." *Mississippi Today.* July 17, 2020. https://mississippitoday.org/2020/07/17/jay-z-meek-mill-group-wants-mississippi-lawmakers-to-override-reeves-prison-reform-veto/

Peoples, S., A. Fram, and J. Lemire. "Key Democrats Spurn Push to Defund the Police amid Trump Attacks." June 9, 2020. *APNews.com.* https://apnews.com/article/american-protests-donald-trump-ap-top-news-elections-joe-biden-3e6226c495f63ea8551f0d997af9412b.

Perez, A. "Between Radical Theory and Community Praxis: Reflections on Organizing and the Non-Profit Industrial Complex." In *The Revolution Will Not Be Funded.* Edited by INCITE! Women of Color against Violence. 91–100. Durham, NC: Duke University Press, 2017.

Pew Research Center. "Americas Incarceration Rate Lowest Since 1995." 2021. https://www.pewresearch.org/fact-tank/2021/08/16/americas-incarceration-rate-lowest-since-1995/.

———. "US Public Becoming Less Religious." November 3, 2015. https://www.pewforum.org/religious-landscape- study/party-affiliation/.

———. "Budget Deficit Slips as Public Priority." January 22, 2016. https://www.pewresearch.org/politics/2016/01/22/budget-deficit-slips-as-public-priority/.

Pfaff, J. *Locked In: The True Causes of Mass Incarceration and How to Achieve Real Reform.* New York: Basic Books, 2017.

Philip, A. "George Floyd Protests Have Made Police Reform the Consensus Position." CNN. June 9, 2020.

Polletta, F. "Contending Stories: Narrative in Social Movements. " *Qualitative Sociology*, 21, no. 4 (1998): 419–46.

Portner, N. "Top Trends in State Criminal Justice Reform, 2019." The Sentencing Project. 2020.

Powell, J. "Meek Mill Celebrates Recent Award with "Mandela Freestyle." *Revolt.* August 13, 2021. https://www.revolt.tv/new-music/2021/8/13/22624199/meek-mill-mandela-freestyle-video.

Process Editors. "Organizing the Prisons in the 1960s and 1970s: Part One, Building Movements." *Process: a Blog for American History.* September 20, 2016.

Putnam, R. D. "The Strange Disappearance of Civic America." *Policy: A Journal of Public Policy and Ideas* 12, no. 1 (1996): 3–15.

———. "Civic Disengagement in Contemporary America." In *Crime, Inequality, and the State.* Edited by Mary E. Vogel. 92–98. London: Routledge.

Ramirez, M. D. "Punitive Sentiment." *Criminology*, 51, no. 2 (2013): 329–64.

"Randall Stephenson Addresses the Racial Tension in American Society." YouTube. September 24, 2016. https://www.youtube.com/watch?v=ThO74-0Ft_Q&t=48s.

Raphael, S., and M. A. Stoll. *Why Are So Many Americans in Prison?* New York: Russell Sage Foundation.

Red Carpet Report. "Jason Isaacs 14th Annual A New Way of Life Fundraising Gala @JasonsFolly." YouTube. December 2012. https://www.youtube.com/watch?v=j1PZiF6Cojo

Reich, R. *Just Giving: Why Philanthropy Is Failing Democracy and How It Can Do Better.* Princeton, NJ: Princeton University Press, 2018.

Reiman, J. *The Rich Get Richer and the Poor Get Prison.* New York: Routledge, 2001.

Rennison, J., and A. Kasumov. "JPMorgan Funds Invested in Core Civic Debt after Vow to Stop Financing Private Prisons." *The Financial Times.* May 20, 2021.

Rentschler, C. A. *Second Wounds.* Durham, NC: Duke University Press, 2011.

Responsible Business Initiative (RBI). "How to Be a Justice-Engaged Business: A Practical Guide." 2021. https://static1.squarespace.com/static/5ee10a9bb6f25739

Bibliography

6e28e5f2/t/5eef43924ad3f01a104423c4/1592738707483/RBIJ_Criminal_Justice _Toolkit.pdf.

Reuters. "GM Settles with S. Africa Apartheid Victims." March 1, 2012.

Risen, J. "GM to Pull Out of South Africa." *Los Angeles Times.* October 21, 1986.

Rodriguez, D. "The Political Logic of the Non-Profit Industrial Complex." In *The Revolution Will Not Be Funded.* Edited by INCITE! Women of Color against Violence. 21–40. Durham, NC: Duke University Press.

Roelofs, T. "Hell Freezes Over: GOP and ACLU Push Prison Reform." *Bridge Michigan.* August 20, 2015. https://www.bridgemi.com/michigan-government/ hell-freezes-over-gop-and-aclu-push-prison-reform.

Rohrer, G. "Major GOP Donor Urges Governor Scott Clemency." *Orlando Sentinel.* August 25, 2015.

Rojas, P. "Are the Cops in Our Heads and Hearts?" *The Revolution Will Not Be Funded.* edited by INCITE! Women of Color against Violence. 197–214. Durham, NC: Duke University Press, 2017.

Rojc, P. "Quantitative Advocacy: How an Effective Altruist Funder Backs Criminal Justice Reform." *Inside Philanthropy.* April 30, 2020.

———. "Fresh Eyes, Deep Pockets. What a Wall Street Justice Reformer Brings to the Cause." *Inside Philanthropy.* November 18, 2019.

———. "Fault Lines: How a Leading Criminal Justice Funder Is Navigating a Historic Moment." *Inside Philanthropy.* August 25, 2020. https://www.inside philanthropy.com/home/2020/8/25/fault-lines-how-a-leading-criminal-jus tice-funder-is-navigating-a-historic-moment.

Romero, A. "Reimagining the Role of Police." *ACLU: News and Commentary.* June 5, 2020. https://www.aclu.org/news/criminal-law-reform/reimagining-the -role-of-police.

Rubin, M. "Michael Rubin Talks Business Come-Up, Friendship with Meek Mill and REFORM Alliance." YouTube. January 30, 2019.

Safavian, D., and C. Culver. "Is Criminal Justice Reform Dead?" *Washington Times.* July 6, 2022.

Sam, T. "Full Pardon from the President of the United States." Facebook videos. December 23, 2020.

Samee Ali, S. "In Discussing Chicago's Violence, Trump Generalizes about Race." NBC News. October 12, 2016. https://www.nbcnews.com/politics/2016-elec tion/discussing-chicago-s-violence-trump-generalizes-about-race-n660541.

Saxon, S. "What Went Wrong with the #8cantwait Police Reform Initiative." *Colorlines.* June 18, 2020. https://www.colorlines.com/articles/what-went-wrong-8 cantwait-police-reform-initiative.

Schenwar, M., and V. Law. *Prison by Any Other Name.* New York: The New Press, 2020.

Schuppe, J. "Republican States Make the Case against Trump's Drug Policy." NBC News. May 19, 2017. https://www.nbcnews.com/news/us-news/republican-states-make-case-against-trump-s-drug-policy-n761651.

Schwartz, J., and J. R. Chaney. *Gifts from the Dark: Learning from the Incarceration Experience*. Lanham, MD: Lexington Books.

Scott, B., and J. Lewis. "SAFE Justice Act Fact Sheet." n.d. https://bobbyscott.house.gov/sites/bobbyscott.house.gov/files/SAFE%20Justice%20Act%20Fact%20Sheet.pdf.

Segura, L. "The First Step Act Could Be a Big Gift to CoreCivic and the Private Prison Industry." *The Intercept.* December 22, 2018.

Seibler, J. M. "No Jeff Sessions as Attorney General Won't Mean Criminal Justice Reform Is Dead." *Daily Signal.* December 12, 2016. https://www.dailysignal.com/2016/12/12/no-jeff-sessions-as-attorney-general-wont-mean-criminal-justice-reform-is-dead/.

Setaro, S. "How Jay-Z and Meek Mill's Reform Organization Plans to Improve the Criminal Justice System." *Complex.* February 15, 2019.

Siegfried, D. "Anti-Apartheid and the Politicisation of Pop Music: Controversies around the Mandela Concert in 1988." In *Apartheid and Anti-Apartheid in Western Europe.* Edited by Knud Andresen. 139–62. London: Palgrave Macmillan.

Silliman, C. "Verizon Supports Criminal Justice Reform." LinkedIn. December 14, 2018.

———. "Working for More Justice in the Criminal Justice System." Verizon News Center. June 12, 2019. https://www.verizon.com/about/news/working-more-justice-criminal-justice-system.

———. "Supporting the COVID-19 Safer Detention Act to Protect the Elderly." Verizon News Center. July 29, 2020. https://www.verizon.com/about/news/supporting-covid-19-safer-detention-act.

Simon, R. "The Company of Second Chances. Nehemiah Manufacturing." *The Wall Street Journal.* January 25, 2020.

Smith. A. Preface. *The Revolution Will Not Be Funded.* Edited by INCITE! Women of Color against Violence. ix-xi. Durham, NC: Duke University Press, 2017.

———. "The NGO-ization of the Palestine Liberation Movement: Interviews with Hatem Bazian, Noura Erekat, Atef Said, and Zeina Zaatari." In *The Revolution Will Not Be Funded.* Edited by INCITE! Women of Color against Violence. 165–84. Durham, NC: Duke University Press, 2017

Society for Human Resource Management (SHRM). "Second Chance Hiring from the Consumer Perspective." 2021. https://www.shrm.org/hr-today/trends-and-forecasting/research-and-surveys/pages/getting-talent-back-to-work---consumer-perspective.aspx.

Bibliography

———. "Workers with Criminal Records: Consumer and Employee Perspectives." 2019. https://www.shrm.org/hr-today/trends-and-forecasting/research-and-surveys/Pages/Workers-with-Criminal-Records-Consumer-and-Employee-Perspectives.aspx.

———. "Workers with Criminal Records." 2018. https://www.shrm.org/hr-today/trends-and-forecasting/research-and-surveys/Pages/Second-Chances.aspx.

Somin, I. "Conservatives Rethinking Mass Imprisonment and the War On Drugs. The Volokh Conspiracy." January 28, 2014. https://advance-lexis-com.ezproxy.wpunj.edu/api/document?collection=news&id=urn:contentItem:5BC S-VC71-JCMN-Y0K7-00000-00&context=1516831.

Spearie, S. "Former Illinois Innocence Project Head: Porter Case Was 'Pivotal' in Death Penalty Abolition." *State Journal-Register.* July 11, 2021. https://www.sj-r.com/story/news/2021/07/11/anthony-porters-case-led-abolition-death-penalty-illinois/7910773002/.

Stolberg, S. G., and A. W. Herndon. "'Lock the S.O.B.s Up': Joe Biden and the Era of Mass Incarceration." *The New York Times.* June 25, 2019.

Stoll, J. D. "Corporate Activism Gets Its Day. Ben & Jerry's Has Been at It for Decades." *The Wall Street Journal.* June 5, 2020. https://www.wsj.com/articles/corporate-activism-gets-its-day-ben-jerrys-has-been-at-it-for-decades-11591365921.

Street, J. "Celebrity Politicians: Popular Culture and Political Representation." *British Journal of Politics & International Relations* 6, no. 4 (2004): 435–52.

Strickland, E. "The New Face of Environmentalism. *East Bay Express.* November 2, 2005. https://eastbayexpress.com/the-new-face-of-environmentalism-1/.

Sullivan, B. "CBS Backtracks on 'The Activist' after a Backlash, Including from One of Its Hosts." NPR. September 16, 2021.

Sullivan, L. E. *The Prison Reform Movement: Forlorn Hope.* Woodbridge, CT: Twayne Publishers, 1990.

Sutherland, B., and B. Chappatta. "Why Jamie Dimon, McDonald's, and Walmart Want to Hire Ex-Convicts." *Chicago Business.* April 26, 2021.

Targeted News Service. "NAACP Report Ties State Spending on Prisons to Low Education Achievement." March 29, 2011.

Tomaselli, K. G., and B. Boster. "Mandela, MTV, Television and Apartheid." *Popular Music and Society* 17, no. 2 (1993): 1–19.

Travis, J. "Reflections on the Reentry Movement." *Federal Sentencing Reporter* 20 (2017): 2.

Travis, J., A. Crayton, and D. A. Mukamal, 2009. "A New Era in Inmate Reentry." *Corrections Today* 71 (2009): 6.

Trejo, D. "Vote Yes on Prop 25." Facebook. October 22, 2020. https://www.facebook.com/watch/?v=826226388144076.

Tufekci, Z. "'Not This One': Social Movements, the Attention Economy, and Microcelebrity Networked Activism." *American Behavioral Scientist* 57 (2018): 848–70.

———. *Twitter and Tear Gas: The Power and Fragility of Networked Protest*. New Haven, CT: Yale University Press.

Up to Speed. "Criminal Justice Reform." Podcast. July 8, 2020. https://uptospeed podcast.com/website/next20-criminal-justice-reform.

US Chamber of Commerce (USCOC). "Letter Supporting the Bipartisan First Step Act of 2018." November 20, 2018. https://www.uschamber.com/letters-con gress/letter-supporting-the-bipartisan-first-step-act-of-2018.

———. "U.S. Chamber Launches National Initiative to Address Inequality of Opportunity." Press release. June 5, 2020.

———. "U.S. Chamber Calls on Congress to Pass Bills to Address Race-Based Opportunity Gaps." Press release. August 4, 2020. https://www.uschamber.com/ press-release/us-chamber-calls-congress-pass-bills-address-race-based-oppor tunity-gaps.

US House Committee on Financial Services Subcommittee on Diversity and Inclusion. "Access Denied: Eliminating Barriers and Increasing Economic Opportunity for Justice Involved Individuals." Testimony of Jeffrey D. Korzenik. September 28, 2021. https://docs.house.gov/meetings/BA/BA13/20210928/114089/ HHRG-117-BA13-Wstate-KorzenikJ-20210928.pdf

Van Krieken, R. *Celebrity Society*. London: Routledge, 2012.

Vazquez, Y. "Crimmigration: The Missing Piece of Criminal Justice Reform." University of Cincinnati College of Law and Scholarship. 2017. https://scholar ship.law.uc.edu/cgi/viewcontent.cgi?httpsredir=1&article=1346&context=fac _pubs.

Vera Institute of Justice. "The Bigger Picture." September 2021. vera.org/justice-in -focus-crime-bill-20/the-bigger-picture/marc-levin.

The View. "Kim Kardashian West on Motivation Behind 'Justice Project' and Prison Reform." YouTube. March 31, 2020. https://www.youtube.com/watch?v=6 x2pTIBQIrc.

Waldrop, T. "'Free Rodney Reed:' Celebrities Use Star Power to Try to Stop Execution of Man on Death Row in Texas." CNN. November 4, 2019. https://www .cnn.com/2019/11/04/entertainment/free-rodney-reed-petition-stars-trnd/ index.html.

Walker, K. "A 'First Step' towards Criminal Justice Reform." Blog. December 20, 2018. https://www.blog.google/outreach-initiatives/public-policy/first-step-to wards-criminal-justice-reform/.

Wall Street Journal Editorial Board. "A Prison Reform Opening." November 16, 2018. https://www.brennancenter.org/our-work/analysis-opinion/how-first-step -act-became-law-and-what-happens-next.

Bibliography

Walmart. "Criminal Justice Grants." https://walmart.org/center-for-racial-equity/center-for-racial-equity-grants.

Walsh, K., Hussemann, J., Flynn, A., Yahner, J., and Golian, L. "Estimating the Prevalence of Wrongful Conviction." National Institute of Justice. 2017. https://nij.ojp.gov/library/publications/estimating-prevalence-wrongful-convictions.

Weston, D. "How Gay Rights Went Mainstream—And at What Cost." *The Washington Post*. June 30, 2019. https://www.washingtonpost.com/outlook/2019/06/30/how-gay-rights-went-mainstream-what-it-cost/.

Wheaton BCG Archives. "Records of Prison Fellowship Ministries—Collection 274." n.d. https://www2.wheaton.edu/bgc/archives/GUIDES/274.htm#4.

Wheeler, M. *Celebrity Politics*. Malden, MA: Polity, 2013.

Wilson Gilmore, R. "In the Shadow of the Shadow State." In *The Revolution Will Not Be Funded*. Edited by INCITE! Women of Color against Violence. 41–52. Durham, NC: Duke University Press, 2017.

Winston, D. "How Gay Rights Went Mainstream—And What It Cost." *The Washington Post*. June 30, 2019.

Whitlock, K., and Heitzig, N. A. "Billionaire-Funded Criminal Justice Reform Actually Expands Carceral System." 2019. https://truthout.org/articles/billionaire-funded-criminal-justice-reform-actually-expands-carceral-system.

Wolf, S. "Beyond Nonhuman Animal Rights: A Grassroots Movement in Istanbul and Its Alignment with Other Causes." *Interface* 1, no. 7 (2015): 40.

Wolfe, D. "Funders Are Backing a Push to Clear Criminal Records. For Many Involved, It's Personal." *Inside Philanthropy*. March 25, 2021. https://www.insidephilanthropy.com/home/2021/3/25/funders-are-backing-a-push-to-clean-criminal-records-for-many-involved-its-personal.

Wright, P. "Victims' Rights as a Stalking Horse for State Repression." *Journal of Prisoners on Prisons* 9, no. 2 (1998): 17–22.

Yakowicz, W. "Billionaire Charles Koch on Why Cannabis Should Be Legal." *Forbes*. July 27, 2021. https://www.forbes.com/sites/willyakowicz/2021/07/27/billionaire-charles-koch-on-why-cannabis-should-be-legal/?sh=284c79b74a73.

Yang, J. "The Problem with the Genius Billionaire Philanthropist Superhero." *The New York Times*. June 20, 2021. https://www.nytimes.com/2021/06/20/opinion/rich-musk-gates-bezos-comics.html.

Young, D. "Van Jones Is Aaron Burr." *The Root*. August 28, 2020.

Zhang, M. "Koch-Backed Group Joins Marijuana Push after Zoom with Snoop Dogg." *Politico*. April 6, 2021. https://www.politico.com/news/2021/04/06/charles-koch-snoop-dogg-marijuana-legalization-479148.

Zimring, F. E. 2007. *The Great American Crime Decline*. New York: Oxford University Press.

INDEX

Abbott, Gregg, 57

abolitionism: and the term reform, 22; framing of criminal justice system, 38, 152; goals, 177; organizations and individuals, 50, 77, 88, 156, 173, 208n30; place in the larger reform movement, 48–49; public reception, 178. *See also* "defund the police"

accelerators: Amazon Black Business Accelerator, 224n11; Justice Accelerator Fund, 68, 169; Justice Capital, 224n11; meaning of, 169; Unlocked Futures, 168

acknowledgment: definition, 28–29; in the mainstreamization process, 29–30; widening of after 2000, 32–36, 54, 114, 181

Adams, Eric, xi, 178

advocacy groups: bipartisan convergence and, 133–35; centering of criminal justice reform in, 46–47; FIPs

and, 169, 172; FSA and, 5, 139–48; foundations and, 184; friction and lack of cohesion, 135, 158–59, 165, 175; liberal reform group goals, 159, 176; liberal reform group narratives, 152, 155 (fig.), 156; nationalized reform movement and, 21, 46; right reform group goals, 158, 175–76; right reform group narratives, 152–54; state-level reform work, 149. *See also* ACLU; ACU; NAACP; nonprofits

Alexander, Michelle, 38, 42, 127. *See also* The New Jim Crow

Ali, Muhammad, 90, 211n19

Allan, Barbara, 151

Allen, Sue Ellen, 28, 46, 141

Alliance for Safety and Justice, 28, 47, 69, 77, 102, 156

American Civil Liberties Union (ACLU): bipartisan work, 150, 156–57; centering criminal justice

American Civil Liberties Union
(*continued*)
reform, 46, 138; criticism of, 138;
Criminal Law Reform Project, 48;
decarceration goal, 158; FSA and,
5, 141–42, 147; legalization of mar-
ijuana, 159; messaging on reform,
36–37, 152, 155(fig); Open Society
Foundations grant, 46–47; police
reform and, 38, 48, 158; Republican
perception of, 171; Second Chance
Month and, 150
American Conservative Union (ACU),
5, 44, 48, 152, 154 (fig.)
American Correctional Association, 5
American Enterprise Institute, 59
Americans for Prosperity, 150
Americans for Tax Reform, 58, 133, 135,
140
American Legislative Exchange Coun-
cil (ALEC), 5
Anderson, Lenore, 11
Angeles, Weldon, 17, 170, 174
Anti-Drug Abuse Acts, 9
Arnold, Laura, 59, 67, 68, 70–71, 73,
160. *See also* philanthropists
Arnold Ventures: algorithmic in-
strument, 71, 74; data and, 71–72;
description of focus, 73; entry into
reform and expansion, 69; FSA
support, 82; grants, 69–70, 73;
influence, 59, 68; LLC status, 70;
Proposition 25, 102; Public Safety
Assessment tool, 74. *See also* Laura
Arnold
Artists & Athletes Alliance, 86
Arquette, David, 86, 99, 212n37
assessment: Arnold Ventures' Public
Safety Assessment pretrial risk
assessment tool, 71, 74; CORREC-
TIONS Act and risk assessment, 15;

FSA's PATTERN risk assessment
tool, 15–16; Prop 25 and algorithmic
risk assessment, 102; risk assessment
tool bias debate, 144–45
attention: as capital, 98, 106; celebrities
and, 88, 91, 94, 96–97, 100, 105, 184;
competition for, 88–89; corporations and, 106, 129; movement
strategy and, 94, 98, 105. *See also*
branding
Austin, Jr., Roy, 126
Aziz, Malik, 166

Baez, Joan, 89, 211n10
bail reform: funders push for, 187;
pushback against, xi; rural support
for, 35
Bail Project, 68
Bank of America, 26, 115, 168
"banning the box", 109, 128
Bay Area Police Watch, 132
Beacon of Hope Business Alliance, 117.
See also Nehemiah Manufacturing
Belafonte, Harry, 89
Ben & Jerry's, 115, 126–27
Beyonce, 93
bipartisanship: Bipartisan Criminal
Justice Reform Summit of 2015,
132–33, 140; convergence and,
178; criminal justice reform as
bipartisan political issue, 11(table),
13–14, 14(fig.), 133, 136, 148; critique
of, 156, 162; fraying of in reform
movement, 158; FSA final vote and,
148; meaning of, 146, 151; national
criminal justice organizations and,
134–35, 139; opportunities for in
criminal justice reform, 160; praise
for FSA and, 3, 5–8, 109–10; state
level victories and, 149; Van Jones'
leadership of from the left and, 132;

White House roundtables and, 141. *See also* strange bedfellows

Black Lives Matter (BLM), 39, 79, 101–2, 125, 171

Bevin, Matt, 1, 3

Biden, Joe, 25

billionaires in criminal justice reform: critique of involvement in reform, 83; entry into reform, 60; 184; funding of reform; 61; impact of, 62, 65; REFORM Alliance and, 66. *See also* elites; Arnold, Laura; Deason, Doug; Loeb, Dan; Novogratz, Michael

branding: individual activists and, 77; celebrity, 89, 105, 184; corporations' use of, 84, 106, 112, 127, 129; nonprofits and, 168

Brando, Marlon, 89

Brandon, Adam, 58

Branson, Richard, 59

Brennan Center, 141, 144, 147

Brown, Michael, 68

Bono, 89

Booker, Cory, 3, 15, 220n26

Books not Bars, 132

Butterball, 115, 184

Boudin, Chesa, xi

Bureau of Prisons (BOP): clemency and, 18, 65; CORRECTIONS Act and, 15; early release pilot program, 18; earned time provisions and, 19–20; FSA assessment system and, 15–16; interpretation of FSA, 200n39; personal identification documents, 18

Burton, Susan, 92, 95

Bush, George: and Second Chance Act, 43–44, 114; and State of the Union 2004, 114

Bush, Wes, 110

Business Roundtable (BRT), 5, 110, 115, 120, 122, 125

businesses. *See* corporations

Cannabis Freedom Alliance, 159

Californians for Safety and Justice, 47

Carlson, Tucker, 143

Cartagena, Juan, 33, 47, 51–52

capacity building, 168, 185

capital: celebrity, 91–94, 96–97, 102, 105; corporate, 106, 126; cultural, 30; 105–6; philanthropic, 66, 69, 80, 184; political, 23, 92, 108, 119, 126, 147, 182; social, 92–93, 182; symbolic, 92

Capital One, 115

capital punishment: as sub issue in criminal justice reform, 48–51; retention of, 32; corporations and, 126, 158; innocence advocates and, 170

careerism in criminal justice reform. *See* professionalization of nonprofit sector

Carter, Jimmy, 113

celebrity: celebritization of advocates; 95; "celebrity capital" 97, 106; criminal justice reform movement and, 98, 100, 103, 106–7; #cut50 use of, 94; linkages with elites in philanthropy, politics, corporations, 127; networked microcelebrity, 209n45; post-democracy and, 93, 182, REFORM alliance use of, 94–96; social movements and, 98; Van Jones and use of, 93; 'voice' and, 99. *See also* brand; platform

Center for American Progress, 150

Chamber of Commerce (USCOC), 110, 115, 125

Chan Zuckerberg Initiative (CZI), 26, 68, 74, 169, 202n6
Charles, Matthew, 6, 164–65
Chauvin, Derek, 124, 158
Chettiar, Inimai, 141, 144, 147, 221n44
Christian beliefs: Christian conservatives, 220n27; Nehemiah manufacturing and, 116; Prison Fellowship and, 13, 42; redemption story and, 43, 152; second chances and, 43–44, 150
civil rights movement, 79–80, 161
Clemente, Rosa, 5
clemency: Alice Marie Johnson and, 86; Bernard Noble and, 63; BOP and, 65.
Clinton, Bill, 11–12(table), 132
Clyde Court #REFORM sneakers, 127–28(fig.)
Coalition for Public Safety, 133, 156
Cobb, Bill, 37, 46–47, 78–80, 138, 147, 156–57, 165–68, 173, 186
Cohen, Steve, 59
collective acknowledgement. See acknowledgment
Collins, Doug, 2–3
Colson, Chuck, 44, 219n13
Comey, James, xi
Common Justice, 160
compassionate release, 18–19
Comprehensive Crime Control Act, 9(table)
conservatives: CPAC poll of membership, 137; identity vouching and language, 139–40, 148, 159; "mass incarceration" and, 42; race and advocacy, 157; second chances and, 42–43; Van Jones' alliance with, 136. See also Christianity; libertarians; Prison Fellowship; right; redemption story; Republicans

consumer politics: and the gay rights' movement, 185; as post-democratic, 127. See also branding; post-democracy
convergence. See bipartisanship
convict leasing, 112. See also prison labor
Cook-McCormack, Jeff, 59
CoreCivic, 109–10, 126
Cornyn, John, 14(fig.), 15, 57
corporate social activism (CSR), 107, 111–12, 124, 127. See also corporations
corporations: anti-apartheid movement and, 94, 111, 214–15n15; anti-death penalty policy and, 126; capital and, 106; Citizens United v. FTC and political expenditures of, 62; civil rights movement and donations to, 79, 214n13; "credibility" for causes via corporate endorsement, 129; donations to reform organizations from, 128; entry into reform, 84, 106, 114–15, 124–26; FSA support and, 108, 110, 112; mainstreamization and, 9, 127, 129; prison labor and, 112–13. See also BRT; Chamber of Commerce; corporate social activism; fair chance hiring; Jamie Dimon; JPMorgan Chase; Nehemiah Manufacturing; second chance hiring; Verizon
CORRECTIONS Act, 14
Corrections Corporation of America. See CoreCivic
cost: as a frame, 37, 162, 164; of mass incarceration on economic growth, 115
Cotton, Tom, 143, 146
Council on Criminal Justice, 112
COVID, x, 20–21, 85

Cox, Hannah, 8, 50–51, 139, 151, 220n27
Craft, Robert, 66
credibility of formerly incarcerated advocates, 171. *See also* lived experience
crime and arrest rates: arrest rates by race, 33; crime rate post 2020, 10–11; historical crime rate, 170–71
criminal justice reform. *See* reform, criminal justice
criminal justice reform movement. *See* reform movement, criminal justice
crimmigration, 49–52
Critical Resistance, 21, 77, 152, 155(fig.), 208n30
Cruz, Ted, 1, 3
Cuban, Mark, 5
cultural shifts: away from harsh punishment, 8, 27, 183; corporations and, 111; "heart and minds" and, 35–36, 170; institutionalization of, 185; mainstreamization and, 8, 46; second chances and, 150
#cut50: FSA
CVS, 115

Dagan, David, 159, 161
data: Arnold Ventures' focus on, 71–72; 50 State Blueprint tool, 158; importance of versus lived experience, 76; measuring impact with criminal justice data, 174–75; missing information about the incarcerated, 19; use in assessment tools, 74
Dave's Killer Bread, 5, 108
Davis, Angela, 77
Deason, Doug: arrest, 56; criminal justice reform support, 56–57; First Step Act involvement, 55, 57–58, 138; First Step Act signing, 2; future of reform, 180; pardon endorsement, 63; partnership with Jared Kushner,

137; relationship with Mark Holden, 108; Trump campaign support, 55, 57
death penalty. *See* capital punishment
decarceration: as a meaning of criminal justice reform, 22, 31, 48; celebrity activism and, 88; conservatives and, 135; corporations and, 183; federal acts and, 8; numeric goals for, 158, 176; philanthropy's impact on, 65; public opinion and, 83; resistance to, 179; state reforms and, 12, 25–26; violent offenders and, 159
decriminalization of drugs, 27, 49–50, 52, 126, 156, 159, 176
"defund the police," xi, 124, 127, 158, 178
Democrats: at FSA signing, 2; at White House summit on criminal justice, 57; bipartisan support with Republicans on reform, 5, 13–14; cosponsors of FSA, 5; Dear Colleague letter on FSA, 143; in story of FSA passage, 137, 140, 142, 146–47; presidential candidates and pledge to cut incarceration, 158; SRCA and, 15; support for policing among, 178; tough on crime legislation and, 14. *See also* liberals
Department of Justice (DOJ): FSA draft suggestions, 142; required reports for FSA, 16; rule on FSA, 20; selection of Hudson Institute for FSA assessment tool, 200; White House FSA summit representation, 57–58
DeRoche, Craig, 2, 36, 44, 58, 150, 168–69
DeSantis, Ron, 57
Deskovic, Jeffrey, 93, 151, 170–71
Dignity Act, 14(fig.), 15, 18
Dimon, Jamie, 110, 119–20, 122–24, 180

directly impacted people. *See* formerly incarcerated people

divisions in the movement, 10, 30, 91, 103, 106, 141, 143, 151

Downey Jr., Robert, 102

Dreisinger, Baz, 31, 40, 96, 167, 189

Drug Police Alliance, 143, 156

Due Process Institute, 58

Durbin, Dick, 14(fig.), 58, 143, 220n26

Dutton, Charles, 88

DuVernay, Ava, 40, 42, 59

Dylan, Bob, 89

earned credit. *See* earned credit *under* First Step Act

Eddy, Thomas, 60

elites: access to power, 62, 93; bipartisanship and, 162; criticism of FSA passage as elitist, 143, 83; divide between elites and voices from "below", 103, 105; influence of, 184, 188; influence of rhetoric on public opinion, 7; interest in criminal justice reform, 60, 189; movement elites, 76, 135, 137–38, 140, 162; post-democracy and, 83, 88, 182–83, 188. *See also* billionaires; post-democracy

Ella Baker Center for Human Rights, 132, 211n22

evidence-based: assessments, 161; FSA programming as, 16; practices advocated for in penal reform history, 179. *See also* assessments; data

"evolving standards of decency," 183. *See also* cultural shifts

fair chance hiring, 113, 120, 215n21. *See also* second chance hiring

Fair Sentencing Act, 13(table), 14, 17, 19, 136

Faith and Freedom Coalition, 2, 58, 148

Families Against Mandatory Minimums (FAMM), 5, 79, 142–43, 145–46, 170, 221n37

Federal Prison Industries. *See* UNICOR

Federal Prison Reform Act, 14(fig.)

First Step Act (FSA): advocacy groups and, 139–48; BOP and, 200n39, 201n44; celebrity activism and, 86–88, 100, 105–6; corporate social activism and, 108–11; correctional reforms; 15–17; DOJ rule and, 20; earned time credit, 16; FIPs and, 6, 163–65; good time credit, 16; House vote, 146; impact of, 20; opposition to, 144–46; philanthropists and, 59, 82, 108; provisions of, 15–19, 108; Senate legislative influences on, 14, 14 (fig.), 15; Senate vote, 148; sentencing reforms, 17; signing, 1–4, 4(fig.); supporters, 5, 220n26; symbolism, 8–10. *See also* compassionate release; #cut50; Deason, Doug; Kushner, Jared; Jackson, Jessica; Jones, Van; juveniles; 924c; PATTERN; safety valve; Second Chance Act; UNICOR

Flom, Jason, 62–63

Floyd, George, 10, 40–41, 68, 112, 124–25, 128–29, 158, 178

Ford Foundation, 68, 73, 79, 133

Forman, Jolene, 74–75, 160, 169

Formerly Incarcerated Convicted People & Families Movement (FICPFM), 166–67, 169

formerly incarcerated people (FIPs): celebrity FIPs, 26; celebritization of, 95, 95(fig.); employment and educational attainment rates and, 114,

121; FSA and, 6, 144–46, 163–65; leadership in reform movement and, 165–74; mainstreamization, 173; nonprofit leadership; voice of, 88, 90, 99, 101, 167–68, 172–73, 187. *See also* Cobb, Bill; Hoskins, DeAnna; JLUSA; FICPFM; Holt, Rayshun; Khan, Adnan; Mendoza, Michael; Mill, Meek; reentry; Saldana, Jose; Sam, Topeka; Second Chance hiring; Trejo, Danny; voice

Fortune Society, 77

foundations. *See* philanthropy

Fraternal Order of Police (FOP), 2

FreedomWorks, 2, 17, 43, 58, 98, 134, 136, 138, 140, 150

funders. *See* philanthropy

gala events, 92

Galaxy Gives, 59, 66, 68, 78. *See also* Michael Novogratz

Galvin-Almanza, Emily, 177

Gay, Kevin, 141

gender-nonconforming people. *See* LGBT issues

Geo Group, 109–10, 126

Gill, Molly, 146

Gilmore, Ruth Wilson, 77

Gingrich, Newt, 132–33, 140

Glover, Danny, 88

good time credit. *See* good time credit *under* First Step Act

Google: Google trends data on mass incarceration and related searches, 40, 41(fig.), 42(fig.), 45(fig.), 46(fig.), 86, 109

Grassley, Chuck, 1–2, 4, 14

Green, David, 179, 182

Greene, Cory, 164

Guenthner, David, 150

Gund, Agnes, 59

Harris, Holly, 8, 35, 90, 97–98, 133, 145–48, 159, 174

Harris, Kamala, 42(fig.), 143, 148

Hart, Kevin, 88

hedge fund approach to philanthropy. *See* hedge fund approach to philanthropy *under* philanthropy

Henderson, Norris, 166

Heritage Foundation, 11, 58

heroin epidemic. *See* opioid epidemic

Higginbottom, Heather, 119–20, 122, 123(fig.), 180

Hininger, Damon, 109

Hochschild, Arlie, 9, 21

Holden, Mark, 58, 108

Hollins, Tinisch, 52–53, 182, 185, 187, 189

Holt, Rayshun, 115–16, 118

Home Depot, 115

Hopwood, Shon, 2, 7, 164

Hoskins, DeAnna, 34, 79, 81, 99–100, 104, 144–45, 166, 172, 181

How Our Lives Link Together Altogether! (HOLLA!), 164

Hudson Institute, 200n35

Hull Family Foundation, 208n30

Human Rights Watch, 143

Hussle, Nipsey, 88, 103

Hutchinson, Asa, 56

identity vouching, 139, 139–40, 171

ideology, 36, 204n44. *See also* ideologically resonant stories

ideologically resonant stories: definition and role in mainstreamization of reform, 29–30, 37; exodus story, 124–25, 152–53, 156, 173, 178, 182; Francesca Polletta on exodus and redemption, 37; redemption story, 44, 115, 120, 124–25, 134, 142, 152–53, 182

immigration: advocacy and criminal justice advocacy, 47, 51–52; federal criminal justice reform legislation and, 12(table); Trump discourse on, 1. *See also* crimmigration
Incarceration Nations Network, 31, 167
incarceration rate, 10, 176
Independent Review Committee (IRC), 15–16, 200n35
influencers. *See* celebrities
Initiate Justice, 88, 186–87
inmate labor. *See* prison labor
Innocence Project, 62, 69
International Association of Chiefs of Police, 2

Jackson, Jessica, 2, 5–6, 78, 82, 87, 132, 140–43, 147–48, 164
Jackson Lee, Sheila, 143
Jacobson, Michael, 7, 28, 78, 84, 135, 175
James, Andrea, 165
Jay-Z, 64, 66, 88, 91, 94, 104, 106. *See also* Roc Nation
Jealous, Ben, 47, 134
Jeffries, Hakeem, 143
JEHT Foundation, 67–68
Jindal, Bobby, 62–63
Johnson, Alice Marie, 2, 6, 109, 164, 174
Johnson, Lyndon, 11(table)
Jones, Van: advocacy history, 132, 212–13n22; bipartisanship and, 132–33, 135; criticism of, 135–26; #cut50 founding, 132; FSA advocacy, 82, 87, 131–32, 142, 145; FSA signing and, 2–3; on corporate actors in reform, 111; REFORM Alliance and, 66–67(fig.); support of celebrities in reform, 93, 100. *See also* #cut50; REFORM Alliance

JPMorgan Chase, 26, 115, 119–24, 180, 184
JPMorgan Policy Center, 119–20, 124. *See also* JPMorgan Chase
JustLeadershipUSA (JLUSA), 47, 143–44, 147, 158, 169
Just Mercy, 40
Justice Accelerator, 68, 169. *See also* Chan Zuckerberg Initiative
Justice Action Network (JAN), 8, 35, 63, 149–50
Justice Fellowship, 2, 36, 150, 219n13
Justice System Improvement Act, 113
Juveniles: FSA and, 18; Proposition 21 and, 212n34

Kennedy, John Fitzgerald, 89
Kerik, Bernie, 2–3, 164, 174
Khan, Adnan, 74, 99
Kim, Jenny, 107–8, 111–12, 117, 119, 121, 126
King, Alveda, 2
King, Jr., Martin Luther, 89
Koch, Charles, 56, 108, 159
Koch Industries, 5, 68, 108, 112, 115, 120, 126, 133, 174
Korzenik, Jeff, 112, 114, 215n21
Koufos, John, 2, 164
Krasner, Larry, 83, 159
Kroger's, 118
Kushner, Charles, 57, 174
Kushner, Jared, 2–3, 57–58, 139–42, 165

labor shortage, 29, 116–17, 121–22, 125, 178
Ladies of Hope Ministries (LOHM), 2, 33, 168
Larson, Brie, 86
LatinoJustice PRLDEF, 33, 47, 52, 143
"law and order", xi, 44, 52, 132, 142, 178, 199n15

Index

257

Leahy, Patrick, 14
Lee, Mike, 1
left. *See* liberals
LCCHR. *See* Leadership Council on
Civil and Human Rights
Leadership Council on Civil and
Human Rights, 143–44, 150, 159,
221n45
legalization of drugs. *See* decriminalization of drugs
Legend, John, 26, 88, 168, 184
Levin, Marc, 35, 80, 138, 141, 160, 171,
176, 180
LGBT: place in criminal justice reform
movement, 49–50; rights movement success, 185; trans issues, 50,
188
liberals: critiques of FSA, 144; critiques
of philanthropy, 82–83; critique of
Van Jones, 136; in FSA-supportive
advocacy groups, 141; reform goals,
159–60, 176; reform narratives, 42,
46, 152, 155 (fig.), 156, 157–58; White
House summit on FSA and, 139. *See
also* ACLU; abolitionism; advocacy groups; Critical Resistance;
Democrats
Libertarians: FSA and, 2, 58, 100;
reasons for reform support, 35, 176;
reform narratives and, 42; right
and, 243, 220n27. *See also* Freedom-
Works; Koch, Charles; Koch Industries; Lee, Mike; Cox, Hannah; Pye,
Jason
Liguori, Serena, 34, 36, 97
lived experience, 81, 162. *See also*
credibility
LL Cool J, 93
'lock 'em up' attitudes, x, 25, 54. *See also*
harsh punishment attitudes. *See also*
"tough on crime"

Loeb, Dan, 48, 59–60, 62–63, 65–66,
70, 72–73, 81, 168
LUSH cosmetics, 127

MacArthur Foundation, 68, 133, 167
mainstreamization: celebrities and,
88, 90, 105; corporate activism and,
127–28; definition, 8, 27; evidence
of, 26; FIPs and, 173; model of and
components, 28, 29, 29(fig.)–31;
normative and structural aspects,
46–48; philanthropy and, 60, 70;
political opportunity and, 73, 139,
162; reform movement and, 21–22,
27; relationship to post-democracy
and philanthrocapitalism, 183
Maloney, Cliff, 34–35
Mandela, Nelson, 131
Martin, Glenn, 48, 164
Mass incarceration: acknowledgment
of problem with, 26, 33; as focus
of civil rights organizations, 47,
138; "ending mass incarceration"
28, 175–76; federal criminal justice
legislation since, 10–13; formerly incarcerated activists and ending, 173;
magnitude of, 32–33; phrase usage,
39–43; public opinion and rise of, 31;
racial justice and, 40, 124
Mauer, M., 161, 219n13
McConnell, Mitch, 35, 59, 144, 148
McMullin, Rodney, 117
Mendoza, Michael, 51, 76, 79, 172
Messaging. *See also* frames; ideologically resonant stories; story
Meyers, Dan, 117
Microsoft, 78, 102, 115
Milano, Alyssa, 26, 38–39, 85–88, 94,
100–1, 103–4, 184
Mill, Meek, 26, 63–64, 66, 88, 91, 93,
96, 102–3, 127, 184

Monroe, Marilyn, 89
Morgan, Dominique, 50, 172, 177, 188
Mukamal, Debbie, 111

narrative. *See* ideologically resonant stories
National Association for the Advancement of Colored People (NAACP): donations to, 79, 124, 129; defund language and, 158; Smart and Safe Campaign, 135; and the FSA, 5, 143, 147; 2015 conference, 133; work on criminal justice reform, 47, 134, 138, 159
National Association of Criminal Defense Lawyers, 67
nationalization of the criminal justice reform movement, 22, 48, 127, 136–37, 164, 175, 182–83, 188. *See also* mainstreamization
National Latino Evangelical Association, 5
National Legislative Exchange Action Council, 5
National Organization of Black Law Enforcement Executives, 5
National Sheriff's Organization, 5
National Urban League, 5, 57–58, 134, 138–39, 143
Nehemiah Manufacturing, 115–19
"networked microcelebrity activism", 77, 209n45
New Hour for Women and Children, 34, 97
New Jim Crow, 38–40. *See also* Alexander, Michelle
A New Way of Life, 92
New Yorkers United for Justice, 63, 168
1994 Crime Bill. *See* Violent Crime Control and Law Enforcement Act
924c provisions. *See* stacking provisions

Nixon, Richard, 44, 89, 136
Noble, Bernard, 62–63
Nolan Center for Criminal Justice Reform. *See* Nolan Center for Criminal Justice Reform *under* American Conservative Union
Nolan, Pat, 2, 163–64, 171, 220n32
nonprofit industrial complex, 76, 81
nonprofits: alliances with celebrities, 93; capacity building in, 185; competition for funds among, 77–78; corporate funding of, 129; FIP leadership and, 169; fundraising and, 92; growth in sector, 209n50; nonprofitization of the reform movement, 76–77, 83. *See also* advocacy groups
Norquist, Grover, 58, 135, 140, 220n32
Northrup Grumman, 110
Novogratz, Michael, 59, 61, 66, 68–70, 72, 81, 91, 161, 181, 184, 188

Obama, Barack, 11(table), 92, 133, 136
O'Brien, Soledad, 92
Ofer, Udi, 36–37, 49–50, 149, 158
Omnibus Crime Control and Safe Streets Bill, 9(table)
Open Philanthropy, 68–69, 78
Open Society Foundations, 46–47, 67, 138
Operation New Hope, 141
opioid epidemic: and conservatives, 34–35; FSA provisions for treatment, 18; racialization of, 34
"overincarceration": usage of versus "mass incarceration," 39–43. *See also* mass incarceration

pandemic. *See* COVID
Papa, Tony, 63
parole: federal reforms of, 11; FSA and, 17; Louisiana reforms and, 149;

Progressive era reforms and, 75; Promise app and, 104; REFORM Alliance and, 66, 91; reform of as a sub movement, 49

penality in the US, 179–80

Pence, Mike, 1–2

Pepsico, 115

Persistent Surveillance Systems, 69

philanthrocapitalism; coincidence with post-democracy, 22; celebrities and, 84; definition and characteristics, 9, 80, 111; in criminal justice reform, 61, 80–81, 88, 184; influence on nonprofits, 70, 173; influence on philanthropy; 70–73; rise of, 61, 78

philanthropy: critiques of, 82–83; discovery goal of, 74, 184; eighteenth through twentieth century involvement in reform, 60; FIPs and, 166–69; FSA and, 58–59; funding of reform, 26, 61, 66–70; hedge fund approach to philanthropy, 70–73; power and, 79–80. *See also* Arnold Foundation; Arnold, Laura; billionaires in criminal justice reform; Deason, Doug; Galaxy Gives; Loeb, Daniel; Novogratz, Michael; philanthrocapitalism; REFORM Alliance

Porter, Laura, 158

Portman, Natalie, 92

post-democracy: characteristics of, 8, 62; celebrities and, 88–89, 93; 182–83; civic disengagement and, 77, 177, 186; criminal justice reform's embeddedness in, 183; countering by movement actors, 187; elite power and, 83, 88, 90, 174; philanthropy and, 73, 80

Prejean, Helen, 93

prison abolitionism. *See* abolitionism

prison labor: as punishment, 112; businesses and, 112; capitalist work ethic and, 112; convict leasing, 112; labor contracts, 113; New Gate prison in, 60; Penal Code of 1786 and, 32

Prisoner Assessment Tool Targeting Estimated Risk and Need (PATTERN), 15–16, 200n36. *See also* assessment; Hudson Institute

Prison Families Anonymous, 151

Prison Fellowship, 5, 36, 43–44, 58, 134–35, 138, 152, 153(fig.), 163, 219n13

Prison Litigation Reform Act, 12(table)

Prison Rape Elimination Act, 12(table)

prison reform movement: early philanthropic involvement, 60; progressive era, 75; role of professionals in, 75. *See also* reform, criminal justice

private prisons, 25, 109–10, 152–53

probation: as Progressive-era reform, 75; Meek Mill and, 64; Promise app and, 104; Proposition 21 and, 212n34; REFORM Alliance and, 66, 91, 96; reform of, 49

professionalization of nonprofit sector, 76–77

progressive prosecutors, xi, 83

progressives. *See* liberals

Promise app, 104, 106

Proposition 21, 93, 212n34

Proposition 25, 101–2

proximity to the carceral system, 32–35, 55, 59, 64, 206n1

Prudential, 115

public opinion: celebrities and, 84; elite rhetoric and, 7; in 2022, xii; mass incarceration and, 31, 84; police reform, 26; responsiveness of criminal justice system to, 177; support for criminal justice reform, 26, 54 public safety: assessment tools and, 74, 101; conservative concerns and, 152–54; defining of, 189; Eric Adams' platform, xi; public messaging and, 161; reduced recidivism and, 120

PUMA, 26, 127, 128(fig.)

Punitiveness: culture of punitiveness, 33, 170, 179, 181; elite discourse and impact on public opinion, 7, 88; of 1970s–1990s, 26–28, 83; public opinion and, 83; reduction of in the post-2000 reform era, 8, 22, 29, 31, 150; sex offenses and, 53

Pye, Jason, 17, 43, 58, 98, 100, 136–37, 140, 220n32

Quakers: advocacy for humanitarianism in prison, 32; American Friends Service Committee history and advocacy, 219n13; hard labor penalty introduction, 32, 112; Philadelphia Society for Alleviating the Miseries in Public Prisons, 32

racial justice: ACLU objective and, 158; celebrities and, 96; Common Justice and, 160; criminal justice reform and linkage to, 68, 124, 129, 156; conservatives and, 157; exodus narrative and, 126, 152–54, 156, 178; "mass incarceration" and linkage to, 40; prison uprisings and, 166; organizations focused on, 101

racism: corporations' opposition to, 124–25; in assessment, 102; 2020 protests against, x; prisoners' rights movement protests and, 166; structural/systemic, 34, 75, 124, 156, 158

Reagan, Ronald, 11(table)

redemption story. *See* redemption story *under* ideologically relevant stories

Reed, Rodney, 93

reentry: as focus of criminal justice reform movement, 51; CORRECTIONS Act and reentry programming, 15; FSA and grants for reentry, 18; Louisiana reforms and, 149; Prison Reentry Initiative, 13(table); 114; private prisons companies and, 109; reentry movement, 22, 36, 113; Second Chance Act and, 13(table); second chance hiring as extension of, 113

REFORM Alliance: founding and founding partners, 66–67(fig.)

reform, criminal justice: abolitionists and term, 22; federal legislation, 10, 11(table), 12(table), 13, 13(table); meaning of, 22, 27; state-level initiatives, 149–50; usage of, 44, 45, 45(fig.), 46, 46(fig.). *See also* FSA; state-level reforms

reform movement, criminal justice; goals of, 176–77; mainstreamization and, 28, 29, 29(fig.)–31; post 2020 and, ix–xiii; structural characteristics, 27; study of as a movement, 20–21; submovements, 48–54. *See also* advocacy groups; capital; collective acknowledgment; ideologically resonant stories; mainstreamization

registry. *See* sex offenses

rehabilitation: post-2000 discourse and, 182; pre-1970s policies and, 17; Progressive era ideals and, 75

Reinventing Reentry, 28

Releasing Aging People in Prison (RAPP), 156, 173

Index

Reseda, Richie, 88, 186–87
resources. *See* capital
restorative justice and groups, 49, 52, 159, 187
Re:Store Justice, 53, 74, 99
Rhianna, 93
right. *See* conservatives
Right on Crime, 58, 134, 149, 171, 176
Ring, Kevin, 39, 158, 164, 170–71, 222n37
risk-taking in philanthropy, 74. *See also* hedge fund approach to philanthropy
Reich, Rob, 73, 79, 84, 184
Roc Nation, 64, 104, 106. *See also* Jay-Z
Rooks, Robert, 52, 77, 134, 138, 154–56, 166–67, 185, 187
Roosevelt, Franklin Delano, 89, 201n42
Rubin, Michael, 59, 63–64, 66, 96

Safavian, David, xiv, 2, 82, 137, 145, 153–54, 157–58, 164, 171, 173–74, 178, 180
"safety valve" on mandatory minimums, 17, 14
Saldana, Jose, 156, 173
salience: of crime, ix, 137, 179–80; of the reform movement, 8, 17, 35
Sam, Topeka, 3, 33, 63, 86, 164, 168, 172
Sarandon, Susan, 88, 93
shackling. *See* women's issues in prison
Schad, Katie, 117–19
Schwartz, Gina, 169
Scott, Bobby, 2
second chances: corporate activism and, 124; motive for reform support, 56, 116, 153, 165. *See also* Christianity; redemption story
Second Chance Act, 18, 32, 108, 114, 163, 201n44

Second Chance Business Coalition (SCBC), 26, 122–23. *See also* fair chance hiring; second chance hiring
second chance hiring, 107–8, 113–15, 117, 119, 121–22, 123(fig.), 180
Sengor, Shaka, 219n17
Sentencing Project, 19, 69, 161, 219n13
sentencing reform: as sub movement in criminal justice reform, 27; in SRCA, 144; state-based reforms, 32. *See also* sentencing reform *under* First Step Act
Sentencing Reform and Corrections Act (SRCA), 14(fig.), 14–15, 144, 147, 218n6; Sessions, Jeff, 11, 142
sex offenses: and 1994 Crime Bill, 12(table); movement to reform sex offender laws, 49; Sex Offender Registration and Notification (SORN) laws, 53–54
Sinatra, Frank, 89
Smarter Sentencing Act (SSA), 14, 14(fig.)
Smith, Robert, 66
social movements: celebrities and, 90, 98–99; merging with consumerism and politics, 111; "nonprofitization" of, 76; story in the context of, 37
Society for Human Resource Management (SHRM), 121
Soros, George, 46–47, 67, 138
Southern Poverty Law Center, 143
stacking provisions, 17, 140, 148, 170, 220n31
Standing Together to Organize a Revolutionary Movement (STORM), 210–11n22

state-level reforms: Florida and, 7; Louisiana and, 149; Michigan and, 149–50; post-2000 initiatives, ix, xii; relationship with federal-level reform, 12; wrongful conviction legislation and, 151

Stewart, Julie, 170

story: definition and importance to politics, 37; clash of stories, 160–61; formerly incarcerated advocates and, 170–71; Hoschchild on deeply felt stories, 160. *See also,* exodus story; redemption story

Stephenson, Randall, 125

Stevenson, Bryan, 40, 206n1

"strange bedfellow" consensus, 8, 129, 132, 134, 150–51. *See also* bipartisanship

survivors. *See* victims

Tankleff, Marty, 171

Tea Party, 134, 150, 220n27

Teles, Steven, 159, 161

Texas Public Policy Foundation (TPPF), 156

theories of change, 168, 188

13th documentary, 40, 59. *See also* Ava DuVernay

Tides Foundation, 47

tight labor market. *See* labor shortage

tipping point, ix, 32, 178–79

Tollman, Brett, 148

Tonry, Michael, 159, 162

"tough on crime," 7, 11(table), 13, 28, 30, 52

trans issues. *See* LGBT

Travis, Jeremy, 35–36, 49, 74, 206n73

Trejo, Danny, 86, 88, 102–3

Trump administration, 82, 137

Trump, Donald: death penalty, 50; First Step Act signing, 1–4, 5; meeting with Kim Kardashian, 87, 93; pardons, 63, 174, 198n11; Prison Reform Summit, 142; rhetoric in presidential candidacy, xiii, 7, 136, 199n15; State of the Union, 165; support for First Step Act, 142–43, 147

Trump, Ivanka, 2–3, 86–87, 136

Tufekci, Zeynep, 98

UNICOR, 18, 201n42

"unlikely allies." *See* "strange bedfellow consensus"

Urban League. *See* National Urban League

USCOC. *See* Chamber of Commerce

Vargas, Taina Angeli, 81, 186–87

Verizon, 109–10, 115, 124, 126, 184, 217n62

victims/survivors: place in reform movement, 49–50, 52–53, 187; victims' rights movement, 52–53

Viguerie, Richard, 220n32

Violent Crime Control and Law Enforcement Act, 9–10, 25, 44, 215n52

violent offenses: drop in during 1990s, 39; hiring and working with people with, 118; historical rates, 176; increase after 2020; x, xi; Violent Crime Control and Law Enforcement Act, 11(table), 217n53

Virgin, 59, 115

Visa, 115

voice: lack of prior to mainstreaming of movement, 46–47; of the incarcerated and FIPs in the movement and controversies, 88, 90, 99, 101,

167–68, 172–73, 187; post-democracy and limiting of, 62, 83; research and, 75; victims/survivors and, 52

Walmart, 26, 115, 126, 184
Ward, Andre, 77–78, 81, 99, 167
Warren, Elizabeth, 14(fig.), 15
Watterson, Billy, 68–69
Weiker, Rebecca, 53, 177
Wells Fargo, 126
West, Kanye, 6, 86
Whitehouse, Sheldon, 2, 15, 57, 220n26
Williams, Tom, 117

women's issues in criminal justice: A New Way of Life's work, 92 #cut50 Dignity campaign, 87; FSA provisions, 3, 15, 18; New Hour for Women and Children, 97; sub movement, 49; trans women, 50, 188
Work Opportunity Tax Credits (WOTC), 113
wrongfully convicted advocates, 170
Wu Tsai, Clara, 66

Zuckerberg, Mark, 70. *See also* Chan Zuckerberg Initiative

Printed in the USA
CPSIA information can be obtained
at www.ICGtesting.com
JSHW080707020823
45818JS00001B/1